GRAVEN IMAGES

Audrey Thomas was born and raised in New York state but has lived and worked on Canada's west coast since 1959. Her previous novels include *Latakia*, *Mrs. Blood*, *Songs My Mother Taught Me* and *Intertidal Life*, which was nominated for a Governor General's Award and won the B.C. Book Prize. She is also the author of a number of widely acclaimed short story collections, including *Two in the Bush and Other Stories*, *Real Mothers*, *Goodbye Harold, Good Luck* and *The Wild Blue Yonder*, which won the Ethel Wilson Fiction Prize. Audrey Thomas is also the recipient of the Canada-Scotland Writer's Literary Fellowship and the Canada-Australia Literary Prize. She lives on Galiano Island, B.C.

Audrey Thomas

GRAVEN IMAGES

Penguin Books

PENGUIN BOOKS
Published by the Penguin Group
Penguin Books Canada Ltd, 10 Alcorn Avenue, Toronto, Ontario,
Canada M4V 3B2
Penguin Books Ltd, 27 Wrights Lane, London W8 5TZ, England
Penguin Books USA Inc., 375 Hudson Street, New York, New York 10014,
U.S.A.
Penguin Books Australia Ltd, Ringwood, Victoria, Australia
Penguin Books (NZ) Ltd, 182-190 Wairau Road, Auckland 10,
New Zealand

Penguin Books Ltd, Registered Offices:
Harmondsworth, Middlesex, England

First published in Viking by Penguin Books Canada Limited, 1993

Published in Penguin Books, 1994

1 3 5 7 9 10 8 6 4 2

*Publisher's note: This book is a work of fiction. Names, characters, places and inci-
dents either are the product of the author's imagination or are used fictitiously, and
any resemblance to actual persons living or dead, events, or locales is entirely coinci-
dental.*

Manufactured in Canada

Canadian Cataloguing in Publication Data
Thomas, Audrey, 1935 -
Graven images

ISBN 0-14-017472-9

I. Title

PS8539.H62G7 1994   C813'.54   C92-095680-7
PR9199.3.T45G7 1994

To Stephen O'Shea, Bill Schermbrucker and Bob Sherrin: les beaux chauffeurs, *("without whose help . . .")*

Acknowledgements

This novel was begun with the financial assistance of the Canada Council.

I would also like to thank Ken and Sylvia Mounsey for their generous assistance with certain details about World War II, Carole Robertson, my cheerful typist, and Marie and Ken Hardy for celestial and earthly help.

Audrey Thomas

GRAVEN IMAGES

In 1892, five years before my mother was born, Julian Huxley sent a letter to his grandfather, Thomas Henry Huxley, asking about water-babies. There was a picture in Kingsley's book of T.H.H. and Professor Owen examining a water-baby.

DEAR GRANDPATER HAVE YOU SEEN A WATER-BABY? DID YOU PUT IT IN A BOTTLE? DID IT WONDER IF IT COULD GET OUT? CAN I SEE IT SOME DAY?
YOUR LOVING
JULIAN

There was rubble everywhere along Euston Road and King's Cross Road and metal signs twisted and crumpled into odd shapes. October 16, 1987. Trees with their medusa roots showing. Broken pavement. Danger signs: KEEP CLEAR. I had twisted my ankle the night of the Captain's Farewell Party and I walked carefully so as not to twist it again.

The meal had begun with Barszcz Czerwony Z Pasztecikiem and ended with Lody Bomba-Victoria, with many courses in-between and a great deal of champagne, paid for by Lydia and me. I tripped going up the stairs from the dining saloon, turned my ankle and received a deep gash as well, from the metal edging that kept the carpet in place. The next morning Lydia insisted I go to the infirmary, which was presided over by a large woman in white who was knitting a sweater out of porridge-coloured yarn. The yarn must have once been another sweater, it was so curly; it looked as though she were knitting up those Japanese noodles that come with little foil packets of broth. She did not seem to speak English and our Polish Fun Class ("Ten Words of Polish a Day") had not covered a visit to the infirmary, so I simply took off my shoe and held up my foot. She nodded and motioned me to sit down. From a glass cupboard behind us — a cupboard full of brown and white bottles with indecipherable labels — she selected one. It was iodine, applied liberally while Lydia smiled encouragement and said "*cholera, cholera*" under her breath.

The fourth night out we had seen a romantic movie in which this word (never translated in the subtitles) kept appearing. Our teacher told us, when asked, that Poles are not given to swearing, that "*cholera*" is a mild epithet, something like "damn." We did not believe him but decided to adopt the word as a private swear word of our own. Iodine on an open wound was definitely a *cholera* situation.

After a gauze dressing was put in place, the nurse wrapped my ankle in an elastic bandage.

"Thank you," I said in Polish. "Lovely weather. Would you care for another cake?" Or that's what Lydia said I said. I thought I was asking her how much I owed her. The nurse smiled and shook her head.

"Iodine," I said to Lydia, when we got back to the grand lounge, where the Silesian band was playing its final concert. It was eleven-thirty a.m. and time for morning coffee, or perhaps something stronger considering what I had just been through. "I didn't know anyone still used iodine, except in salt. My whole childhood flashed before my eyes. Proust had it easy with his tea and bun."

"Mercurochrome for the small scrapes," she said, "iodine for the more serious stuff."

"It's the smell, isn't it, not just the sting; it smells as though it's going to hurt."

We gave our order to the moustached waiter. Or one of the moustached waiters. Most of the men on the ship, with the exception of the captain, looked like Lech Walesa — or had his moustache. Which came first, we wondered, the man or his moustache?

"My aunt drank iodine once," I said. "My grandfather offered my grandmother first choice of the Christmas turkey so my aunt jumped up from the table, ran into the bathroom and drank the bottle of iodine from the medicine cabinet."

"Did she die?"

"My grandparents went into their bedroom and shut the door, after telling my mother to call a doctor and call the State Hospital to come and get her. They stayed in their room until the doctor was finished with her and the ambulance had carted her off to the loony-bin. My mother had to deal with it all."

"I didn't know you had an aunt."

"I still do. But this was a long time ago — they were just young women then. Before that my aunt stood on a window-ledge in New York City, threatening to jump. They put her in Bellevue for observation. My mother had to deal with it that time as well. She says, 'Poor Betty, poor Betty' when she tells me these things, but she always has a smile on her face. Are you sure you want to find your relatives?"

"I'm sure."

❧

In London everyone was reading a newspaper, and I saw the headlines as I walked along:

WORST STORM IN RECORDED HISTORY
ONE DEAD IN LONDON
KEW IN SHAMBLES
CITY BROUGHT TO A HALT

I stopped to buy papers at a tobacconist's and turned the corner, heading for Mecklenburgh Square. My heavy bag, strapped to one of those wheeled luggage carriers, kept turning over because of the uneven pavement. I travel a lot, and I long for the day when I can figure out how to travel with one notebook, five pens and some sort of lovely, seamless, all-purpose garment. It was tiring and somehow humiliating to be walking along a thoroughfare dragging a suitcase behind. Immediately I was a stranger, not "one of us." Another bloody Yank.

(At the first Polish Fun Class we went around the room saying who we were, where we came from and what was our occupation. A blonde woman named Bobbi announces that she is a writer.

The Entertainments Officer, who is our teacher, stares at her, is silent for several seconds and then asks:

"What kind of a *wry*-ter, Madame?"

"Newspaper articles, travel pieces, that sort of thing."

"No, Madame," he says, "you are not a *wry*-ter, you are a *journalist*. In Poland we make a distinction between a real *wry*-ter, someone who creates *literature*, and a journalist. *You* are a journalist."

Lydia looks over at me and smiles her "innocent" smile. I fear that she is going to tell if I don't. She says "housewife" and gets praised for it, as she knows she will be. I make a note to find out how to say "servants" in Polish, how to say "liar."

I am the last person to speak.

"Charlotte," I say, "Canadian," I say, "Vancouver," I say. "Writer."

I get the stare. He is tall, dark-haired, with blue eyes and a long straight nose. He has an M.A. in English from the University of Warsaw.

"Real writer," I say in a very small voice, my face burning.

It's not true. Yet.)

My mother lives in a senior citizens' home in Massachusetts. She moved there at age seventy-two and has now been a resident for eighteen years. I live in another country and thousands of miles away. I like it that way; I like to keep distance and a border between my mother and myself. I am no longer afraid of her; my heart no longer pounds when I hear her high, rather nasal voice on the telephone, nor do I feel anxious and afraid when one of her letters arrives in the mail. I used to leave them unopened for hours, even days, especially the ones with PLEASE DESTROY just below her name and return address. "Sticks and stones may break my bones," we used to chant in the schoolyard, "but names will never hurt me." I didn't believe it then and I don't believe it now, but I have acquired a certain distance on it all. As I say to my friends, I have realized she is quite democratic with her abuse — she hates everybody. There's no need for me to take it personally when she is in one of her rages. I have even grown rather fond of her and trot out her sayings at dinner parties. I refer to her as the Aged Pea. Having a ninety-year-old mother gives me a certain cachet. There was someone in the family who lived to be ninety-nine. I don't know about old men but I have a theory about cantankerous old women. I think all that nastiness acts as a kind of emotional Drāno, clears out the pipes the way acid clears the drains. We even acknowledge this in a way when we refer to caustic remarks, although here, I suppose, the acid is supposed to splash on the receiver, not the giver.

Mother would argue this. She constantly says she mustn't get upset: "I might get a shock." She means a stroke. She doesn't care, however, if others get upset. Presumably their constitutions are not so delicate as hers. For example:

"If I'd had a son," my mother says, "I wouldn't

be in this fix." She wants to move to another place; she feels she's too old to cook now. She has just vacuumed, in honour of my visit, and has worn herself out. The vacuum stands in the corner, like some strange life-support system. She says she's too tired to put it away.

"Why is that?" I ask.

"Well, at fifty-plus he'd be successful, established. He'd look after me."

"You're sure of that are you? What if he were unsuccessful? Always mooching off you?"

"There wouldn't be much to mooch," she says.

As usual, I am saved from complete fury by my mother's strange sense of humour. In spite of the fact that she is "tuckered out," she's looking very nice. She is wearing a pale pink duster, which suits her pink-and-white look. ("Your sister knows I never wear anything pink, but I kept it so her feelings wouldn't be hurt.") She looks soft, like a decaying angel, with her pink, wrinkled skin and her white white hair — exactly like the angel hair, the real stuff, made of spun glass, which our father put on the Christmas tree each year, the dog locked in the basement so she wouldn't get it up her nose. I loved it, and in spite of not being a successful son who does right by his mother, in spite of the accusatory vacuum cleaner in the corner ("I just ran out of steam") I am feeling very kindly towards my mother, even if I know in my heart she is like those awful medieval statues of Frau Welt, lovely on one side but serpents and toads behind.

"Your hair looks lovely," I say, "and now that your hair is white I think pink suits you."

"The hairdresser pulled my hair," she says. "She's very overweight and I think she has personal problems. I told her that she has such a pretty face, she'd be a knockout if she'd only lose some weight."

"Did you tell her this before or after she pulled your hair?"

It is because of my mother that I found myself, in October 1987, walking through a London that looked in places like the set for a sci-fi movie, *The Kraken Wakes* or something like that. It is because of me — or my persuasion — that Lydia, at the same time, was speeding by train towards Birmingham in a seat facing the engine, in England for the first time since she set sail in 1942, in a convoy of ships headed for Halifax, Nova Scotia. (She doesn't count the VIP lounge at Heathrow. Whenever she and her husband have had to change planes in England she refuses to leave the airport. Or refused, up until now, to set foot on English soil.)

I stood in line with her at Euston Station, and when the barriers opened and the crowd surged forward I gave her a kiss on the cheek.

"The best of British luck," I said. "Remember, no harm can come to one who has been kissed by the Witch of the North. And call me if you need me."

"Charlotte," she said quickly, "do you remember the used Kotex that fell out of your cardigan pocket one day in music class?"

"I remember."

"I put it there."

I smiled and shook my head. "Heather put it there."

She brightened. "That's right — it was Heather. I forgot."

Not that Heather changed all that much, except

in name (and hair colour), later on, but I didn't want Lydia to go off on her quest feeling blue.

I met Lydia Sørenson when we were seven years old and she was little Heather Fulford, a child evacuee who had been brought over from England to America by one of the richest families in our town. They owned the bread factory and sponsored a Saturday afternoon program of light classical music. Someone had made up a lyric to the music from "Tales from the Vienna Woods."

The famous Armstrong Bakery
The name that stands for quality
Invites you to try
Invites you to buy
Delicious and fresh
Armstrong Bread

The day before, our teacher had told us she had a surprise for us: we were getting a new classmate, a little girl who'd come all the way from England. We were to be especially nice to her and not to call attention to her if she cried.

She had straight brown hair and rosy cheeks and talked as though she had a permanent head cold. And she did cry — a lot — even though she had been given a pony and a puppy and a new two-wheeler and a wrist-watch. Nearly everyone wanted to be her best friend. Not me. I longed to be sent away and adopted by a nice couple who didn't shout at each other every night or throw things or live in such emotional chaos. I couldn't see what she had to cry about. She was an exotic misfit, romantic even.

The entire school was very romantic about the war. Most of us girls had dolls named Elizabeth or Margaret Rose; most of the boys raced through the playground shooting down Jap Zeros or German Messerschmitts with their water-pistols and pea-shooters. All of us pulled wagons around our neighbourhoods collecting tinfoil and fat, which could be redeemed for savings stamps. When you had twenty-five dollars' worth of stamps you could buy a Liberty Bond. We could also do our bit for the war effort by being nice to Heather.

My birthday was in late November, and the year that Heather joined our class my mother got it into her head that I should have a birthday party. I said no. She said why not? I said no one would come. I had never announced my birthday at school the way the other kids did, with hand-made invitations for some, not all, given out at recess. But teachers had all that information: I discovered this in kindergarten. After that, I managed to be so sick early enough and forcefully enough, on the day, that I didn't go to school. My mother said that if I wanted friends I was going to have to make an effort. *She* was prepared to make the effort, why wasn't I?

I thought I was the only child in the school whose parents fought, whose parents couldn't pay their bills, who told lies on the telephone to the milk company, the electricity company, the telephone company itself. My mother was a good cook. I knew she would make something nice and no doubt spend a lot of time thinking up games and prizes. The games would be too young and the prizes would be too expensive. I would also be treated to a new velveteen dress to be bought on account at one of the three department stores, the one where we owed the least that year. I had not yet read Lawrence's "The Rocking Horse Winner" but I had a terrible fear that the walls of our house, which had heard all, would somehow repeat all: the accusations, the counter-accusations, the terrible noise like Donald Duck that my father sometimes made to drown out my mother's voice: *qwack, qwack, qwack, qwack* — that my schoolmates would hear it and repeat it to those who weren't lucky enough to have been invited. They would know — the whole town would know that we might go to the Poor House any minute. I was like someone in a fairy-tale with a secret, hidden deformity. So long as she stays clothed and covered no one will know that she is the witch's child (or even the witch herself). I could manage to appear normal most of the time ("You never seemed normal to me," says Lydia, "but then I wasn't normal") but trying to put on a normal party in the witch's house defeated me.

My mother, looking around at the plaster flaking off the ceiling, the wallpaper faded to a splotchy brown, thought I was ashamed of the house. I was — but there was a deeper shame.

"You're right, I was crazy to think of having a party here — right off my rocker." She began to cry. I imagined the fight she would have built up to by dinnertime.

"I do my best, I get no help from your father." And then, "I've already called the mothers." She ran upstairs and locked herself in her room.

In the end, we had the party at my grandfather's house. Seven little girls and me, starched damask tablecloth with party paper plates and napkins, a cake with lemon icing and pink candles. Instead of games and prizes, my mother (with money from my grandfather, I'm sure) would treat us all to *The Wizard of Oz*, which was enjoying a second run at the Riviera. My mother did not drive, but from my grandfather's house it was easy enough to walk along Court Street and across the bridge to the centre of town. I felt weightless, without bones, a creature made of air. Even the birthday presents had been things I secretly coveted: a book called *Little Anne of England*, hankies for every day of the week, barrettes, Carmen Miranda paper dolls. We walked downtown in twos; Heather's arm was linked in mine. ("My mother told me to be especially nice to you," Lydia said. "She said you had a troubled background. It made me want to hit you or do something mean but I wanted to see the show.")

Heather ruined my party. About fifteen minutes into the picture, when Glinda points to the feet of the Wicked Witch of the West, Heather began to scream. She screamed and screamed. My mother hissed "Stay where you are, all of you" and hauled Heather up the aisle and into the foyer. We could still hear her screams on the other side of the heavy doors and velvet curtains. Six little girls sobbed in fright; one sat rigid, staring at the screen, trying to get back inside the picture. None of us knew, then, that Heather's mother had not sent her away, that a wall had collapsed on Heather's mother and granny and grandpa while Heather was on her way home from a visit to her aunt and uncle's. That the bomb that killed her mother was a fluke meant for Wolverhampton and not the slums of Birmingham. Heather had seen not the Witch of the West but her mother's body being pulled feet first from the rubble.

"She always wore socks," Lydia said (we were doing our morning promenade before breakfast), "because the house was drafty and her feet were always cold. I didn't actually see her body, you know. I just imagined it."

"Where was your father?"

"I don't ever remember any father. It didn't seem to matter, though. I know I had a long-form birth certificate, the kind they don't use any more, and it came with me to America. It meant I was illegitimate. It may have had my father's name on it, I don't know. After Mrs. Armstrong died I searched through everything — the safety deposit box, dresser drawers, hat boxes, the backs of picture frames. Nothing. They must have burned it — *she* must have — when I was finally adopted. She was very proper."

"You could have got it from England."

"I could have — and now I'm going to. And find my Mum's grave."

"You said 'Mum.' "

"Did I?" She looked away. "Enough of this bourgeois chit-chat, let's go spy on someone. Did you know the poodle lady brought her own olives with her, for *wodka* martinis? Several jars in fact. Maybe there's no poodle; maybe she just gets sloshed and has a personality change, begins to bark."

We resumed our walk around the deck. Many people were asleep in deck chairs, bundled up in heavy wool blankets, like TB patients in old photographs. A young Polish couple held hands, even in their sleep. We had learned that morning that the word for husband was the same as the word for warrior. Lydia was composing a postcard for Søren made entirely of words we had learned so far. Søren is Lydia's third husband. It's like Goldilocks and the

Three Bears, she says. Larry was too cold, Stephen too hot: this one is just right. How about too big or too little, I say, or too hard or too soft?

&

No matter which way you went, to get downtown from our house you had to cross a river. "Over town," my mother said on my last visit, "I always used to walk over town unless the weather was really bad. I think it kept me healthy."

"Would you like to go for a walk now?" I said. "It's a lovely day. Just for five minutes?"

"Oh, I don't think so. I don't think I'm up to it today."

She goes out of her room only to buy a few things at the residents' store (boil-in-a-bag dinners, for example), exchange a large-print book at the library or see if there's any mail. Most of the time she sits in a chair, like the ancient spider she is, storing up venom, thrumming. She writes letters. I expected at least two to be waiting for me in London.

In any event, to get over town you had to cross a bridge, for our town grew and prospered at the junction of the Chenango and Susquehanna Rivers in western New York State. I grew up there but left as soon as possible. Had my childhood been different, less shameful, perhaps I would have loved the area, for that section of the state is very attractive, the valley of the Susquehanna and the soft, undulating hills beyond. I see myself then as a small, bitter child with eyes permanently cast down, humpbacked with grief. Lydia remembers me as sullen and full of self-pity, "But I always envied your hair. You glittered when you walked."

"Like Richard Cory," I said, "the guy in the poem who put a bullet through his head. *He* 'glittered when he walked.' "

The rivers were just something to cross. I never stood in the centre of the bridge, looking down at the Susquehanna, swollen with the spring runoff. I knew that it originated at Otsego Lake, for our grandfather had taken us to Cooperstown once and shown us the plaque commemorating Clinton's feat, and later he gave us *The LeatherStocking Tales*. I knew the river had an Indian name, that was all — a name my sister and I used in our mystical incantations as we made daisy-chains and soothed the dead babies in the family cemetery at Corbettsville.

"Shh, shh, Susquehanna, shh, shh, Susquehanna."

Most of our branch of the Corbett family was buried there, including our grandmother, with a pink granite stone at her head and our grandfather's name and birthdate already chiselled in. There were Fishes as well, and a few other families, including a very old stone, thin and dark, like a piece of stone toast, with the strange name of Waples Hance. An iron plaque said that Waples Hance fought with General Washington at Valley Forge. We liked the cemetery on those hot summer afternoons. The railway tracks were just beyond the fence and below them, Snake Creek, one of the tributaries of the Susquehanna. In those days my mother never talked about her childhood visits to Corbettsville, where her grandparents had a large house with a tower room and her great-granny lived in the carriage house. We must have passed that house hundreds of times but she never said a word.

The great-granny's name was Juliet Bowes

Corbett. "She always wore a piece of lace over her hair, like Queen Mary." Now, years later, Mother digs out old photos. A woman sits upright in a folding chair, a lorgnette pinned to her blouse. She does look a bit like Queen Mary, but perhaps it is the hair and the lace mantilla.

"She was a bit of a mystic," my mother says. "She had visions, I think."

"Visions of what?"

"I don't know. I don't think we children ever asked."

Neither the great-granny, Juliet, nor her son and his wife, Marshall and Elizabeth, liked my grandfather's wife, Grace Cleary. She was an only child whose father was a bookkeeper for Grace Steamship Lines in Brooklyn. She had never been allowed to go to high school because of the coloured children there. Perhaps the Corbetts did not think she was good enough for their only son.

Although she lived in the coach house, my mother says it was Juliet who ruled the roost. I think of mystics' faces as either soft and blurred, slightly out of focus in the here and now, or very intense, rapt, eyes closed and heads thrown back. This woman stared straight at the camera, clear-eyed and capable, Ira Corbett's widow, a woman of property. It is her house that her son and his family have lived in, *her* house the grandchildren visit, *her* father-in-law who broke off this chunk of the village of Conklin and declared it Corbettsville. When I look again at the photograph, taken in July 1906, I see that this is not a Fourth of July celebration but an event that took place on July 23. "Grandmother's birthday" it says, in *my* grandmother's hand.

"She grew prize asparagus, strawberries, melons, things like that. All the relatives came out to get this stuff, although I don't think any of them ever paid her a red cent." The Matriarch.

My mother's grandfather, Marshall Corbett, her son, wanted to start a dynasty. "*Die-nasty*," my mother said, "is that how you pronounce it?"

"For this family it's perfect," I say.

Ira Corbett
1817–1895
Juliet Bowes
His Wife
1826–1912

In the 1906 photograph they are celebrating her eightieth birthday.

"One day the Fish sisters came to call," my mother said. "They were very hoity-toity old maids, very well-to-do. My mother — your grandmother Grace — opened the door."

" 'We are the Fish sisters,' they said.

" 'No thank you,' your grandma said, 'we don't need any fish.' She grew up in Brooklyn, you see, where people peddled all sorts of things from door to door. The Corbetts liked to tell that story on Mother. They were a cruel bunch."

The Fish sisters lie not too far from my grandmother; but their gravestone is much more elaborate and there is an iron chain around the family plot.

But the graves of the adults didn't really interest us back then, only the graves of babies and young children: Baby Grace, 1901–1902; Fred, 1880–1881; Infant, 1882; Sarah, 1 mo.; Sewell,

6 mo.; Amanda, 8; Julia, 6; Baby Love. It was for these we wove the daisy-chains, sang our incantation, "Shh, shh, Susquehanna," patted the lambs, the small headstones, said "There, there." If we got drowsy and our parents hadn't finished planting and pruning we lay on our backs in the sweet grass, holding hands and watching the flocks of white clouds graze in the blue fields of Heaven. We were believers then; we had no doubt that the dead babies were up there somewhere thanking us for our thoughtfulness.

"I want to get one thing straight," my mother said last year. "I don't want to be buried at Corbettsville. What is it the kids say? No way Ho-Say?"

"But Corbettsville is lovely. Even now that the village is more or less gone."

"I *don't* want to be buried there," she says, red-faced and ready to cry with frustration. "I've left my body to Harvard Medical School and I've told them, when they've taken all the spare parts they can use, they can chuck the rest of it out. Just chuck it out in the garbage."

"Even if they wanted to do that, Ma, I don't think they can. It's against the law." I try to keep from laughing — or maybe I'm crying. My mother's body, sans eyes, sans teeth, sans heart, sans everything, in a bag with bloody sponges, used syringes, God knows what. (I've worked on a hospital ward; I have a pretty clear picture of God knows what, even in the eighties, a more enlightened era than when I was an orderly.) "You still have to be buried." I mean "disposed of," but I can't bring myself to say it.

She starts to fuss and asks me to get down her box of important papers, her fairly large box of papers — letters, insurance certificates, Medicare, pension, last will and testament. She pulls this out.

"I thought I gave you a copy of this."

"You did. It's back home in my safety deposit box."

"You probably never read it."

"I probably never did. I assumed it was to be read in the event of your death."

"Your sister's read it."

"Do you want me to read it? I can sit here and read it right now if that will make you more comfortable." I sound like a psychiatrist or social worker, distanced, professional, uninvolved. This woman drives me nuts, but I obviously don't want to think about her death. Cowardy custard, I say to myself and hold out my hand for the will. She has, indeed, left her body to Harvard and has instructed them to do what they like with what's left over.

That night I call my sister from the airport.

"What would Harvard want with the body of a woman as old as Mother?"

"Just that — she's an interesting specimen. The Corbetts are long-lived. It must be genetic, because she certainly doesn't exercise or eat properly, except for bananas — and that's only because she knows she needs potassium."

"Does she know how many bananas she'd have to eat a day to get all her potassium exclusively from bananas? She'd be swinging from the curtain rods!"

"I didn't know that."

"Well now you know."

"She does try."

"In her fashion."

"Well, I can tell you that Harvard will be very interested to get her body."

"Do they know? Or is it going to be a surprise? She'll be left on the doorstep by a messenger?"

"I'm sure they know. You send in a donor card or something."

"Would you mind checking? And also, on what they do with —" I also find this hard to say "— 'the remains.' "

"Maybe if you donate your whole body there aren't any real remains."

"There's got to be. They're not going to use up every scrap of every body that gets given to them."

"They might — with someone who's as interesting as Mother."

"I think you are overestimating their possible interest. What is *really* interesting, down to the last little neuron, is her mind. It's like one of those elaborate mazes — or maybe the original maze, with something as shameful and scary as the Minotaur at the centre. It's a pity they can't go to work on her mind."

My sister is laughing and so am I, even though our laughter is both spiteful and sad. There's just too much water under the bridge — one of our mother's sayings. I hang up, with her promise to check with Harvard about leftovers. I am pretty sure we are still responsible for burial.

Flying westward towards Vancouver, half asleep from a gin and tonic, wine with dinner and the emotional fatigue that always comes after a visit with my mother, I suddenly see her in our old kitchen, her hands and arms leprous with flour, rolling out scraps of leftover piecrust, cutting them into strips and sprinkling them with cinnamon-sugar. As soon as the apple pie is done, she says, we'll pop these in and you girls can have them with a glass of milk. Using up the leftovers. Eat this, in remembrance of me . . .

> Do you ever think as the hearse drives by
> That it won't be long till you and I
> Will both ride out in the big, plumed hack
> And we'll never, never, never ride back?
>
> Do you ever think as you strive for gold
> That a dead man's hand can't a dollar hold?
> We may tug and toil and pinch and save
> And we'll lose it all when we reach the grave.
>
> Do you ever think as you closely clasp
> Your bag of gold with a firmer grasp,
> If the hungry hearts of the world were fed,
> It might bring peace to your dying bed?

Found in the Corbett papers, probably clipped from a newspaper by Merritt Corbett, my grandfather's uncle, a man rich enough to ship his Duesenberg south every winter, by train, so that it would be waiting for the family when they arrived. His mansion on Riverside Drive was bought by the Catholic Church and became Lourdes Hospital. At age seventeen I had my appendix taken out there, scared to death of the Mother Superior, who looked as though she were wearing a large white sailboat on her head, and of the steady drone of prayers over the public-address system. Priests hurried along the corridors carrying little black cases; I couldn't wait to go home.

❧

I am in England for three reasons: One (the one that pays for two and three), to write up an account of the last transatlantic sailing of the Polish ocean liner the *Stefan Batory*, for the Toronto *Globe and Mail* and for *Departures* magazine. I will also do a series of chats about ocean voyages for the CBC. Two, to try and find the missing link between the Robert Corbett (Corbit, Corbet, Corbin) who showed up in Massachusetts around 1660 and the Corbet/Corbetts back in England. When I have done this the tree is complete, and my mother wants it done before she croaks (her words). I have been making her, with the help of my daughters, a three-dimensional family tree as well as the standard one-dimensional sort. It is papier mâché and has everybody's name on an individual apple. Anyone considered a "bad apple" or a "rotten apple" by my mother gets an apple with a worm peeking out or a withered-looking apple. I hope to be able to give it to her for Christmas.

The whole family history thing started as a make-work project for her — "Tell me everything you can remember about the Corbetts and we'll do a family history of some kind, not just a boring enumeration but something livelier." She was reluctant at first but then became obsessed, with sometimes two letters arriving in a single day. Her memory is excellent and she can also recall things that her mother or even her grandparents told her. Very early on I decided that the ancient stuff wasn't as important as what has happened in the last three hundred years, but I'll complete the "tree" if I can.

Three is my secret project, a novel. No one knows about this, not even Lydia, although why I didn't confess to her in our midnight conversations (so satisfying, lying in the dark in our comfortable bunks while the ship sailed on through the darkness) I'll never know. Lydia is very generous — perhaps I was afraid she would immediately want to "help," start talking about agents and contracts when I've only just begun. Perhaps I am afraid I'll fail. Every night I must repeat to myself, I'm a *wry*-ter, I'm a *wry*-ter, I'm a real, real *wry*-ter, the way we used to say I must, I must, I must increase my bust. And every day I must do what the real *wry*-ters do — put aside the outside world and write. The novel will be about my mother.

"Watch out!" my mother said. "Don't run, you'll fall." "Don't talk to strangers." "Don't kiss me, you might get my germs." As I grew up — and away — it seemed to me that my mother saw the world as a sinister and frightening place, and I puzzled over this. Given her unhappy marriage, I could see more easily why she feels she has had a difficult and unrewarding life. But I have always felt that she was unhappy long before she was married and produced ungrateful children. Perhaps she was born unhappy, I thought. Was that possible? To float in the womb in a bath of bile, not benevolence?

And then, on my last visit, she said:

"I saw something."

"When?"

"When I was small. Eight, maybe nine years old."

"What did you see?"

She turned her head away. "I talked about it once and it got me in hot water. Why should I talk about it now?"

"Because I'm curious. You did bring the subject up — that you saw something once, when you were a child."

Her mouth was set in a grim line. "I'm not supposed to get upset."

As soon as I was back home I went to the stationer's and bought two large spiral notebooks and a box of pens. I knew she would tell me eventually and I wanted to be ready. I didn't have long to wait.

❧

In London I stay at a house for overseas graduates, William Goodenough House. I like it not only because it's cheap and safe and comfortable but also because it's in Bloomsbury. I hear voices all around me — Dickens up in Doughty Street, Eliot at the bank where I cash my traveller's cheques, Virginia Woolf and all her friends. Virginia used to live in the same square in a house no longer standing. I was assigned a room in the annex, a pretty room in a new wing. Pale-blue carpet, blue curtains, blue coverlet. Outside a room just down the hall was a daunting collection of milk bottles. Most of this wing consists of flats, for families who are here for a year or more, and I wondered how many children lived — and shrieked — behind that innocent-looking door. I have had my share of children; I know how mothers build up a tolerance to shrieks and shouts, to the point where the noise is actually missed when the children are at school and they have to keep the radio turned on. But I was going to need to concentrate, for I had allowed myself exactly three weeks.

I unpacked my case, put my unopened duty-free bottle of *wodka* (Bison brand) on the top shelf of the cupboard, next to the opium. As we were packing on the afternoon of the last night, Lydia handed me a small, white, paper bag. Inside was a bottle of tincture of opium.

"I almost forgot to give this to you."

"You wonderful person. How did you manage to get it?"

"It wasn't that difficult. Søren said he was going to China and needed some in case of diarrhoea. It isn't as much as you wanted, sorry."

"It will do. I'm going to mix it with Madeira and spices anyway, not take it straight."

"Open it," Lydia said, "and smell."

It smelled like liquorice. It smelled comforting. I like liquorice and anise-flavoured drinks: ouzo, pernod, pastis. I still buy liquorice whips and eat them when nobody's looking. I like to hang them out my mouth and reel them in slowly. I like Bassetts' Allsorts.

"Do you think it was always in a liquorice-flavoured base?" I said.

"Didn't you ever have paregoric when you were a kid? For 'summer complaint'?"

"I don't remember that. I remember a doctor coming to the house but I think it was winter. He had his doctor's bag with him and all the little phials of pills. He poured some into a small envelope. They were oatmeal-coloured and dusty to the touch, like chalk. But they smelled of liquorice."

"I sniffed that stuff and I immediately remembered paregoric — which is what this is: camphorated tincture of opium. I remember that nanny my mother hired giving me some."

"Laudanum."

"I think they're the same thing."

"Lydia, my mother said Grandma was very fond of liquorice, that she said it was her one weakness. I knew she took laudanum but I didn't make that connection until just now." I put some on my tongue.

"Stop that, Charlotte. I don't want you nodding off in some corner with a stupid smile on your face instead of drinking *wodka* up on deck and watching the lights of Cornwall."

"I just wanted to have a taste, to see what it tasted like."

"That's what Eve said."

"Don't worry, I'm saving it for a special occasion."

"What?"

"I don't know yet, but I'll know it at the time."

On the desk, which faced a window overlooking the square, I placed the bits and pieces I had brought with me from home: two flat, grey stones from up Snake Creek, the box of my mother's letters and her will ("I, Frances W. Callahan, being of sound mind"), a small gold pencil, a brass button or coin, I wasn't sure which, my new notebooks with their bright covers and blank pages and my old ones, already filled. An envelope full of old photographs and what I had come to refer to as "the Book of Begats," a genealogy of the descendants of Robert Corbett of Weymouth, Massachusetts. I had only recently received this from a cousin I hadn't seen in thirty years. His father was my mother's brother: they didn't speak. I also had *The Anglo-Saxon Chronicles*, two books on the Normans and the Battle of Hastings and a red brick. There were no letters for me at the desk, no messages and the telephone lines were down. All of a sudden I missed Lydia and the ship. No doubt she felt the same — or would when she finished unpacking at her bed-and-breakfast in Birmingham.

I opened the window and decided to take a little nap before I went exploring, sightseeing among the ruins. Even the papers could wait until later. My tape-recorder wouldn't work but the radio part was fine. I fell asleep to the sound of a chainsaw somewhere nearby and a doctor on a woman's program saying something about *mean-o-pause*. I had just enough energy to reach over and turn him off. Why was there no letter from my mother or any of my daughters? Perhaps my mother was already on her way to Harvard; perhaps my daughters were sitting together drawing up an outline for a Mommy Dearest book. Perhaps I should just go to sleep to the gentle rocking of this lovely bed.

Had the ship sailed already, on the turn of the tide, the Silesian band up on the Promenade Deck playing the Polish national anthem, which sounds so much like a song we used to sing in kindergarten?:

> Down by the station
> Early in the morning
> See the little puffa-bellies
> all in a row
> See the engine driver
> Pull a little lever
> Puff Puff
> Choo Choo
> Off they go.

And off I went, to an uneasy sleep.

Mother couldn't remember the name of the hired girl that summer. In my novel I'll call her Edna.

"Your mother's lying down," the hired girl said. "Hush." Her name was Edna and she was very

pretty in a speckled sort of way, like an egg. Mama had to rest a lot so Edna came to stay with them that summer. They got her from the County Farm. Frances said it must be awful to be an orphan and live at the County Farm, which was just a fancy name for the Poor House, but Mama said it used to be worse, when girls and boys were auctioned off, like slaves, and sold to the highest bidder. Things were more civilized now. Edna was so pale she had to wear a big straw hat when she went out in the sun, even just to hang up the clothes. Her skin was pale blue and covered in tiny freckles. Edna was a Roman Catholic and she told them that if a Catholic cut his finger off, or any part, he had to keep it with him always so it could be buried with him when he died. Otherwise, on Resurrection Day, he wouldn't be made whole.

"What happens if you're not a Catholic?" Frances said.

"I don't know, I only know what happens to Catholics. Protestants is damned anyway, so I guess it doesn't matter."

"Are we Protestants, Edna?"

"You are. Your grandpa can carry on all he likes with his morning prayers and evening prayers and all the rest of it, but it won't do him a lick of good."

Frances wasn't sure. If Catholics were so wonderful, why had Edna been forced to live at the County Farm? Grandpa had built a whole church and he had a big Bible with pages edged in gold. Her name was in there and Betty's and Lawrence's and Mama and Papa and a whole long list of people going way way back.

"You're a liar," Frances said. "You're just the hired girl, you don't know anything. I'm going to

tell my mama what you said. You'll be back at the Poor House before you can say Jack Robinson."

Edna was really frightened, Frances could see that. Good.

"Don't upset your mother, girly, please. She's been so poorly. Go find your sister and we'll go berry-picking. Then we'll come back and make a pie, all right?"

Frances thought about her mother. "All right," she said, "but you better be careful what you say to me."

"That's a good girl; leave your mama to sleep this afternoon. You can help me make her a special supper."

❦

When the tail end of the hurricane struck, my small, maroon tape-recorder — a present from Søren and Lydia after a trip to Hong Kong — flew off the chest of drawers, where I'd left it in order to catch the first sounds of docking in the morning. It missed my head by inches and crashed into the bulkhead beside my bunk. The crossing had been so calm, so amazingly calm for October, said all the old-timers, myself included. Lydia had pronounced it, at the Farewell Banquet, "disappointingly calm." I think she felt a little cheated. We had had lifeboat drill, of course, very early on, and a notice in our cabin told us that when the alarm sounded we were to go to PUNKTZBORNY #1. Lydia thought PUNK-TZBORNY sounded like the name of a Polish heavy-metal band, and during the drill everyone joked and laughed and had pictures taken in their life jackets by the ship's photographer.

The people whose cabin we were in had cancelled the day before sailing. Something to do with their dog biting someone and their being sued. Years from now, will they tell the story to their great-grandchildren, of how Doggy (let's call him Prince) saved their lives by his naughtiness? Petted and pampered, overfed on steak and Gravy Train and Milk-Bone biscuit, Prince will grow fat and lazy and die early of a heart attack. But his memory will linger on. Perhaps they will even have him stuffed or made into a rug to go in front of the fire. A woman I know told me how her grandparents, when they left Norway for the New World, shot their beloved wire-haired terrier and had him made into a rug. She remembers the rug very well, although not the name of the rug.

My grandfather Corbett had a sitting room full of stuffed animals, most of which he had shot: a pheasant, an opossum with its tail like a rope clothesline, a grouse, a deer head over the mantel, even a rattlesnake made into an ashtray. I didn't like them, and his various housekeepers hated to dust them, but none of them had been pets. We buried our pets, as decent people do, or had them "put down" and disposed of for us. I don't think, after all, that they will stuff Prince — a large colour photograph on the mantelpiece will do.

I was wearing a cotton nightdress. If I tumbled into the sea and drowned, the nightdress would most probably ride up around my waist. I would be an indecent corpse and not exactly a mermaid — the old waist isn't what it used to be. Not a mermaid but a merlady, a merwoman, a merperson. A mere corpse if you come right down to it. I wanted to get up and put on my corduroy trousers and a blouse — clothes kept out for tomorrow morning, now this morning, surely, as we didn't go to bed until after one. Lydia was all right; her sensible night-attire on the voyage had been track-suit pyjamas. She would remain discreetly covered (elastic at ankles and cuffs) while I . . . yanked up out of the drink by a grappling hook or discovered by schoolboys, as I bobbed, bobbed, bobbed against a piling. I did not want the pitiless stare of bargers or boys or loungers to feast upon my naked body. I did not want the men from the tabloids shouting to one another, calling for photographers. It would be bad enough being dead. And if we were actually in the Thames, which is where we should have been, but where I doubted we were, I might conceivably bob bob bob all the way to Windsor where the Queen, out walking her Corgis by the riverbank (Lydia says the Queen loves dogs and horses because they do not know she is the Queen), peers into the water and sees a very lumpen, or two very lumpen, bits of the lumpenproletariat — well, even if one can't manage a hat or a curtsey, one still wants to be decently covered up.

"Lydia," I said, "wake up."

Just then I heard a dog bark, somewhere near. This had to be the dog in the Frenchwoman's cabin. The dog was supposed to be up on the Sports Deck (called by Lydia and me the Dog Deck) with all the other animals, but the Frenchwoman kept it in her cabin. It was a toy poodle, and the gossip was that every day it was given a plate of food, money for the dining-room steward left discreetly under a starched white napkin. One day we listened outside the cabin door. The dog gave a couple of yips and the Frenchwoman said "*Tais-toi, tais-toi.*" And when it barked again she said in a fierce whisper, "*Tosca, ça suffice!*" In the mornings there was always an empty champagne bottle in a bucket outside the door. Perhaps the poodle had a postprandial glass of champagne with her mistress every evening, along with certain others we had seen going in at midnight. We didn't really know that it is a toy poodle for we had never seen it. What is the Sherlock Holmes story about the barking dog?

I wondered, if I were to yell at the wind, "*Tais-toi, tais-toi,*" or "*Ça suffice!*" if it would stop its howling. Or what about "Sweet Thames! run softly, till I end my Song"?

In the years when I was a Christian, the years of my youth, before I put away childish things, I remember colouring in a Sunday School picture of Jesus calming the waves. He is standing up in a small boat and the others with him are cowering in fear. I coloured their faces green. Underneath it said:

"And the wind Ceased, and there was great Calm."

However, I can't remember what He said to achieve that end. I do remember feeling quite superior to the Disciples because I learned to row a boat very early in my life, around the age of five. Of course I had never been in a small boat on the ocean; I had not even seen the ocean. I think I coloured their faces green through instinct, rather than experience of storms at sea. When *I* was sore afraid, which was often and had nothing to do with boats, I threw up.

If the *Batory* had been a hotel there would have been a Gideon Bible in the dresser drawer. But it was not a hotel — it had only been pretending to be a hotel. Now we were faced with the truth. A ship is nothing but a wood-and-metal box and we were

about as safe as chickens in a crate on the open
water. What we had been living for the past nine
days was a lie, or at best an illusion. We were cavort-
ing on the back of a wild beast who was only biding
his time, her time. Now he was tired of our tickles
and prickings; now he would show us who's boss.

"Lydia?"

"Hmmh?"

"Lydia, wake up. I think we should get dressed.
The alarm bell is going to ring at any minute. Lydia,
I'm afraid."

"Don't be afraid," said the calm, sepulchral
voice of a person deep in sleep. "It's only the champagne and vodka. Just close your eyes."

"Lydia! We have to get dressed!"

There was a long silence as the room hurtled
back and forth like something being played with by
a giant cat. Then the calm voice spoke again:

"Charlotte, how does one dress for drowning?"

I think we must have still been drunk, for with
great difficulty we got up, cursing and swearing as
we dropped things or banged our arms and legs. We
put on our party dresses — Lydia's a silver lamé
skirt and top, mine a thin red wool with large
buttons down the front. I held my small torch while
she put on her make-up; she did the same for me. It
was impossible to write any last words, and the tape
part of the tape-recorder no longer worked, so we
each scrawled "love you" in lipstick and put the
papers in a plastic bag. Each promised the other that
should she survive she would carry messages to the
loved ones.

We sat all the rest of the night with our warm
blanket and our life jackets at the ready but the
alarm bell never rang. We sang songs.

Old Aunt Jemima, how's your Uncle Jim?
Down in the duck pond learnin' how to
    swim
First he does the side-stroke, then he does
    the crawl
Now he's under water doin nothin' at all
        Glug Glug

After remaining silent all night the public-address system began to broadcast announcements, first in Polish, then in English. "We would like to inform all passengers. . . ." Breakfast, which had been pushed forward for the projected early docking, was now set back to 8 a.m. first sitting, 9 a.m. second. "You always ask for second sitting," I told Lydia, showing off. "That way you aren't rushed by the dining-room stewards and can linger over your coffee and dessert." We had asked for second sitting, no smoking, preferably with some Poles. It appeared that Poles either smoked or stayed together. We were put at a table for six, with three strange men and a widow who had at least married a Pole. None of them drank — at least until the Captain's Farewell Dinner, when Lydia and I went wild and said we would treat everyone to champagne. They had been a pretty grim bunch until then. The widow danced on the table. She was a heavy woman with exquisite ankles, like a piece of Victorian furniture.

Now passengers were requested to stay off the open deck. Passengers were requested to be careful of stairs and sills. Ladies were requested not to wear high heels. Parents were requested to keep careful watch over their children. No explanation was offered for the tempest in the night. The wind had ceased its howling but was still very strong, as we discovered when we made the mistake of opening the porthole a few inches and were pushed right off Lydia's bunk, where we had both been kneeling. Lydia, who had already changed back into sensible clothes, had to go and find our bedroom steward to help us shut it again. He came back a few minutes later with coffee and biscuits.

"Little Tongues with Jam," Lydia said, which was what they had been called on the menu. "Little *langues des chats*," she said. "Up until this morning, somewhere in the Thames, I had never seen the connection between language and tongue, although God knows I've said 'My mother tongue is' often enough at receptions."

"My mother-in-law used to cook tongue, right from scratch, as it were. She'd bring it home wrapped in butcher's paper and simmer it with peppercorns and bay leaves and vegetables. Then she'd skin it and serve it cold."

"So this was not your mother tongue but your mother-in-law's tongue."

"Very funny. The Europeans are so much less squeamish than we are, they'll eat anything: tongue, kidneys, sweetbreads — whatever they are — hearts. She also made stuffed heart."

"Blood puddings," Lydia said.

"They were on the menu the first time I sailed for England. The steward kept threatening to bring us some."

"I think I had them as a child."

"No wonder you're so strange. They sound like something made from leftover placentas. By the way, in my last talk with Mother she mentioned

Baby Grace, my grandmother's favourite child, who only lived six months. Then she said there was another baby. 'A still life, is that what you call it?' she said."

"Your mother amazes me. Not Mrs. Malaprop at all."

The sun was shining and the sea — the river — was gently heaving in long rolls scalloped with foam. It looked like moiré silk. It was a strange colour, a yellowish silver, and as we proceeded towards Tilbury we saw freighters and smaller vessels broadside to the shore. The water was full of debris.

" 'Sweet Thames! run softly,' " Lydia said. "Did you really think we might drown?"

"Yes. And I kept hoping I'd be brave."

"I sometimes think," she said, "that bravery is simply lack of imagination. Courage anyway — physical courage. Bravery probably has a moral component. Well, we'll be able to dine out on the story for weeks to come. I wouldn't have missed it for the world."

In the end we docked at noon. The sightseeing tour of London, for those going on to Rotterdam and Gdynia, had been cancelled so that the ship could sail with the tide. The baggage in the customs shed was piled up any old way, Bs and Cs and Js and Ss side by side with Ws and Ls. The busy porters told us there were no trains running from Tilbury to London but the company had ordered buses. There were precious few trains running anywhere, they said, except to the north. Worst storm in living memory. On the south coast, where I wanted to go the next day, millions of people had awakened at 3 a.m. to find themselves in the middle of a nightmare.

"D'you know Sevenoaks, love?" one of the porters said to me.

"It's in Kent somewhere, isn't it?"

"Right. Bloody One-oak it is now. Thousands of trees down — London's a mess. You'll see."

I felt a little better hearing all this; I was not getting old and neurotic — that really was an awful storm. I had been right to be afraid of that dreadful howling.

❧

I woke up from my nap feeling as though I had been wrapped in wet cotton wool. Not jet-lag this time, but a reaction to the excitement (and the *wodka*) of the night before. The first thing I wanted was a bath. Our "superior" cabin on the Boat Deck ran only to a shower. The soap was the size of two dominoes stacked on top of one another and good only as a souvenir. "SBS," it said, "SZCZUCZYN." It smelled like laundry soap. We had, thank goodness, each brought a new bar of very expensive, smelly soap, but we missed a bath. Lydia decided she must have a bath before the Farewell Party and descended to B Deck in search of a stewardess. Passengers on B Deck had told us there were lovely baths to be had below. One informed the stewardess, who unlocked the bathroom, drew your bath and ten minutes later knocked on your door with an enormous bath towel over her arm. One sat in the steamy comfort of a huge old-fashioned ship's bathtub while not too many feet below fishes and whales frolicked in the icy waters of the Atlantic. One felt united with all creation and arose, dripping and pink-cheeked, renewed and refreshed.

Lydia came back fuming. "She says it's not possible."

"All booked up?"

"No. We're on the wrong deck."

"We can't have a bath because we're on the Boat Deck?"

"That's right. I even resorted to bribery. You would have thought I'd offered her a dead toad. 'You have privates,' she said. 'That's just the point,' I wanted to say, but I know she meant private facilities. It seems all the other cabins on this deck have baths, not showers. We are the poor relations of the Boat Deck; the others probably think we smell."

"Maybe that's why the dog lady didn't invite us to her private cocktail parties. Tosca would have sniffed at our privates and embarrassed everyone."

So in Mecklenburgh Square I luxuriated in my first bath since leaving Canada, stayed a long, long time until there was not a discreet but an irate knocking on the door, a pounding, and a very *academic* voice calling out, "May I remind you that there are others waiting to use the bath!"

When I finally emerged from the bathroom I came face to face with "the others," a small woman in a dressing gown. This was obviously the pounder. Everything about her was sensible — her haircut, her washable terry-cloth slippers, her navy corduroy bathrobe, her leatherette sponge bag. I tried to guess what she was doing here in London — it's a game I play when I see someone who is so obviously a type. Sometimes I am quite surprised at how wrong my guess is. Perhaps this woman is not working on the conditions of distressed gentlewomen in the eighteenth century at all but a major — and brilliant — new deconstructionist analysis of the plays of Oscar Wilde. Nevertheless, I was glad I was wearing my Japanese kimono with dragons and chrysanthemums and that my feet were bare. My toenails were shiny with red nail polish, "Wet and Wild." Lydia and I had done each other's toenails before the Farewell Dinner.

"Sorry," I said, and she hmph'd past me and bolted the bathroom door.

I dressed and went out to see if any phones were working nearby, and also to have a look at the damage in the immediate neighbourhood. The private gardens in the square itself ("Apply to Receptionist for key") were temporarily closed. Through the wrought-iron fence I could see workmen already busy with the clearing up, the gathering of branches, the sawing of felled trees. It was strange to hear country sounds here in the centre of London. The pavement was covered with branches as well, and sodden brown leaves. I picked my way around them, around the square itself, along Mecklenburgh Street and out into Guildford Street, where I stopped in front of the gate to Coram's Fields. "In Coram's Fields the children go:" that phrase came to me; this was a playground for children, and no adult would be admitted unless accompanied by a child. Today the gate was shut, the playground closed "until further notice." I could see why. A huge tree had come down — "come up" might be more accurate — in the centre of the playground, right on top of a little round-about. It was a giant of a tree, and lilliputian workmen in blue overalls were roping and measuring it almost as though it were alive — something they had captured — and they were cowboys or big-game hunters, not members of the Borough of

Camden Parks Department. They were calling to
one another about the way to cut it up. Perhaps they
would go through some ceremony — eat the heart
first before they began lopping off head and limbs. I
stood in a little crowd of adults-in-the-company-of-
children temporarily barred from their rightful
garden and agreed, yes, it was a blessing the tree
came down at night when the playground was
closed. I couldn't help thinking that here we had a
kind of reversal of the situation in Eden: the tree
fell, not man. Nevertheless, the result was the
same: we were all shut out.

"What does 'temporarily' mean?" said a small
boy in short pants and a blazer.

"For a little while," said his mum, and led him
away. They would have to find something else to do
on this Friday afternoon.

On the other side of Guildford Street a mother
was pushing a child in a wheelchair. A young, dark-
haired nurse, who looked like the Cherry Ames,
Student Nurse of my girls' books, walked to the side
and slightly behind, holding an intravenous drip.
The child wore a pink woollen cap pulled down low
over her forehead. I say "her" because the cap was
pink, but really it was impossible to tell — the face,
except for the eyes, was completely covered in bandages. Her head was at an impossible angle, like a
bird with a broken neck, and her legs didn't look
right either. She must have been a patient at the
Institute for Sick Children or at Great Ormond
Street Hospital, just a block away. At lunchtime
and in the evenings young doctors and nurses fill
the pubs on Lamb's Conduit Street and, on nice
evenings, spill out onto the pavements. One of
these pubs is supposedly Dickens' favourite pub,

The Lamb. The street is named for a man, not the children, but the name is singularly appropriate as the street starts directly across from the front gates of Coram's Fields. In the eighteenth century, cows would have been grazing on either side of the street. From here on it was country.

> Little Lamb, who made thee?
> Dost thou know who made thee?
> Gave thee life and bid thee feed . . .

What happens to orphans these days? Where do they go? This was once a place famous throughout the United Kingdom, maybe even the world. Hogarth designed the children's uniforms; Handel donated his manuscript of the Messiah; Dickens created a sad and bitter composite child from the orphans he saw on Sundays in the chapel. All because a retired sea-captain named Thomas Coram saw babies thrown away on dung heaps and resolved to do something about it, bullied and badgered and cajoled until he had a royal charter for the first Foundling Hospital in Britain.

Not the first in the world: that was started by Pope Innocent III. After the fishermen who fished the Tiber complained of catching too many babies in their nets.

I waited in the telephone queue for a while then gave up and went over to Marchmount Street, where there was an Indian restaurant I liked. It was cheaper to eat at London House, in the square, but I felt too tired to be sociable, to ask people where they were from and what they were working on. It was still early and the restaurant was nearly empty. I ordered my favourite, Sag Gosht, only I said it wrong, thinking of other things. Lydia says Freudian slips are very important. I would have to tell her about this one. "I'll have a half-pint of lager," I said to the waiter, "a small dish of steamed rice and the Sad Ghost."

ॐ

In the fifth grade, after Christmas, Heather was skipped to 6B. She had shot up and was the tallest kid in the class, taller than the tallest boy. Mr. Armstrong, after suffering two heart attacks, died in his sleep. Mrs. Armstrong became a vegetarian and was considered very strange. She wore only black and devoted herself to good causes. This seemed to involve sitting at her desk and writing endless letters on heavy, cream-coloured stationery. The usual birthday party took place, and this time I went. We were even allowed to ride up and down on a seat that was attached to the banister and had moved Mr. Armstrong from one floor to another after he was forbidden to climb stairs. Heather had new friends, sixth-grade friends, who talked about boys and getting the Curse and how their breasts hurt.

A girl named Carla Van Horner gave me something to eat she said would taste really good. It smelled like onions and I said I didn't want it. "It's delicious," she said, "go ahead. You have to chew the whole thing."

"Eat it," Heather said, "or I won't be your friend any more." I put it in my mouth and chewed hard. Then I threw up.

My mother said, "Daisy Armstrong gets more and more strange. What did she serve you anyway? You smell like an Italian."

I didn't know what it was called; my mother

never used anything as exotic as garlic. Most of the mothers didn't. I wouldn't have told on anyone, even if I had known the name. What would have been the point? And when school let out in June, Heather went away to a different summer camp this time and then to boarding school. We lost touch. I don't think I saw her again until my first day of college when, late and humiliated (I hadn't known to change trains at Springfield and sat in an empty compartment on a siding until a train man came along and told me I should have got on the train to Northampton fifteen minutes before, now I would have to wait two hours), I walked into Chapin House and stood uncertainly in the hall, looking around for the housemother.

There were girls everywhere: girls lying on their stomachs in the enormous living room, reading sections of *The New York Times*; girls chatting with one another on sofas; two sets of girls playing bridge; a girl playing the piano, head down, intent upon the keys. It was like a hive of girls, all of them pretty, all of them self-assured, all with friends. The place gave off a contented hum.

A girl near the archway turned and saw me.

"You must be Charlotte," she said, coming forward. "Where've you been? They were about to call your parents."

"I missed the connection," I said, "and had to wait."

The hum stopped as the room looked carefully at the new girl. Everyone called out greetings and welcomed me, except for the girl playing the piano. There was something about the back of her head, her neck. I went closer.

"Heather?" I asked, not sure.

The girl whirled around.

"Heather is at its loveliest just now in the Scottish Highlands!" She jumped up and grabbed my arm above the elbow. She pinched me, hard.

"Good heavens, it's little Charlotte." ("My name is *Lydia*," she whispered, "and my hair is naturally this colour. Understand?" Another hard squeeze. I nodded.)

"We were in grade school together," she announced to the room. "Mrs. Jenks told us you were coming but somehow I just didn't make the connection. How long has it been? Eight years? Seven years? A long time anyway. I'll show you your room; you can meet everyone in a few minutes, at dinner. Did you bring a napkin ring?"

I nodded. I had borrowed one from my grandfather.

"Good," she said, "good." Keeping a firm hand on my arm she led me upstairs to my room and shut the door behind us.

"Do you still throw up when you're upset?" she said. "Because if you do, maybe I should take you down the hall first, to the john."

"Not so much any more."

"Okay. There's fifteen minutes until dinner. We have to talk."

❧

From the *Atlantic*, July 1988

In the space of eight hours, between midnight and daybreak on October 16, 1987, Kew, one of the oldest botanical gardens in the world, was torn apart. A storm of a severity essentially unheard of in Britain swept in from the southwest, and its winds cut like Paul Bunyan through woodlands and across the width of Britain.

An ill wind
The axe of God

Just when I am looking for inspiration along comes Nature and with divine afflatus blows down half a million trees between bedtime and breakfast. Notice how the storm becomes a foreigner, a mythological Yankee, not a British storm at all. Barbaric. Hurricane Len.

The only orphanage in our town — or the only one I knew about — began in the mid-1800s as a small wooden building at the corner of Leroy and Oak Streets. By the time I was growing up this had been replaced by a spacious red-brick building with extensive grounds. This was St. Mary's Orphan Asylum, run by the Sisters of St. Joseph. About one hundred orphans lived there and went to St. Pat's parochial school when they were old enough. Sometimes on our way to the doll hospital, where we took our babies to be restrung and repaired, we saw a serpentine of children walking two by two with a black-and-white nun at their head. Because I was fascinated by the eyes on my dollies, and was always poking away at them, trips to the doll hospital usually meant I had once again poked too hard and the eyes of one of my babies had fallen back inside her head. Mother hurried us past St. Mary's.

I gathered from my mother that all orphans were Catholic. It had something to do with the Pope. "What about Heather?" I said, but she said that was different. Heather was an orphan of the storm in Europe, a different thing altogether. She had had loving parents but they were dead. Orphans were unwanted children — children left in baskets on the doorsteps of churches, or even in garbage cans or cardboard boxes. A few lucky ones were adopted but most went to the orphanage and then to the County Home out in the valley.

Moses was a baby in a basket; I had coloured him at Sunday School. I gave the Pharaoh's daughter a blue-violet gown and red hair.

After we had been on one of these excursions to the doll hospital I would lie in bed, listening to the angry voices of my parents rise up through the hot-air registers, and wonder if it was really so terrible to be an orphan. Look at Lydia, she'd done all right. Look at Moses. God seemed to favour orphans.

"God!" Lydia said, when I confessed this to her in the darkness of our cabin. "I missed my mother so. I missed the neighbours, the markets, the voices. I missed my granny hugging me. I even missed the horrible privy we shared with other families. I missed all the stuff I couldn't remember after the bombing! And those kids you saw — they probably had no idea who their parents were; they'd spend their lives wondering why they were abandoned. You don't know what you're talking about, Charlotte; I hate that kind of self-pitying romanticism."

"I'm only telling you what I thought then. You didn't have a monopoly on pain, nor did they. You didn't hear your parents quarrel every evening after dinner, listen to the threats and counter-threats and sometimes screams and broken glass. I would lie awake wondering if they were going to kill one another, and if they did what I would say when I called my grandfather and then the police. I never saw my sister doing this, for some reason, even though she was older and had more presence of mind. It was always me."

"Self-dramatization."

"Maybe." Given her censorious mood I didn't tell her that I even thought about what I would wear to the police station when they took us down for questioning and what flavour I would order when they gave us ice cream to comfort us. Maple-walnut.

I said that we made our trips to the doll hospital in order to get our babies restrung. All of a sudden I hear my mother saying to me, about herself as a small child, "I was too high-strung and so was your Aunt Betty." Circumstances, or heredity, like a bad doll-maker or a naughty child, pulls our elastic bands too tight until we're in danger of snapping and flying apart. "Your aunt went to pieces," my mother said to me. "She tried to do too much on too little money and she cracked up."

In our fourth year at college both Lydia and I enrolled in a course in Anglo-Saxon language and literature. We had never really become friends in my first two years. She wanted very much to be different from all the other girls — wore full skirts instead of Bermuda shorts like everybody else, swore, cut classes, wrote poetry on such intimate subjects as finger-fucking, refused to knit squares for refugees, got drunk on Mountain Day. I wanted nothing more than to conform, to never stand out in any crowd, never say or do anything that would call attention to myself. My junior year at a Scottish university changed all that, but I was still wary of Lydia when I saw her again in the autumn of 1957. She had spent her junior year at the Sorbonne, now wore black skirts and stockings and sprinkled her sentences with French swear words. She let it be known she was no longer a virgin.

"How was Scotland?" she said the first day. "Were you able to get under any of those kilts?"

She rarely called me Charlotte. It was Harlot or Harlotta or Lotte Lena or Vacant Lottie. We were taking some of the same classes and we lived in the same residence but we weren't exactly friends. "Lydia" wasn't exactly friends with anyone.

"I liked making you angry," she said years later. "I guess I despised what you were trying to turn yourself into. Or maybe I was just mean and spiteful. I was pregnant at the beginning of that term and didn't know what to do about it. I needed to lash out at somebody — I wanted you to get mad at me and yell so that I could have a legitimate excuse for a really good cry." She smiled at her choice of words. "I wasn't really so sophisticated after all."

She went to New York one weekend, all by herself, and had the abortion. The nurse made her leave when she was barely awake and she stood at the foot of the steep stairs, in the rain, trying desperately to flag a taxi, blood running down the insides of her legs and into her heavy black stockings. At the beginning of the second term she dropped out of school to marry a poet from Yale, Larry, husband number one. In a strange way I missed her. We had both discovered that we liked studying the language and literature of that old, far-off world. Lydia, who had beautiful handwriting, copied out "The Wanderer" and "The Seafarer" and had them framed for my birthday. We felt that the *Beowulf* poem, with its emphasis on a powerful female as well as a male, might, like the *Iliad* and the *Odyssey*, have been written by a woman. Lydia wrote a bizarre paper on Grendel and Hamlet which she turned in just before Christmas vacation. It had to do with mother love — Grendel's dam being a better mother than Gertrude or something like that — and was pretty far out in its thinking. She told me she was considering going on to graduate school and doing some work on women as avengers. Then she met Larry at a house party in New Hampshire.

"I knew by then I didn't have the talent to be a good poet," she said, "nor the patience or humility to be merely adequate. Larry was good — I could see that right away. We seemed to like the same things. He thought my past was romantic. He said he could see in my face that I was a woman who had suffered. Charlotte, nobody had ever called me a *woman* before. Nobody had ever said they could see that I had suffered. And I thought I could care for him, be his helpmate — all the stuff Smith was really programming us to be."

"Wives of great men oft remind us, we can make our lives sublime . . ."

"Exactly. I told him about my trust fund on the second day."

"Oh Lydia. He must have felt like one of God's chosen."

"He already felt like that, my dear. What he saw in me was material plus material goods."

"Plus somebody to wash his socks."

"Yes, that too."

"Did you love him?"

"I persuaded myself that I did. But the sex was never any good. After we had sex he would get up immediately, take a shower, brush his teeth, put on his dressing gown and go to his desk. I was both hurt and flattered. Maybe this was what great men were like. Then when his book came out — well, I never went back to the apartment after the book came out. Just got on the train to New York and left everything behind."

I remember that book very well, although I can't remember the title. The poems could never be called intimate. They were detached, clinical, quite terrifyingly so. *Glumdalclitch*. Yes, that was the name. Larry describes Lydia's body and her physical actions and reactions as though he is Gulliver married to a Brobdingnagian. Every mole, every smell or excretion — it's all there. He won a National Book Award for those poems; Lydia won a nervous breakdown.

"Fortunately," she said, "before I broke down completely I managed to get to the lawyer who handled my trust fund and annul my will. I was so sure I was going to die — from shame if not from suicide — and I didn't want Larry to share in my estate. The lawyer was very nice — doddery, but nice — kept sending his secretary out to make more tea — but he did say I should name somebody, or some institution, as my beneficiary."

"Did you leave it all to Smith?"

"Oh no. I left it all to you." She smiled. "Of course that was all changed long ago. And anyway, you've done all right without it."

Lydia never contacted me when she was in hospital, or later, from the convalescent home she went to somewhere on Long Island. I wonder if she saw anyone at all, except for nurses and doctors and other patients, during those bleak months. Those were not the days when it was possible to get a divorce on the grounds of mental cruelty but somehow she managed it. Money, I suppose, but I don't begrudge her that. It's strange to think that if Lydia had died during that year I would have been heiress to a million dollars. All that bread, all those doughnuts. Would my life have been any different? No, Lydia says. I would have given it to my parents in the hopes that the money would make them happy and when this didn't work I would have blamed myself.

On the day that Lydia left the book party and boarded the train for New York I was on a ship going back across the ocean to England.

❧

My grandfather had a stereopticon and a box of views. On rainy afternoons at his summer camp in the Adirondacks I would sit for hours looking at these pictures, sliding the crosspiece up and down until the view suddenly jumped out at me, became three-dimensional, and the Champs-Élysées or the Grand Canal or the Appian Way invited me to enter: come in, come in, we are real. Grandpa had never been to Europe, but he said his parents went once, with his youngest sister Mabel, and did the Grand Tour. This must have been the time she danced with the Prince of Wales. My grandfather sat in his large leather easy chair, fiddling with the radio, which promised, on its shortwave band, news from London, Paris, even, I seem to remember, Cairo. Because of the mountains all we usually managed to get was Utica, New York. Whether those afternoons had anything to do with it or not, I don't know, but when I was fifteen I wrote away to such giants as the United Fruit Company and Cunard, to see if I couldn't get taken on as a stewardess on a freighter or passenger liner. It surprises me now that these companies bothered to reply, but they did, very courteously, regretting the fact that I was too young or that I would have to join the San Francisco Cooks and Stewards Union and that would cost a lot of money. Perhaps it was just that I wanted so badly to get away and the life of a stewardess seemed glamorous and exciting. Even the radio seemed to push me in that direction. "I'd like to get you," Frankie sang, "on a slow boat to China."

One day, after I had been a stewardess for a while and proved my worth, I would let a few tendrils of my beautiful hair escape from underneath my kerchief and some wealthy young coffee-planter would look at me and smile: "You have a smudge on your nose," he would say, and reach up with a perfectly manicured finger to wipe it off. That would be the start. I had read several historical novels about such things as glove marriages and was sorry I lived in such a restricted time and place. The word "Europe," the word "abroad," beckoned to me the way train whistles called me on autumn nights. I felt about travel the same way I felt about sex: excited, frightened, anxious to get going.

It wasn't long. By scrimping and saving (working summers in the state mental hospital, getting scholarships at college), I gathered together enough money. I think even the D.A.R. kicked in with a few dollars. My mother, through Robert of Weymouth, is a Daughter of the American Revolution. My parents actually encouraged me in this adventure — I think I was meant to do their living for them. My grandfather told me never to sleep with a man unless I was willing to marry him. He laughed at my embarrassment and gave me fifty dollars for emergencies. I didn't know the girl I was travelling with very well — it had been her idea, really, to find a university that would accept us for one year, so that our parents would agree to us going so far away. Our college had a junior year abroad but I couldn't afford that and didn't want to be so chaperoned. I could imagine a bunch of girls, like a gaggle of geese, being shown the Bernini Doors, the Tate Collection, the Jeu de Paume. Living all together somewhere, "never being allowed to explore the back alleys of experience," as I put it to myself. I was nineteen years old, a virgin and ready to meet Mr. Right or Mr. Wrong, whoever showed up first.

Everybody — nearly everybody — travelled to Europe by ship in those post-war years. We could have sailed on one of the Holland-American ships, the student ships, but that was not what we wanted either. I found something else, a Furness-Withy ship, the *Nova Scotia*. Boston, Halifax, St. John's, Liverpool: the smallest passenger ship that crossed the North Atlantic.

When we arrived in Boston we were told that the longshoremen were on strike, but that the ship would sail on time if passengers would carry cabin baggage on for themselves. A photographer from the Boston *Globe* approached and asked if I would mind carrying my suitcase up the gangway while he took a photo from above. "College girls forced to carry own luggage during walk-out," or something like that. I actually went up and down four or five times before he was satisfied with the result, other passengers glaring at me as they were held up at the bottom of the gangway. But as a result I, who am not much of a picture taker, have a five-by-eight glossy of myself setting off on my first great adventure. I am wearing a sort of pilgrim get-up, a black cotton dress with a large white linen collar. My hair looks as though I had peroxided it in front, but I don't remember doing that, and I am wearing far too much "Fire and Ice" lipstick. My half-slip, true to its name, has worked its way down some time during the photography session so that several inches of lace border are showing beneath the hem of my dress. Never mind: I have only to look at that photo and my stomach starts to churn with excitement. I'm smiling up at the photographer and my back is turned resolutely against my family, the City of Boston, the Commonwealth of Massachusetts, the United States of America in general, and I suppose, AUTHORITY.

I did not know then that somewhere around 1660 a man named Robert Corbett had sailed into Boston Harbour on a ship that would have taken anywhere from forty-seven to one hundred and thirty-eight days to cross from England, and established himself in a place called North Purchase. I am his great-great-great-great-great-great-great-great-great-granddaughter, and, as I have said, the ostensible reason I was on TS/S *Stefan Batory* on the night of October 16, when the hurricane struck the south of England, was to try and find out more about him, where in England he sailed from if possible, the name of the ship he sailed on, and, most importantly, why he came. No one, in the seventeenth century, crossed what is still in the twentieth considered the most dangerous stretch of ocean in the world for pleasure. He came as an immigrant, that is understood, but was he fleeing? Were his reasons political or personal? Was he a Cavalier or

Roundhead or neither? A younger son with no prospects, an adventurer, a bastard? 1660 was a pivotal year in British history; this fact might make my task more difficult. In 1675 and '76 Robert Corbett was a soldier in King Philip's War and saw service on the Connecticut River, but this does not necessarily prove that he was friendly or unfriendly to the idea of kings. King Philip was an Indian, son of Chief Massasoit, and Robert fought against him.

I didn't know about any of this in 1955; had I known I doubt I would have cared. So why did I care now? Would my life be changed in some way if I found out the reasons for his leaving England? I don't believe in biological determinism; if I did I might slit my throat. And I really don't care whether we are descended from noble blood or not. Blood's blood. Being bopped on the shoulder — Arise, Sir Knight — or granted vast estates doesn't make the blood better, although there are those who would like to think so. Mother would like to know, but so what? I could make up any old thing about this Robert — the missing link — and she would never know. *She* wants to know who he was and *I* want to know why he left. That's a completely different thing, although the second depends upon the first. Perhaps I think that if I find out why he left I'll know why I'm so happy when I'm on a journey, why I devour books by intrepid women like Mary Kingsley and Isabella Bird, why, for me, "getting there" really is half the fun. Not by airplane. Never by airplane except of necessity. Did anyone ever send you flowers when you left on a holiday by plane? I mean a bouquet, not an orchid. Telegrams, chocolates, fancy soap? When I am over the mid-Atlantic on a plane I don't even think about it, except to wish we would hurry up and get there. This generation of travellers has missed out on something special.

In the old days there were people — especially women — who spent their declining years sailing on the same ships, over and over. Some of them no doubt died at sea. The stewardess would knock gently, then enter with the morning tea. The old lady does not respond to the usual greeting. The stewardess quickly draws the curtains, bends down and then goes to fetch the doctor. The captain performs a short and tasteful service; the passenger, lying in a canvas shroud, is gently lowered over the side. The resident orchestra plays her favourite hymn.

> All things bright and beautiful
> All creatures great and small

I have been on two ships where someone died, and the body was not sent over the side; perhaps the family was going to meet it at the other end. The body was put in the deep-freeze.

"Now the milk will go off, worse luck," said our steward.

"Why will the milk go off?" said one of the children, I forget which one.

"Because that's what they take out to make room for the body. Drink up, lovey, while it's still fresh."

In the days of sail the sailmaker did a "nose-stitch" after the body was in the canvas. One firm stitch joining nose and canvas — so that the body wouldn't slide to the bottom of the sack. In the days before refrigeration; in the days when there wasn't any choice. Down to Davy Jones's Locker. Full fathoms five.

In 1955, when the last ropes were unwound from the capstans and a satisfying stretch of water appeared between the pier and the ship, I felt as though I too had been set free from America and the great burden of my parents' misery. It crossed my mind that if I was lucky, if I "played my cards right," an expression my mother often used although she never touched a card (the games my mother plays are not listed in the book of Hoyle), I might never be coming back. This idea filled me with such intense joy I burst into tears and saw the receding port of Boston and the white handkerchiefs of our waving friends through a watery blur. I was to return to America one more time, in fact, but that day marked the beginning of my real life. Everything up until then didn't count. Or so I thought.

Even the awful old Fish sisters had to admit that Mama had brought her girls up right. Their elocution was so good they could have gone on the stage. Frances was often called upon to recite "The Death of Little Nell," which moved everyone to tears. "The Death of Little Nell" was one of the pieces in the Elocution book, second series.

The ladies all wept and then they all had raspberry vinegar and big scalloped buttermilk cookies baked by the hired girl that morning.

As for the boys — Lawrence and his cousin Marshall — they were allowed to run wild in Corbettsville. That summer they came to breakfast in their underwear and straw hats. Edna said, "You boys go back and put your clothes on," but Papa and Mama had already breakfasted so they paid no attention. Sometimes the boys didn't even say grace. Frances was sure that if they got struck by lightning they'd go straight to Hell.

They ate towers of pancakes, calling for more butter, more syrup.

"Are those boys giving you any trouble?" Mama said.

"They're just boys," Edna said, laughing. "You know what boys are."

❀

"Were there ever snakes in Snake Creek, Mother?"

"I don't remember any snakes but there was an eel-weir."

Lawrence and his cousin came upon the little girls playing by the creek, making posies.

"You girls, look what we've got!"

They unbuttoned their flies, something dreadful hanging out, with teeth, with eyes. "Touch it," they said, "touch it or we'll push you in the creek."

She abandoned her sister, the dollies and ran, screaming, towards the house. Mama, Mama!

Edna met her at the door, "Hush hush your Mama isn't well, she's lying down. Don't come around here with that racket." Then, "Where's your little sister?"

Betty found, they clung to Edna; Frances told.

That night, from the woodshed, the sound of beatings. They put their hands over their ears.

Lawrence and Cousin Marshall came into the bedroom late at night. Out of the darkness they hissed at her — "We'll get you for this, you stupid tattle-tale."

Frances kept her eyes shut in case they did it again, in case they came right up to the bed and made her touch it.

"I did a dreadful thing," my mother said, "I've never forgiven myself. I left Betty to fend for herself and I ran and ran. It was only an eel, and dead at that. I was stupid to be taken in by them. I think Betty started to go queer right after that."

"Did they make her touch it?"

"I don't know. She wouldn't say. All she said was 'I hate you, I hate you' when the hired girl and I went back for her. I was her older sister and I let her down."

"It's understandable."

"Is it?"

"Did you tell on the boys?"

"Of course. And that was a mistake too. My father took them out to the woodshed, separately, and gave them a licking. After that they never missed a chance to torment me."

"Sounds pretty normal to me," I said, brotherless, but imagining always that this was what brothers did.

"Oh no, it wasn't. We weren't a normal family. No way Ho-Say."

☸

When I got back to Goodenough House on Friday evening the receptionist stopped me to say I did have some mail and some messages, they had been put in the wrong box. I hurried to my room. Letters from family ("Dear Mom," "Dearest *Marmie*," "Hi Mum"), a letter from an English friend, a note from the reference library at the Greenwich Maritime Museum. A message to call Lydia in the morning. I was loved after all, and thought about. I read the letters twice, had a shot of vodka in my toothbrush glass and fell asleep to the strangest dream.

❧

I dreamt of trees, Disney trees like the ones in *Snow White*, whose knotholes became eyes and round, toothless mouths. The dream was full of blue smoke and twice I woke up thinking Goodenough House was on fire. I am used to sleeping in strange beds but I was overstimulated and my ankle throbbed. I wondered if there was an all-night chemist's in this area. The first time I ever went to a chemist's in England was in 1955, on a walking trip with my roommate, before we went up to Scotland. In Stratford-upon-Avon I had terrible cramps, absolutely debilitating. I couldn't remember ever having anything like this and the landlady in the place where we were staying suggested I trot along to the chemist. I was embarrassed to tell him what was wrong but I managed it by concentrating on the second button of his white coat. "One moment please," he said, just like a telephone operator. A fat lady was sitting on a chair, drinking down some milky-looking stuff the chemist's assistant had handed her. Did anyone ever take their medicine right there, at a drug-store back home? Was I going to do the same?

The man in the white coat came back with a small round box of red-lacquered cardboard. He handed it to me and asked if I had an NHS number. I didn't know what he was talking about. He charged me five shillings and I took the box away with me. On the top he'd affixed a white label, on which he had written FEMALE COMPLAINTS. His penmanship was impeccable.

❧

I woke up late the next morning, the smell of woodsmoke coming through the open window. This is a smell I have always loved, spicy, autumnal. People back home don't burn piles of leaves anymore the way they did when I was a child. We raked the leaves into huge crackling mounds, then jumped in them or buried ourselves in their spicy dustiness. Autumn was always my favourite season. If the leaves had been pushed over the curbs mothers stood in doorways, aprons on, wooden spoons in their hands, yelling warnings about kids who got run over doing just that sort of thing, and anyway, it's time to wash your hands and face for dinner. Before the leaves turned completely brown we went along the streets of the neighbourhood looking for perfect specimens to take to our teachers. At least one week of art lessons would be based on leaves.

In our town, in the autumn of 1794, just before Robert Corbett, great-grandson of Robert of Weymouth, moved up across the state line into New York state, there was a flooding of the Susquehanna River that was known as "the Pumpkin Freshet." The current of the river rose way above its usual height and came sweeping down the valley with such energy that it carried away with it the produce from nearly all the fields along its banks, including thousands of pumpkins. How I wish I had seen it! What a wonderful thing, as though the big, golden October moon herself had given birth to a vast tribe of little moons or thousands of Dutch cheeses, tumbling over each other as they headed down the great river to Chesapeake Bay and ultimately out to the sea.

I can think like this because I am a *wry*-ter, not a farmer. The Susquehanna was not always kind to farmers and settlers. Six years before the famous

Pumpkin Freshet a remarkable ice freshet destroyed the sown fields, and in 1789 there was a famine so great that featherbeds were exchanged for bread.

In the fifth grade we were asked to compose a letter to send to England, describing our lives, our town, our block, our house. I decided to write about leaves. Only one "official" letter was to go to some class at a school in London; the rest would simply be marked for penmanship, spelling, grammar and ideas. I worked very hard; I was good at writing, all my teachers said so, even the ones who found me "difficult." I talked about the way the leaves, as they knew they were dying, decided to go out with a splash. No old lady pastels for them but reds and oranges and yellows, the colours of fire, of warmth, and not the colours of winter. I talked about how many of the autumn fruits and vegetables contained these colours and how I never felt sad in autumn. I even used the word "melancholy" because I had got it right in a spelling bee the week before. My handwriting was never very good so I copied the letter three or four times until I was sure it looked as good as I could make it. We handed the letters in first thing Friday morning.

On Monday the teacher announced that she'd read all the letters and had decided on five finalists, but now she wanted us to help her make up her mind. The five letters would be read out by their writers and the class would vote. I read mine last. I knew it was much better than the others ("My name is Bobby French. I have an older sister who plays the piano and a little brother who's a pain. I collect baseball cards. Do you have baseball in England? My Dad's going to take me to a Yankees game." "My name is Shirley and I like to play dolls.

My father was in the war and he came back with a lot of medals and a German gun.") but I knew I wouldn't win. I had put in ideas and feelings, imagery. Even as I read I cursed the very sentences I was reading. Some of the children laughed when I said the bit about old lady colours. I struggled on to the end.

When the letters were handed back mine had an A and "good work" written at the top. I could see, very faintly, where the teacher had erased the words "Send to England."

Looking back now I think I side with the other children. My letter was a show-off letter, "poetic" in a sickening way, meant to impress teachers, not communicate with kids in another country. What would my classmates have thought if I'd written:

"Hi, my name is Charlotte. Last night my parents hid in the bathroom while a bill collector pounded on the door. Can I come and live with you?"

The words my parents shouted at one another were stones, sticks, knives, shards of glass, and although the quarrels usually began after my sister and I had gone to bed, the words bounced off the walls of the dining room downstairs, flew up the hot-air ducts and into my room where I lay still as a statue underneath the bedclothes.

I slept in a room at the top of the stairs; my sister Jane slept down the hall. I never thought to get up and go to her. Even now we do not talk about those days; we talk about Mother, "what to do about Mother," but we rarely go back to our childhood.

Once, fairly recently, I tried. I was visiting my sister and her husband was out for the evening.

"Now," I said to myself, "do it now."

"Let's talk, really talk," I said.

"Let's get comfortable first," she said, "put on our bathrobes and have a nightcap."

When we were settled again she began to flip through the *TV Guide*.

"Have you seen *Norma Rae*? It's just beginning."

I hadn't seen it but I wanted to talk.

"Let's just watch the first bit," she said. "I love it when Sally Field gets up on the table and gets them organized."

"I can see it some other time," I said.

The scene on the table does not occur near the beginning of the picture and my sister fell asleep long before then.

She hugs people a lot these days; I think she feels she has to — to make up for lost time. I tend to wait until someone hugs me first. (Except with my children; with my children it was always easy — hugging, kissing, holding. I had not known I had so much love in me, waiting.)

"We never talked," I said to Jane as I stood at the door of her apartment, waiting for the taxi-driver to buzz.

"Talked about what?" said her husband.

"I was really sorry when Sally Field and Burt Reynolds split up," my sister said.

The taxi-driver buzzed; we hugged.

I had just been to see my mother. It was Easter-time and the flower-seller outside Park Street Station had a special offer on daffodils and paper narcissus. I bought four bunches; people smiled at me on the train.

"Lovely flowers."

"Yes, aren't they?"

A poster in Spanish and English told you who to call if you were pregnant and alone.

The dutiful daughter, the daughter from "out west," arriving with her arms full of flowers. How can you hug when your arms are full of flowers?

"Don't kiss me," she said, "I have a cold."

Sometimes I would stare at myself in the old, wavery mirror in our bathroom and the face of the child who looked back was like the face of a child who has fallen through the ice. There she is, just beneath the surface, her mouth frozen in a howl of pain.

"Cold," my mother said to me, "Charlotte, you're cold." She marched me to the mirror. "Look at yourself, you're cold." ("You'll catch my cold.")

If a child has fallen through the ice is it fair to accuse it of being cold?

❧

I'm not quite clear about what happened to Lydia after she got out of the convalescent home. I think she hung around in New York for a while working at this and that. At one point she was a waitress at Schraffts, wearing the little black dress and white apron like a French maid and living at the Barbizon Hotel. She didn't have to work — she was worth more than a few million, thanks to her lawyer's shrewd investments — but she had no idea where to go from there. She stayed away from the Beats and Bohemians in case she bumped into Larry, whose book of poems was a big success as books of poetry go. She saw it in bookstores everywhere.

One day she thought of at least one thing she could do with her money; she arranged, anonymously, to buy up as many copies of *Glumdalclitch* as her representatives — sworn to secrecy — could ferret out. Larry's agent, his publisher, his family even — for he was well-endowed in the money department himself, though nothing like so rich as Lydia — everybody tried to find out who was this mysterious fan.

"What did you do with all the books?"

"Well there weren't that many. The *Yale Younger Poets* doesn't print thousands, you know, even today. I rented a small locker at a warehouse in New Jersey and left them there. I paid for twenty years' storage space and arranged that my lawyer would pay for twenty more when that ran out. Sort of like perpetual care at a cemetery."

"Why didn't you just arrange to dump them in the river?"

"I'm not sure why not. Even after years of therapy I'm not sure why not. Because that was *me*, inside those pale-blue covers, I guess — or one version of me. I was still outraged at what he had done — the poems were terribly cruel. This was before Betty Friedan, before The Enlightenment, if you like, and I had no idea why this man that I loved should have turned on me like that. And then to take me to that book party, to dedicate the book to me — 'without whose inspiration . . .'

" 'Rivers of blood flow from her glumdalclitch thighs —' *God!*

"I was taller than he was, if you remember, and so I always wore flat shoes — those Capezio ballet slippers with my black bohemian stockings. One poem began — 'She's grown again, while I was sleeping, in the night.' He asked me not to wash, said he loved the smell of me. Asked me not to shave my legs or under my arms, loved — or so he

said — to make love to me when I had my period.
And yet he didn't like sex, hated being dirty
himself. All the time observing me, taking notes,
telling me I couldn't see the manuscript until it
was done. At least I was saved the labour of typing
it, like other writers' wives. But I walked into that
book party with him, so proud, still not having
seen a copy. Obviously he had had his author's
copies sent somewhere else. To his mother,
perhaps.

"The trouble was, Larry was good — as a poet I
mean. He was young and good-looking, had longish
hair at a time when long hair on men was very
suspect — he had the right *image*. Nevertheless,
although the book got rave reviews, people were
uneasy. Even the critic in *The New York Times*
mentioned a certain coolness which bordered on
the pathological. I wondered what Larry said when
people asked him where his charming wife had
gone."

On the basis of the sell-out of the first edition a
second was printed, and a third, something Lydia
hadn't anticipated when she bought up all the
remaining copies of the first. Larry was up for all
kinds of awards — he gave lectures and taught at the
Bread Loaf writing program. He wrote a second book
but it was more or less a rehash of the first; he took
a teaching job at Yale. He didn't fulfill his early
promise.

One day Lydia saw his mother lunching at
Schraffts with another woman. Lydia went into the
kitchen of the restaurant, said she had a splitting
headache and had to go home. That night she took
the train to California, where she got a job in a half-
way house. In 1964 she joined the Peace Corps.

✿

Special to The Globe and Mail, *London, England*:

Under a heavy brown rug, in the mid-Atlantic in October, you sip bouillon and doze, gently rocked from one side to another. Down below someone else is preparing lunch. There will be choices. Some of the choices on the *Batory* don't translate all that well, but they are nevertheless delicious when they arrive: "noodle dumplings with lard," "boiled with green parsley," "little tongues with jam." Pampered. That's how one feels aboard an ocean liner. As though — whatever the water temperature, whatever the temperature of the air — one were immersed in a warm bath of benevolence. Does a child feel like this in the womb?

I knew they wouldn't accept that. Womb is not a word commonly used in the travel section of a newspaper. Cradle of Civilization, yes, but not womb. Start again. Write about the iceberg, bigger than a city block, off the coast of Labrador. Small turquoise chunks were breaking off, and Lydia impressed us all by knowing they were called "calves."

"All that picture needs," she said, "is 'Lawren Harris' scrawled in the right-hand corner."

Write about the Tall Ship appearing out of the mist, heading towards Quebec City like a ship in a children's book, a ship in a dream.

Write about the Entertainments Officer who

said, on the last day, "My job is all lies." What will happen to him now?

Write about Talent Night. Amuse the readers, make them sorry they weren't on board.

Write about the storm. Begin there.

Special to The Globe and Mail, *London, England*:

Wodka: We received our diplomas from the Polish Fun Class this afternoon before dinner. They certify that we have "studied in depth the Polish language at the rate of 10 words a day (Captain's estimate) and [are] now competent to order a glass of *WODKA* without danger of receiving a glass of *WODA*." The words "in depth" and "WODA" now seem prophetic. We might soon be studying the fishes in depth (what fish are left in the polluted Thames) and there is entirely too much angry WODA outside, demanding to be let in . . .

As I dressed to go over to breakfast I wondered what was wrong with the child I had seen being wheeled along Guildford Street. They do wonderful things now to cancel out nature's stumbles and fumbles. New hearts. New kidneys. New faces. They can, I am told, even operate on a fetus in the womb. Soon there will be no excuse for imperfect bodies. Soon every child will have straight limbs, clear eyes, perfect teeth and a sound heart. Every child in the western world, that is. No doubt, in other less fortunate places, there will always be Bottle Babies. These are not aborted fetuses on a laboratory shelf or infants born to drunks, but certain babies in Calcutta who are deliberately deformed from birth, placed in jars or large containers for part of every day. A beggar child has a better chance of alms if it is dragging a twisted leg or has one arm bent behind its back, like a broken wing. The child's chances of survival lie with its disfigurement. (Little Crooked Lamb, who made thee? Does thou know who crooked made thee?)

The trouble is, there are too many babies. There have always been too many. "Don't let anyone ever tell you you weren't wanted," wrote my mother in a recent letter. (Nobody ever had.)

❧

I called Lydia's number from the phone booth in the main building — my phone still wouldn't work — but she was out. On my way downstairs to the courtyard I had noticed all the empty milk bottles were gone. The new ones must already be inside and the children up and out for I heard no noise. I left a message to tell Lydia I would call again and then I stepped outside. The sun was shining and there was no wind. I decided that after breakfast, instead of going back to my room to work on my *Batory* piece, I would visit Portobello Market. The receptionist had said the trains were still not running to the southeast so why not have a day off? Go With the Flow. Well, we'd almost done that two nights ago.

London House residence (for men and some married students — without families) was just across the square. Its cafeteria would never make *The Good Food Guide* but it was cheap and clean and I liked sitting at the long oak tables with people from all over the world. You made your own toast and waited in line to punch the coffee machine.

Some of the poorer students — either on small fellowships or at the end of their year — brought their own boxes of cereal and sticky jars of marmalade full of crumbs. And not all of the diners were young; professors on sabbatical, usually accompanied by their wives, shared the morning papers with young men and women in their early twenties. The dining room was large, wood-panelled and well-proportioned, so that the noise of a hundred or so diners never became unpleasant. Enormous portraits of stern, uncompromising men in robes looked down on us as we ate. I was just finishing when I looked up and saw, several tables down, the back of a head I recognized. I got rid of my tray and went over and tapped him on the shoulder.

"Robert?"

He stood up and hugged me. An old friend from the West Coast, a poet. He was spending a few days at a branch of the British Museum before heading off to Italy. Something to do with bones and a recurring motif in Italian art. For a new book of poetry, he said.

I told him I'd just come from a crossing on the *Batory*, and that I too was looking for bones, in a way. I said I had told the Polish teacher on the ship that I was a writer — a real one.

"You could be, if you'd stop this travel-writing nonsense."

"Maybe. I've certainly got hold of the tail of something interesting."

"What is that?"

"I can't say yet — I'm scared to talk about it, as a book I mean."

"Would you like to have dinner tonight or tomorrow?"

"Tomorrow I think. I have some stuff I need to do tonight. Tomorrow around half-past seven?" I could feel him wince at the expression "stuff."

He walked away, a tall man whose red hair was gradually fading. He reminded me of Abraham Lincoln or one of the prophets of old and I liked him very much. A good man, dedicated, somewhat of a loner but always a pretty, intelligent woman in the background, adoring him. I liked making him laugh.

Travel-writing, the kind I do — for travel magazines and in-flight articles — is not unlike writing fiction. You have to select and arrange. However, unless you are being humorous, you always present the best side of a place. You didn't talk, in the late seventies, about bodies of young girls being washed ashore at Goa or dwell on the fact that the Taj Mahal was built to commemorate a woman who died in childbirth. You didn't mention the lepers in Mombassa, the dogshit on the streets of Paris. (I once heard a woman walking behind me with her little boy refer to the street we were on as "*rue Merde*.") It's like postcards. You want your friends to envy you, not pity you. You want your readers to call up their travel agent right away.

I'm tired of it, actually. I'm not sure I can do it any more, whatever happens with the novel. "Nuns fret not at their convent's narrow room," said Wordsworth, trying to find an objective correlative for the restrictions of the sonnet form. Well, I'm fretting, I'm fretting. I've had enough of clear blue skies and clean beaches. I want to *sprawl*, I want to *let go*.

The papers were full of photos from the aftermath of the storm: collapsed walls, twisted scaffolding, huge holes left by uprooted trees. There were forty trees on the railway line on the stretch between Tonbridge and Tunbridge Wells in Kent. The ports of Dover, Folkstone and Plymouth were closed, Dover for the first time since 1703. A hundred trees were down around the Albert Memorial. Six thousand calls had come in to the London Fire Brigade on the night of the storm.

On the Tube to Holland Park and on the streets everyone was talking about the storm. People love a crisis situation, especially when the crisis is more or less over. And only one dead, an old vagrant who took refuge under a tree at the Inns of Court. "It's a miracle there weren't more."

Hurricane Len. In the name of equality hurricanes are now named after men as well as women. Soon he would be downgraded to a tropical storm. Meanwhile, Britain was out with chainsaws and green wellies, coping.

The tree the vagrant chose to shelter under blew over and crushed him to death. What would Dickens have done with this? — a marvellous beginning for a novel, the old man with his bottle, sitting underneath the huge tree, thinking that way he'll keep dry. Perhaps he is so drunk he falls asleep in spite of the howling wind. How long does it take a tree like that to fall? Wouldn't there have been a cracking sound as it came loose from the earth?

At Dover a small freighter capsized just outside the harbour entrance. Imagine Lydia, safe in Birmingham, reading the morning papers and marvelling, "We came that close. We really were in danger." No doubt she is smiling and clipping out bits to show back home.

Or is she sitting somewhere on a bench, too stunned to move, with memories flooding in, drowning after all.

❧

I am not a serious collector of objects of any kind. If I were, I would have been up at dawn, not ambling along Portobello Road at 10 a.m., having stopped en route to have another cup of coffee and another look at the papers. But you never knew what you might find in the way of Christmas gifts or old bits of jewellery. Lydia told me that, when asked to describe me once, she said, "She gives good presents." That may be so, but if I do it's because I get so much pleasure in the finding of things, inexpensive things, at markets wherever I go. Bags of spices in Athens, weighed out on a finger-scale, beautiful paper in Japan, toys in Denmark or Sweden, a bit of coral, even, picked up on a beach in Africa. I have a drawer back home — my present drawer. Sometimes I have no idea who I'm buying for until much later. It should really be labelled "my future drawer." Sometimes, when I'm too reluctant to part with something, I realize that the present was meant for me. Usually nothing very large — whatever I buy has to fit in a suitcase or a poster tube. Jewellery, I thought that morning, jewellery as presents and maybe a set of bone-handled fish knives and forks for me.

What they sell on Portobello Road are pieces of the past — mourning rings, nanny brooches, pudding moulds of such elaborate design I can't help thinking what lovely sand-castles they would make. Antique ribbons and laces, stained glass from stately homes and deconsecrated churches, junk. I wandered up and down, enjoying the crowds and envious, a little, of the camaraderie among the various proprietors of the stalls. It's a whole world, self-enclosed, somewhat amused and slightly contemptuous of the people who come to pick and choose. I bought a tartanware pin-cushion, a garnet ring, a silver brooch that said "MOTHER." Then, because my ankle was hurting, I went upstairs in one of the arcades and had a coffee and a cheese-and-tomato roll. An East Indian girl with a sad face served me from behind the small counter. I wanted to say to her, "Cheer up, things will look brighter next week." The Brits are not particularly friendly towards East Indians. Even the most enlightened will cheerfully refer to the "Paki store on the corner." I look at the bus conductors, the railway sweepers, the lavatory attendants: their faces are all various shades of brown. Would these people have been happier in the old days? A British passport gives you the right to come here and be sneered at. I had my first child in England. When I went for my check-up at the hospital the woman in front of me came storming out after only a minute. She said she refused to have a black doctor put his finger up inside her. Red-faced and furious, she told the nurse she wanted an appointment on the day a proper English doctor would be there. "The very idea," she said, and looked at me. I suppose she was waiting for the rest of us to get up and leave. The Brits don't like anybody who isn't British. Actually, it's the *English*. As my father-in-law used to say "Wogs begin at Calais."

I couldn't help noticing the girl because everyone else around was so cheerful — exchanging information about mutual friends, minding each other's stalls while so and so nipped out for a few minutes.

On my way out I saw, high up on a shelf above a jumble of old tins and dolls and Coronation mugs, a biscuit tin with the picture of a liner on it. That would make the perfect present for Lydia. I approached the two elderly women who were sitting side-by-side, knitting (they were obviously sisters, possibly twins) and asked if I could see the tin.

"You might want to know how much it is, dear, before I climb up and get it. I mean, I'll tell you the price and then we'll see if you're serious." She smiled. No offence meant, but the tin was on the very top shelf and the ladder didn't look as if it would bear her weight.

"How much is it then?" Was I willing to go as high as twenty pounds for something I was sure Lydia would love? ("She gives good presents.")

"Seventy pounds, love." She looked at my face. "Yes, I thought you might not be interested."

"It seems rather a lot for a biscuit tin."

"It's the *Lusitania*, dear. Only a few of those tins remain. They were all called in by the manufacturer after the tragedy."

I told them about our trip on the *Batory* and how I had thought we might capsize and drown. They were most interested but did not, as I had hoped, come down in price. Some American would buy it, eventually; they could wait.

What else could I buy Lydia, something that would amuse her. Nothing really caught my eye. And then I saw a strange porcelain doll. Not for Lydia — there was something creepy about this doll — maybe not even for me. But I was curious. The glaze was dead white, like marshmallow sauce, and the doll, in fact, was white all over, except for the face, which had been hand-painted and was quite lovely. I had never seen anything like it before.

"What's that?"

"Oh, that's a Frozen Charlotte, dear. A very nice specimen, isn't it, Dulcie?"

"Not in mint condition, but few of them are. They used to be sold for pennies in the old days."

"Is it a toy?"

"Once upon a time. German they are. Funny to think that sort of body was the fashion once. Whatever would they have thought of Twiggy?"

"A Frozen Charlotte? Is that what she's called?"

"They're all called that, dear, I've no idea why. Dolls like this are always Frozen Charlottes."

"That's my name," I said, "Charlotte."

"Fancy," Dulcie said, not missing a stitch.

"It's not cheap, dear. Fifty pounds."

"I call them water-babies," Dulcie said.

"It's very strange. I don't exactly like it but I must have it. Frozen Charlotte!"

They didn't take cheques, not even traveller's cheques — "No cheques of any kind, dear, unless you're a dealer and known to us" — so I went over to the Midland Bank on the corner and stood in a line made up of Americans who had relied on their American Express cards. Why do Americans talk so loudly? I would put it down to the first settlers, to seafarers shouting above gales or over long distances in the forests, but they all do it. I wished I had a maple-leaf pin to pin in my lapel. The quickest and easiest way for Canadians to define themselves is to say they're not Americans. When my turn came I cashed a lot of money. I'd buy the biscuit tin as well, why not?

I went back to the sisters and climbed the ladder myself. The Frozen Charlotte had cost me the equivalent of one hundred Canadian dollars. I told myself

I must be mad. It was bizarre. I'd have to keep it in my bathroom — it was the same colour as my claw-foot bathtub. I had spent, on my second day in London, a week's money. And just because it had my name. "Water-babies," Dulcie had called them. She couldn't know that the favourite book of my mother and her sister was Kingsley's *The Water-Babies*. I own it now; my mother gave it to me. I had it with me on the desk in my room at Goodenough House.

Things were connecting up in ways that were beginning to scare me. I had forgotten all about the fishknives and forks. I went to find the woman who sold pudding basins. She had the largest collection in the world. Perhaps she would let me interview her. I might be able to sell a piece like that to *Gourmet* magazine and offset the cost of my extravagance. And I hoped my mother would like the brooch. She always says, "Don't buy me any presents this year, I'm too old. I'm not giving any presents and I don't want any." I don't listen, neither does my sister.

"I like buying presents," I say to my mother. "It gives *me* pleasure." Once, from Syria, I sent her a wooden box, elaborately inlaid with mother-of-pearl, and filled it with sweetmeats wrapped in brilliant colours: magenta, turquoise, gold. A year later I peeked into the box and the sweets were still there.

"You didn't eat the candies I sent you." (She is very fond of candy.)

"No. Well. I don't want to put on any more weight."

"That's too bad. I tasted some while I was in the shop and I thought they were delicious. Made with apricot paste and figs and chocolate — things like that."

"It worries me when you go to these strange places," she said.

I dropped the subject; I realized she hadn't eaten the candies because she didn't know what dark hands might have touched them. Like my ex-father-in-law, like the woman at the postnatal clinic, my mother has certain problems concerning skin colour.

"Why don't you take those candies with you," she said as I was leaving, "since you liked them so much."

"They're over a year old now, Mother, why don't I just dump them in the trash?"

I worry about my mother. Even as I was enjoying the October day and Portobello Road I was worrying about her, sitting alone in her one-room apartment, chewing on stale grievances. Why had I received no letters from her? Had I done something (recent) to offend? Was she dead (passed away, gone to her reward)? Had she shaken off these mortal coils? Had she croaked? Had she kicked the bucket? "Peacefully, in her sleep . . ." Would you know if it happened in your sleep? Would it be like one of those dreams of falling; would you thrash about and try to wake yourself up? This is a woman who has never been at peace, not even in her sleep. From her bedroom, where she slept alone, came sounds throughout my childhood of my mother screaming, yelling, calling out in some guttural language. She always locked herself in so it was no good going to her, but we would pound on the door, Mother Mother wake up. Mother you are having a bad dream. Our father slept in another part of the house, with two doors between him and our hallway. "Because of his asthma."

Now, years later, she tells me that she used to sleepwalk as a child and was always afraid it might start again. "Once, at Corbettsville, they found me on the roof."

Perhaps she will sleepwalk after she is dead, appear some midnight in her old blue satin nightgown outside my bedroom door. Sad ghost.

[What is that noise?
It is the cry of women, my good Lord]

❧

Everywhere there were warnings: be careful, careful, careful. If enough branches are lopped off the uprooted tree it may, like a dancer, spring back into position, crushing your dog, your small son or daughter playing in the hole.

DANGER
KEEP CLEAR

The pavements upheaved as in a horror film: *The Trees That Walked.*

I wondered about the trees at Kew, the ones that had spent their lives in the glasshouses like that poor boy in America whose immune system was so deficient he had to live in a plexiglass bubble. When he came out he died. Were the glasshouse trees keeling over, biting the dust? Perhaps temporary coverings have been thrown over them (my father in an oxygen tent) to help them to breathe. Hurricane Len, like a small boy with a million stones.

Sticks and stones. Why had I received no letters from her? Had I done something to offend her? I do this often; my mother is easily offended. When I was growing up, it was a rare day that my mother was on speaking terms with the neighbours on either side of us. "I'm not surprised," I said to her last year, "that the Corbetts were in the acid business. Sometimes I think they were all dipped in acid." I had just been reading some Corbett wills: ". . . and only if my son should mend his intemperate ways." Cooper Corbett Senior on his son.

"If my said son shall so reform as to become a temperate man, by abandoning the use of intoxicating drink as a beverage, and shall continue to live in a temperate manner" for one year . . . for two years . . . for three . . . for four. Adding, "But in case my said son does not reform . . ."

The name Cooper Corbett never appears as a family name again. The black sheep. The white sheep, his brother Ira, my great-great-grandfather, received one hundred and two acres, "more or less" situated in the Town of Conklin.

Cooper, son of Cooper, is not buried in the cemetery at Corbettsville. Nobody seems to know what happened to him.

As it says in *The Water-Babies*, "those that would be foul, foul they will be."

"Your grandfather only got in on the end of that business," she said, "just as the whole thing was collapsing."

"You know what I mean."

I smiled and said "They" — so she laughed.

I had lunch in a pub and then took the Tube to Russell Square. I had decided to spend the rest of the afternoon in the British Museum. If I was going to play hooky, I would play hooky until suppertime. By then I would be ready to retreat from the city for a while and work on the Book of Begats. It occurred to me that I should have asked the pudding-mould woman the official definition of a Charlotte. Was the Charlotte who gave the name to the pud the same as the Charlotte who gave the name to my doll? Was she Charlotte Sophie or Elizabeth Charlotte of Bavaria? When a woman is pregnant the Brits say, "She's in the pudding club."

❧

Whenever I go to London, which has been fairly frequently in the last five years, almost the first thing I do is pay a visit to the British Library Galleries in the British Museum. Here one can find, in the first gallery, Grenville Library, illuminated manuscripts, both English and Continental in origin, and, in the next, a wealth of English literary autographs. An autograph, in this case, doesn't mean a signature you begged from Bob Dylan or Madonna, but rather a working draft, a fair copy (that's when you copy it over again, the way you want it to go to the printers), a proof copy (with your corrections), a letter, a typescript (especially interesting if it has been scribbled on and shows mysterious water marks that could have come from whisky or from tears), a musical score, even a shopping list.

I always spend some time in the first gallery marvelling at the old manuscripts displayed there in heavy, glass-topped wooden cases: psalters, Books of Hours, Astronomical Treatises, works featuring such delights as an Annunciation from Central Italy in which God appears to be shooting Mary in the head with a golden pea-shooter or an Apocalypse (French) where the angels, with their multihued wings, seem not unlike some of the kids walking around outside, kids with tipped, dipped, outrageously coloured hair. I love this room and like to think of those long-ago monks in their drab habits in chilly scriptoria, having renounced the world and its vanities, dipping their quills into pots of brilliant colour, creating fabulous birds, beasts, initial letters, angels, indulging themselves in colour and in gold (lots of gold — that provides the "illumination"). Brother Aiden whispers to Brother Anselm: "Do you think those serpents could do with a brighter green?"

But unless I have all day, I hurry to the next gallery, the Manuscript Saloon, my real goal, where I can gaze down at the handwriting of John Donne, Milton, Andrew Marvell (who would have earned a gold star from my grade three teacher in Binghamton — she was a stickler for penmanship), Byron (dashing in handwriting as well as looks), Robert Burns (blots), the Brontës, Jane Austen, Virginia Woolf and James Joyce (side by side in the same case, although the Hogarth Press wasn't keen on *Ulysses*), Lewis Carroll (who wrote in notebooks in purple ink and agonized over what to call his "fairy tale": *Alice's Hour in Elf Land*? *Alice's Adventures Underground*?), Philip Larkin, The Beatles. Such a show of "hands"! So many cross-outs, hesitations, second thoughts. John Lennon writes that he's worried about some lines in "Penny Lane." Take out the bit about his mother and the Welshman. George Eliot crosses out with dark lines, a firm hand. Swift's handwriting in a letter to "Stella" is lilliputian. I came away cheered, uplifted, somehow connected to all these people. Sister, you are not alone. Even real *wry*-ters have to work at it, so get busy.

I don't type — I don't even own a typewriter. I used to say "I can't type" until a friend pointed out that anyone with one or more fingers could type, that I obviously didn't want to type. I like the feel of my pen moving across the paper. I like the near-silence. I like being able to tell what my mood was when I wrote a particular sentence. My poet friend Robert told me once that somewhere in England there is a private typewriter museum, full of ingenious machines. We were discussing whether people twenty, fifty, one hundred years from now will ever stand enthralled in a room full of word-processors and computer printouts. He thinks not. He thinks that someday there will be a museum for that stuff and the people who go to look at it will go because they are interested in displays of industrial design. It won't be the same thing at all, he says, for those machines will tell us nothing about the writer.

I ate a quick supper at London House, sitting next to a Nigerian dentist in an immaculate stone-coloured suit and an old school tie. He told me that he had always eaten here while he was in training. Now he was back in Nigeria but his children, a boy and a girl, were at "the best schools" in England. He said he wanted them to become absolutely fluid in English. I didn't correct him; I like to think that language, like a river, is itself fluid enough to accommodate such minor changes. It wasn't so long ago that the gentry (and others) said "aint."

The dentist gave me his card and asked if I would like to go dancing. I told him about my research, which was going to take up most of my time. I suspected we would not go to an African club but to some quaint place where he could demonstrate his knowledge of the quick-step and the waltz. Perhaps I did him an injustice, but I don't think so. I have met been-to men before.

"Ah yes," he said, "roots, these are exceedingly important!"

"To a dentist as well," I said, and he laughed heartily, showing his immaculate teeth.

When I got back to my room there was a note shoved under the door.

> I'm sorry if I was rude about the bathroom yesterday, but I had an urgent appointment. Would you like to meet me in the reception lounge tomorrow and we'll walk over to breakfast together? Don't bother with an answer. If you're not there by 8:30 I'll start on over. (I'm going to St. Paul's for the 11 o'clock service.)
>
> Your neighbour,
> Dorothy Moore

It bothered me that Dorothy Moore might think I wanted companionship. Perhaps she did, but even so, why pick on me? Did she think I was LIKE HER? The apology was only an excuse; I knew that and she would know I knew. She was going on to Divine Service at St. Paul's. American academic attending High Church in London. The last time I went to St. Paul's was Christmas 1957, and I went with my roommate to hear Handel's *Messiah*. It was so foggy we couldn't see the singers, only hear them, and the effect was eerie, especially during the solos. It was like listening to a mixed choir of angels. Not angels but Angles, of course, but that was the impression we were left with. In the crush of leaving we slipped out a side door and found ourselves in the graveyard. I expected the ghost of John Donne to appear at any moment. It took us a while to find our way out, and I haven't been back since. I don't go to churches or cathedrals any more except to listen to music or look at architecture and stained glass. If I felt impelled to meet Dorothy Moore for breakfast, at least I could say, in all honesty, "I'm not a believer." Meanwhile I would apply myself to the history of the Corbetts once they had crossed the water.

Lydia was out again but our code word — "*cholera, cholera*" — had not been used in the message she left with the landlady so I knew she was all right. She did say she had "phoned family and they know you are okay." What fun it would be if I could have breakfast with Lydia tomorrow instead of Dorothy Moore, show Lydia the Frozen Charlotte and give her the biscuit tin. The tiny doll was lying on my bed; I didn't dare stand her up for fear she might fall over. Besides, she had only one good leg. To get her home safely I would have to wrap her in a face-cloth and put her in my carry-on bag. What would she look like when she went through the X-ray machine? A small homunculus, homuncula. How many more bits and pieces would I have by the time this trip was over? *Viaticum*, the Latin word for voyage. Originally the things one took, provisions for the journey, and now the journey itself. Except in the Catholic Church where the Latin word is still used with its original meaning. When the priest comes with the *viaticum* you know you are probably a goner. The Eucharist is the way into the Heavenly Host. "Open your mouth and shut your eyes." Last rites. But as late as the mid-seventeenth century, as late as the time the first "American" Corbett is supposed to have left England, *viaticum, viatica* was still in use. "Provisions taken for use on a journey."

Via — the road, the way. In Canada, a railway line. What did that Robert carry with him when he left? Any mementoes of the old country? Any family heirlooms? Gold? Silver? Or just the shirt on his back? Silver buckles?

Lydia asked me why I had told Richard I was a real writer and I said because the Corbett material was going to be a book and not a book of journalism. But I didn't say "novel" and I didn't tell her what my mother had written in letter #105 — the few sentences that had set me off:

"I saw a baby in a bucket outside the hired girl's room. The tops of the carrots we had for dinner were floating all around it, like seaweed or ferns. And my father, just closing the door."

❧

They were always searching for the water-babies, ever since Mama read them the book.

"But that was someplace else," Betty said, "that was in England. Maybe there aren't any water-babies in New York state."

"Either there are water-babies or there aren't," Frances said. "If there are, they could be found anywhere; if there aren't, you won't find them, wherever you look."

Lawrence had come up behind them. "That's a silly argument," he said. "Think of penguins. Think of kangaroos. We know for a fact there are penguins and kangaroos but we don't see any in New York state. Anyway," he said, veering off in exactly the opposite direction, "there's no such thing as water-babies. That's a silly book — a book for real babies like you two. When Tom fell in the water he drowned."

"He did not!"

"Did so."

"Did not."

"You are a couple of sillies," Lawrence said and went off to the eel-weir to see if he'd caught any eels.

When he had gone, Betty said, "If we find a water-baby where will we keep him?"

"In the bath," Frances said, but wasn't sure. She'd have to think about it.

"We could give him to Mama," Betty said, "to make up for Baby Grace."

❧

Clutching my relics, laying them out on the desk. The new one, the Frozen Charlotte, shines whitely among the books and papers, the letters, the flat grey stones from Snake Creek. Photos of tents and rivers and factory chimneys, "Dad's own girls" canoeing over from Treasure Island to the Shinhopple store to get the milk and the mail. Silly to lug all this around, this *midden* as Lydia calls it. There is hardly room to write. Would it all come together if I took a sip from the magic bottle up there on the shelf? Two sips? The whole shebang? DRINK ME. But something says "Not here, not yet." I put the bottle back, next to the tooth-mug and the fast-disappearing *wodka*, and begin to read.

"The Descendants of Robert Corbett of Weymouth, Massachusetts." In a way I'm sorry I found out about this book — it might force me to stick to the facts. Facts might have a way of tripping up a novelist, of getting in the way. Facts are like the trees in the old saying "He can't see the forest for the trees." Facts could keep one from the larger view. I know perfectly well that for the purposes of a novel, or even for my mother, if I can't find the original Robert or Roger, or the place he sailed from or the ship he sailed in or (most important) the reason why he left at all, I can easily make them up. "Lies," Richard said, "my job is all lies." In that, the Entertainments Officer is like the novelist. Yet Richard also gave us, in the Polish Fun Class, history and a sense of Poland's past. There are the lies one tells to engage and entertain and there are the facts one uses to instruct. Think of Dante, I tell myself, think of the Beautiful Lie. Think of Dante for other reasons. "In the middle of the journey of our life/I came to myself within a dark wood . . ."

By 1700 the Corbetts, wherever they came from, were well established in Massachusetts, and there they remained up to and during the Revolution. They were there for a hundred years before they moved west to Pennsylvania and later up into New York state. Robert of Weymouth begat Daniel (Elder Daniel), a prosperous farmer and an Elder of the Church. He left his wife £256.10s.1d. in real estate and a negro boy, his bed, bedding, axe and hoe. A man of property.

Elder Daniel begat Deacon Daniel who begat Robert, born February 1, 1745, in North Purchase, Milford, Mass., and buried in Corbettsville, New York. Robert begat Cooper who begat Ira who begat Marshall who begat Lawrence who begat Frances who begat me — if such a term can be used on the female side.

I made a note to slip Elder Daniel's sister Alice into my novel if I could. She married a man named

Dudley Chase when she was twenty, lived near her parents for ten years and then went off with her husband and seven children to settle in New Hampshire on the banks of the Connecticut River. They had seven more children in their new home. Once, she was left alone at an old fort with her little ones for several weeks while Dudley and his men went miles away to make a clearing for crops and a new house. There was nothing between that fort and Canada, and this was 1763. The genealogy says that five of her sons were college graduates and all of the sons were "smart men." Her sons, in later life, spoke of her as their "angel mother," their "saint." What the daughters said is not known. Alice lived to be seventy-nine years old. Her great-nephew, Robert, son of Deacon Daniel and Mary, married Elizabeth Daniels of Holliston, Mass., and either he or his wife gave their children names that hadn't appeared in the Corbett family before: Asaph, Edith, Pruda, "———" (who lived twenty-two days), another Pruda, Ruby, Ruth, Eve, Sewell, Warren and Cooper. The first Pruda died when she was not quite three. I would have been too superstitious to name another child after one who had died so young. As a small child herself, on a horseback journey with her family, Elizabeth had been captured by some Indians and scalped. The Indians left her for dead and she was found by some militia men lying in a bloody heap in the woods. Her parents had a special bonnet made for her and when she was married Robert ordered her a wig. Sometime after they moved to Pennsylvania, she was sitting in her bedroom combing her hair when an Indian snuck up behind her and raised his knife.

Elizabeth saw him in the looking-glass just in time. Without thinking she pulled off the wig, and with a dreadful scream she turned around and threw it at the astonished Indian, who screamed in turn and ran away.

Robert and the children, who had been working in the clearing burning stumps, came running but the Indian had already fled. It was the first time any of them, except Robert, had seen her scalp and the little ones began to cry. Elizabeth just laughed, picked up the wig from where it had fallen, and put it on her head.

What would her scalp have looked like? The scars would be very visible. Nothing would be smooth and shining. There would have been lines and creases, scabs, perhaps folds. I saw it the colour of bubblegum.

I have been to Corbettsville and placed flowers on their graves, Robert and Elizabeth, side by side. Elizabeth lived to be eighty-nine, outliving her husband by seventeen years. Robert's daughter-in-law remembered him as "a small man, very much a gentleman, who dressed well, wore something of a Quaker dress, and shoes with silver buckles." Was Elizabeth buried in her wig?

I was finding it hard to concentrate; the travel alarm by my bedside said it was well past midnight. I got ready for bed, then threw open the curtains and raised the window higher. It was a night of no moon, but the street lights gave enough light to show that the square was deserted. I could hear voices farther away — perhaps up on Guildford Street — and laughter. The air still smelled of smoke. All those pioneer ancestors on the one hand

and on the other, my mother, alone in her L-shaped room. No land of her own, no house even, just a room and a half, rented. We take her cut flowers and sometimes potted plants. She says she's no good at keeping plants alive, don't bring her any more, your father was the one with the green thumb, not me.

"Mother," I said to her once, "why did you name me Charlotte and my sister Jane? Were you reading the Brontës?"

"Who?"

"The Brontës. *Jane Eyre*, *Wuthering Heights*, *The Professor*, *Villette*."

"I never went to college — your Aunt Betty was the clever one, not Frannie."

"Well it's an interesting coincidence — they don't seem to be family names. I just wonder where you got them from, that's all."

"I can't remember. Your father wanted Veronica, I think, for you. I really can't remember."

"Were you awake when we were born?"

"They gave you something to knock you out — I think it was called Twilight Sleep. And they put a thick gauze pad over your eyes, in case there was something wrong with the baby."

"And if there had been, what then?"

"I don't know; I guess they would've knocked me out and taken the baby away."

She wasn't interested in this conversation, I could see that. She doesn't like talking about birth.

Then she perks up, smiling.

"You were nearly born in a snowdrift, did I tell you that? We didn't have chains on and got stuck. A State Trooper came along and helped us out or you would have been born right there."

"Frozen Charlotte," I said to myself now. "Good heavens. No wonder I had to have her." I'd write and tell Mother in the morning. Maybe she had one of those dolls when she was little. Maybe that's where my name came from. Woozy from the Twilight Sleep, not wanting Veronica but still undecided on an alternative, the blizzard, the snowbank, a doll from the past. "Charlotte," she says to the nurse. "Her name is Charlotte."

Thankful
Polly
Betsy
Hephzibah
Beulah
Hopestill
Lovice
Truelove (married twice)
Adaline
Emeline
Amanda
Cornelia
Hannah
Elmira
Aurilla
Fidelia

These are the early names, pre-nineteenth century. What would it have been like to carry the name Thankful all your life? or Truelove? So far I had not come across a single Charlotte, frozen or otherwise.

Names are important to me. The way they sound to the ear. The flowers in the bottle on my desk I bought at Brunswick Market because of their name — gaillardia. And because the flower-seller had kidded me about them being gale-hardy. Which was what Lydia and I were now, after our adventure. They were like punk daisies, flowers that were colourful and cheeky. I could not see their colours as I lay awake in the dark, but it was enough to know they were there. I decided that I would have breakfast with Dorothy Moore and then I would go to Greenwich. The library wouldn't be open on a Sunday, but I could learn something about the kind of ship the seventeenth-century Corbett might have left in. I set the alarm for eight a.m., and this time I managed to sleep without dreaming.

❧

In Cockney slang the Thames was "the Old Mother," from "Mother and Daughter" for "water."

"Use your loaf," my husband Michael would say to the kids. Loaf equalled bread equalled head.

❧

I would like to be a painter and paint her in all her crumpledness — the tallow colour of her skin, the blue veins beating at her temples, the milky-blue of her eyes. But old women, generally, are painted only as character studies and always always clothed. The Virgin Mary is always young. The Holy Ghost appears to have given her eternal youth along with everything else. Even Michelangelo's magnificent Pietà shows a young girl with a full-grown Christ lying across her lap; she can barely hold him. In his vision Christ was allowed to grow, but not Mary.

Old women are suspect, when they are not worthless. Mother worries about smells. If she lets off a little fart she gets out the Glade and begins to spray, as though the fart were a dangerous bug which, left to itself, might hide in a corner and breed. She never says "fart" of course; she says what she has always said: "Pardon me, Mrs. Astor" or "I just disgraced myself." In the old days it was Air-Wick, a green cobra rising up out of a bottle on the toilet tank. We were supposed to think of forests and pine trees. Now the stuff she uses purports to be a meadow. The mist lingers in the small room for ages, gets in my hair, my food. I tell her I would rather smell her farts and she's offended. The old mother, the Aged Pee.

"I'm no spring chicken," my mother said, when I urged her to take more walks.

"Well, you don't want to be a sprung chicken, do you? Get up and move those bones."

"You don't know what it's like, being old," she said.

"No, I don't. But I still think you should get out more. Doesn't this place at least have exercise classes?"

She supposes it does but asks me to imagine her in a leotard now that all her organs have dropped. (She is convinced that all her organs have dropped; maybe they have.)

"You could at least do exercises in your room; I'm sure there's a program or two on TV. Jane said you were very good about doing your physio after you broke your arm."

"That was different. Somebody came in to help me."

"The TV lady can help you. Just do the stretches, not the fancy stuff. Stretches and bends."

"There's hardly room to swing a cat in here."

She's right. Certainly no expanse of floor big enough to lie down on. But room to bend and stretch.

"Remember how we used to go hiking up T-Lake Mountain in the summer? You've always had strong legs — keep using them."

"I'll see."

I send her, once I'm back home, a pair of cotton, footless, tights in royal blue and a black leotard in what I hope is her size, big enough to accommodate the dropped organs without falling off her top. I know she won't use them; I would have to be there, cheering her on. The next time I visit I don't ask and she doesn't mention them.

❧

In 1066, William of Normandy, about to be William the Conqueror, set sail across the English Channel in order to establish his right to be the king of England. One of the lesser-known people with him was a man called Hugo le Corbeau, later anglicized to Corbet and, even later, in the New World, spelled as well as Corbet, Corbitt, Corbin and Corbett, which is my mother's name, and I am my mother's daughter. Hugo the Crow, Hugo the Raven or possibly Hugo Crow-Nose? The Book of Begats tries hard, in introduction and appendices, to trace us back, in a straight line, to Hugo and his two sons, Robert and Roger (*Rho-bear* and *Rhoge-ay*), who were rewarded for their loyalty with vast estates in Shropshire. Other people besides my mother have been anxious to prove this link but so far, no luck.

At the end of the Book of Begats there is a letter, written in 1930, from Sir Archer Corbet to Mrs. Luella Corbett Gault, in Charlotte, Iowa:

It will probably interest you to know that all the Corbetts, whether spelt with one or

two Ts, came from one stock. When you
hear people say that they can trace their
descent direct from the Norman Con-
quest, I might tell you that there are only
about 15 families (or less) that can do so. I
have met many claimants, myself, both
here and in America, but in most cases the
claim falls to the ground.

Clunk. So there. He encloses a page from *Debretts*
(missing from my copy) which shows the coat of
arms and crests belonging to the family, "the raven
of course being the origin of the name (Fr. Corbeau)."

Mr. Fox Davies, one of the best modern
authorities, states in his book that the
Corbets could trace their ancestry for 6
generations in Normandy before they
came to England.
    Reckoning 3 generations for 100
years, this means that they must have
come from Denmark with Rollo the
Norseman about the year 850 A.D. I do not
know on what Mr. Davies bases his state-
ments, but he is regarded as a great authority; now dead two years hence.

(It is always useful in these cases if the great author-
ity is dead.)
    I suppose being Hugo the Raven or Hugo Crow-
Nose is better than being Charles the Simple or
Ethelred the Unready, at any rate.
    Last year I joined Lydia and Søren for a trip to
Normandy. Søren is the Swedish Trade Commis-
sioner to Canada so he travels around quite a lot,

and sometimes Lydia accompanies him. When she does this she says "accompany" is the correct word. She smiles (she has excellent teeth) and wears elegant dresses in dark colours — she sees herself as someone playing the background music to Søren's *lieder*. It's a game and they both enjoy it. In their Ontario farmhouse back home in the Gatineau Hills, barefoot and in jeans, she'll point out the photos of the two of them dressed to the nines in Paris or London or Helsinki.

They knew I wanted to see the place where the Conqueror set off, so we went there; it's not really in Normandy at all, but we ate oysters and drank Calvados en route to St. Valéry.

That last evening, looking out towards England, the angelus ringing in the town behind us, I said, "William arrived first. I've been reading all about it. When they finally did get going they had an excellent crossing. The only ship they lost was the one containing William's soothsayer — which shows he wasn't much good, doesn't it, or he would have stayed at home. William's men gradually gathered behind him and they waited for dawn. I wonder what he said to them, some sort of Norman equivalent of 'God for Harry, England, and St. George!'?"

"No," said Søren, who had spent several years at the London School of Economics, "he said, 'All right men, be prepared for bad food.'"

Grumble grumble, fuck the camp-followers, mend the chain-mail, look at his lordship riding back and forth thinking we'll be cheered up by some old bones in a box. If there were an instrument to measure boredom . . .

The first invasion would have been of St. Valéry itself: 2,002 knights, 3,003 infantry, 2,465 crew,

2,500 horses and 500 ships in the harbour. No doubt the villagers locked up their daughters as soon as it was dark. September 12, 1066, to September 27. In two and one-half weeks a lot of havoc can be wreaked. I live in a port city; I have seen sailors on forty-eight-hour passes. Could the leaders of this army really keep an eye on everyone? Where was Hugo le Corbeau? There are no statistics on the number of babies born in Picardy in May 1067.

Some ships had been lost in bad weather during the move from Dives to St. Valéry; some men had deserted. Duke William increased the daily ration and buried the men from the shipwrecks secretly. Alas poor Henri, alas poor Georges.

"Do you realize," said Søren, looking out the window of the second-storey restaurant where the three of us were sampling *la gastronomie normande*, "that the two greatest defeats the British have ever suffered have to do with the mouth of the Somme?"

On our way to St. Valéry we had stopped several times to sightsee. Once to visit the cemeteries. Everyone so young — nineteen, nineteen, nineteen, eighteen, nineteen. To see a cross that said thirty-nine or forty was a shock. Two wars, so many bones in boxes.

I looked down from the restaurant window at the peaceful scene below. Two men in hip-waders were fishing in the estuary. It was November, just past Remembrance Day, called Armistice Day when Lydia and I were growing up.

In grade five we learned "In Flanders Fields." I liked it for the poetry and sentiment but it was all so far away. No one in our family has fought in a war since Lee's surrender. My great-grandfather

Corbett, Marshall J., fired the first shot on the third day of the Battle of Gettysburg. Then he came home.

"He wanted to found a *die-nasty,*" my mother said. Yet he cut his eldest child and only son out of his will except for a shack on Hawley Street. He died on a train to California.

Everywhere we went there were fresh wreaths at the war memorials: silk ribbons, paper poppies red as blood against the grey stone buildings and the grey November skies. *Mort pour La France.* November. "Blood month" in Anglo-Saxon.

William and his men set sail on the night of September 27. There was a brightening sky, with thin cloud cover and no direct threat of rain. The next day they were on foreign soil with the sea behind them.

Eighteen days later, at the place the Normans later named Battle, "there were six human bodies and a horse for every hill," but the gods stood up for bastards and the Normans won.

"What are *nattes?*" Lydia said. We were at Caen and she was reading from the Michelin Guide, in French. "It says here that Mathilda said she'd rather be a *nonne voilée* than marry that bastard William. But he came back a second time and marched straight into her father's castle, up to her room and dragged her around by her *nattes* until she said yes."

"Waltzing Mathilda," I said.

"Plaits," Søren said, "what you North Americans call braids."

"I hope you're right. It sounds painful whatever they were. And where were the guards, the faithful servants, the aged nurse who would have died rather than let her be mistreated?"

"Where was her Papa," I said, "while all this was going on? He must have been in cahoots with William, don't you think? Where was her Ma?"

"Apparently they lived happily ever after, and he even trusted her to run his dukedom while he was off conquering England."

"Who says they lived happily ever after? The Michelin man? Legend? She may have longed for revenge."

"A Norse woman," Søren said, "would not have put up with that. Norse women were very fierce when they were crossed."

"Is that why you married me?" Lydia said, closing the book. "To avoid having to marry a fierce Scandinavian?"

They smiled at one another, sharing secrets.

"What else does the book say?" I asked. There is a little flame that passes between couples who love and respect one another. Quick as a firefly's wink, but it's there. Two's company, then, but three's a crowd.

❦

I didn't like my grandfather's house in town. It was dark and the ceilings were low. I didn't like the stuffed animals or the pans of rusty water on the radiator. He had a housekeeper named Mrs. Thing. She sang songs in a high, thin voice:

> Ev-ry little white-cap
> Has a night-cap of its own . . .

There were three wooden monkeys on the mantelpiece, one with his eyes covered, one his ears, one his mouth.

Grandpa showed me drawers full of white shirts never worn, neckties, socks, presents from relatives he didn't care about: my mother, her sister, my uncle out in Massachusetts.

He died in a nursing home at ninety-six and is buried at Corbettsville.

"He wouldn't keep covered up," my mother said. "As soon as a nurse came in the room he kicked his covers off. He always was too sexy.

"I hope they shoot me when I get like that," she said.

Just who is "they," I wondered. Shoot her and stuff her and put her over the mantelpiece? "Oh that's just my mother. Her brain of course has gone to Harvard."

"I can't believe I was ever afraid of that woman," I said to Lydia when we were on the *Batory*.

"Think of shadows," Lydia said. "Given the right amount of light a shadow can make the smallest thing look big. Or even look like what it isn't: remember making shadow pictures on the walls at camp? I believe there's a theory that the whole idea of giants comes from infant Neanderthals seeing the giant, flickering shadows of their parents on the walls of caves."

"Of the mothers maybe. The fathers were probably out celebrating their hunting and gathering. And now it's the opposite, with Mother; she's shrunk to the size of little old Mrs. Pepperpot."

"But has she? If that were so would you be crossing an ocean to do her research for her?"

"She's too old to cross an ocean."

"Did you ask her if she'd like to come?"

"I did not. Anyway, she would have said she's too old. Just getting her out the front door of that place requires all my powers of persuasion."

"But Harlotta, did you *ask* her?"

"No," I said, "it never occurred to me."

On Sunday I walked over to Southampton Row to take the bus to Greenwich. Several tourists, with large suitcases on wheels, were waiting for the Airbus to Heathrow. Those suitcases always remind me of dogs on leashes: "Come along now, Jock." The young, who wouldn't be caught dead pulling a suitcase, walk bent over, their eyes on the sidewalk, carrying on their backs enormous packs that look like life-support systems for another planet. I'm just as bad. Under the delusion that I travel light, I carry a small bag, to which I usually have to add at least two more small bags whose zippers break at the last minute so that their contents have to be held in with old belts and those elastic bungies. (One seamless garment suitable for thirty-above or thirty-below, one book, a toothbrush, a notebook and some pens. The book can be exchanged for other books along the way.)

It was hard to tell whether the people waiting had had a good time or not. They looked tired and anxious, their minds already set towards home. But they have their slides to prove that they have been here and their Liberty scarves, their tea-towels printed with a map of the London Underground. Their Burberry scarves and raincoats. I wanted to ask them, "Well, was it worth it?" but for a journalist I am shy about walking up to strangers and asking questions unless they are of a factual nature — "Do you have the time?" "Is this the train for Waterloo?"

They were still standing there, or sitting on those nasty little plastic seats that won't fit any behind over the age of ten, when my bus came along. No one was speaking; not one of them looked radiant or as though he or she had fulfilled a lifetime dream. It seems to me that for a lot of people travelling has become a duty and a chore, not the enlightening experience it was meant to be. I would be going home by plane, nine hours in a seat less comfortable than a dentist's chair, told off by a stewardess if I refused to lower my window shade so that the clouds are blocked out and the sky and we can watch some stupid movie. Nothing with a plane crash in it, of course, or a terrorist attack. All landings are happy in the movies shown on planes. "All happy landings are alike." A good beginning to my novel?

I had never been to Greenwich before, and at first, when the bus let us off in the centre of the town, I thought I had made a bad mistake. The place was crammed with people (in fact my first thought was that this was infinitely worse than Heathrow). To add to the push and shove there was also the noise of chainsaws — trees down here as well — but once I got inside the Maritime Museum itself things quietened down. There was an exhibit of paintings about the conflicts between the Stuarts and the Dutch in the seventeenth century, but I was more interested in the wonderful objects that the mariners used to sail the seas: cross-staffs and astro-labes, long, long telescopes and sextants. I fell in love with the celestial globes. I saw globes without

America on them and the beautifully crafted pocket globes that gentlemen owned in the seventeenth and eighteenth centuries, when, said the placard, "it was considered essential for a gentleman to have the rudiments of astronomy, geography, mathematics and the science of the day." Essential for poets as well? I thought of John Donne with his images of maps and compasses: "She is all states, and all princes, I,/Nothing else is."

Nothing I saw was invented by a woman; indeed, the references to women were few, and then only to queens. The sea herself may be "the mother of all that lives," but that is analogous to the dedications in so many books: "To my wife Laura, without whose patience and support. . . ." The world of Greenwich was essentially a masculine world. The sea is *she*, the ship is *she* and the new lands will be claimed (and sometimes named) for *she*s; but the discoverers, the travellers, the inventors were all *he*s. As were the Royal Astronomers: Flamstead, Halley, Bradley, etc., etc. The Royal Observatory itself was founded by a *he* (King Charles II) and built by another (Christopher Wren): "We built indeed an observatory at Greenwich . . . it was for the observator's habitation and a little for pompe."

I do not understand astrolabes, sextants or celestial navigation, although I'm sure I could if I put my mind to it. When I went over to the old observatory itself, I admired the Airy Transit but I liked even more its name, and while I was standing looking out a back window, standing right where the brass bar of the prime meridian cuts through the building, I noticed a fat English robin hop from right to left, crossing from one hemisphere to another without a moment's hesitation. (At supper Robert said, "And you had to hop, in your brain, from right to left, in order to enjoy and speak about what you saw." There are times when Robert "gives me the pip," as my mother would say. But I just smiled.)

In the octagonal room upstairs the guard told me, "Look through the telescope, love, and you'll see Pluto." I didn't believe him but I looked anyway. Walt Disney's Pluto had been pasted on the lens. The guard twinkled at the joke. "Now don't you tell," he said to me, as a group of children ran up the stairs. I wondered what Charles II would have thought of that bit of nonsense. I didn't know then that Disney's Pluto took his name from the planet. Robert told me.

I ate a sandwich in the tea-room. A man at a table behind me was going on and on about some American tour operator he had met: "I said," "I said," "I said," in a superior English voice.

"She didn't know anything. She said she was going to see Big Ben and I said you can't see Big Ben there's no such thing as Big Ben. I've asked her to send me a letter when she gets back home to America." He wanted to be able to tell from her "choice of words" what sort of education she'd had, how intelligent she was and so on. He went on and on about the stupidity of Americans; he absolutely quivered with outrage. When I stood up to go I was surprised to see that he wasn't much over thirty, yet already a prissy old man. The woman with him might have been his mother. "Yes," she said as he rambled on, "Yes," "Yes," "Quite."

I managed to knock against their table just as he was raising his cup to his lips. "Frightfully sorry," I said, and sallied forth without a backward glance.

I asked about a reader's ticket for the library, which was closed on Sunday, and bought a few presents in the shop — postcards, a book of knots, two enamelled mugs for Lydia and Søren: both said "Captain." I had been tempted to buy "Third Mate" and "Captain" but thought that might be interpreted as mean. I bought a book about passenger liners, *The Only Way to Cross*, presents for the children.

Outside in the park a band was playing in a Victorian bandstand with Chinese decorations. Families lounged on the grass listening to "The Poet and Peasant Overture" and a medley from *Fiddler on the Roof*. Nothing taxing, just music for a Sunday afternoon. The bandmaster wore a heavy uniform and a sword. He told us, at the break, that this was the band of the Essex Yeomanry. My father-in-law was very proud of the fact that he came from "good yeoman stock." I was never quite sure what it meant until I looked it up years later. It turned out to have several meanings, but I assume he meant "countryman of good standing." Here it meant — I think — foot soldiers, like the American infantry. They played well, but they all looked hot.

If I had not arranged to meet Robert I would have gone back by boat, it was such a lovely afternoon. Next time. I made my way slowly back towards the town centre and the bus stop. ("Cruisin' down the river/On a Sunday afternoon . . .")

When I was at the observatory several people asked me to take their picture with one foot in each hemisphere. I had my picture taken as well. If it was any good I'd have it blown up as a present for my mother. She has never been to England. Should I have at least asked her if she wanted to come? On the bus home I tried to imagine her picturing me walking the streets of London. When I was a teenager and yearning to get to Europe I imagined the American Express Company to be full of dark-green steamer trunks. If I said to my mother, "Tell me the first five things that come into your head when I say 'London,' " what would she reply? I would have to try it when I got home. Would she say "bridge"? Would she say "falling down"? Would she say, "I'm too old to play games"?

   meridian — of, or pertaining to, midday or noon. Now rare. fig. pertaining to the period of greatest elevation or splendour (of a person, state, etc.) + consummate — 1734.
   meridian — a midday rest or siesta, 1645 — the middle period of a man's life, his prime.
   "Nel mezzo del camin di nostra vita / Mi retrovai per una selva oscura . . ."

   I became a travel-writer ("You are not a real *wry*-ter, Madame") thanks to the disappearance of Lydia's second husband, Stephen, a journalist who specialized in travel-writing, sort of an early Paul Theroux. He wrote for all the big magazines and was very fashionable, very cynical. Lydia had joined the Peace Corps in 1964 and he met her when she was taking a holiday in Kano, Northern Nigeria. He was older than she was, maybe ten years older, and very dashing with his bush jacket and his camera slung around his neck. He had been in Benin, doing a piece on Concepts of Beauty or something like that for *Horizon* magazine, and now he, too, was taking a break. She let him seduce her that night, in a small African hotel called the Avenida Kingsway, the three-bladed fan in the ceiling pushing the sluggish air around, their bodies so slippery with sweat they seemed to be oiled. Two weeks later they were married in Lagos by the American Consul.

He was warm and witty and very well-read. She could talk about books again, and Africa, which she had grown to love.

"But his worldliness was just a pose," Lydia said to me later. "He was naïve enough to think he could play little games on the side and not get caught."

"Maybe he wanted to get caught and write about it?"

"In that case he was even more naïve."

About eight years into the marriage, Lydia accompanied Stephen on a trip to the Ivory Coast. He was very hot stuff by this time and they were staying at the Hotel Ivoire in Abidjan. Travel in Africa had become his specialty and he might, on the same trip, write an article about a trip as a deck passenger up the Niger to Timbuktu and a stay at a place like the Hotel Ivoire, with its elegant gambling casino (even the sugar lumps were wrapped to resemble dice) and its ice-skating rink. He was also, although she didn't know it then (Lydia hadn't gone to Mali but had joined him in Abidjan), involved in some gun-running for the freedom fighters in Angola and some drug-buying for various buddies of his back home.

"We were sitting in the bar," Lydia said, "talking to a couple of tuna-fish kings who'd come out to buy from the Portuguese ships offshore, arranging a trip for the following day, when the waiter came over to say two men wanted to speak to Stephen. They were waiting at the door.

"Stephen liked his booze — who started the

fashion that you couldn't be a journalist — or a male writer generally — unless you could drink like a fish? — so he was quite merry. 'Tell 'em to join the party' he said, waving his arms. He didn't look up, but I did. Two short, dark men in silk suits were standing at the entrance to the bar. I saw the waiter talking to them, saw them shake their heads, no, they wouldn't join the party.

"The waiter came back and said they wanted Mr. Garwood to know it was urgent and confidential; they needed to speak to him in private.

"'I'll take 'em up to our room,' he said and lurched away from the table. No — that's not true. When he stood up he was immediately sober.

"'Steve,' I said, 'don't go. Please.' Those men were too chunky — too still. I don't know how I knew, but I did, I just knew. After he left the doorway I never saw him again. Nobody ever saw him again."

We had met, by sheer chance — if there is such a thing — on the steps of the Victoria and Albert.

"Lydia?" I said. I was with my two eldest, sixteen and eighteen by then, who were on holiday with me. We'd been at the Science Museum all morning and now it was my turn to choose. We'd stopped to buy iced lollies before going in.

I wasn't sure it was Lydia, this thin, painfully thin woman in black dress, dark glasses. Her hair was black as well, and straight.

"Well, Charlotte," she said, as though we'd just left off yesterday's conversation, as though it hadn't been seventeen years. She looked at her watch.

"Let's leave Arts and Crafts for another day," Lydia said, "and find a pub."

"Oh it's all right Harlotte," she said, "I'm not an alcoholic. But I am a *drinker*. If I can't drown my sorrows at least I can keep them busy swimming desperately towards shore."

"Why did she keep calling you Harlotte?" the kids said later. They hadn't warmed to Lydia, who had virtually ignored them ("I'm sorry," she said, "I don't know how to talk to children").

"It's an old joke," I said, "from college."

"*Harlotte*," said the eldest, with scorn.

"Actually," I said, "I never minded it. It set me apart from all the Buffies and Muffies and the like."

Married for fifteen years to an Englishman (born of good yeoman stock), I find myself saying things like 'actually' or 'iced-lolly' or 'aubergine' almost automatically whenever I'm back in England. The children are bilingual and they say sweets or candy, truck or lorry, biscuits or cookies as the spirit moves them. And they still say "What's for afters?" as their father used to say, if they are still hungry — or want to tease me — at the end of a meal.

Stephen had been missing — and presumed dead — for nearly a year. I had been separated for nine months, the length of time it takes for a baby to be born. Yet I was still swollen with my grief-baby, couldn't let it go and felt as though I might die of it if I didn't yield it up soon. I'd come back to England with the children (we had immigrated to Western Canada in 1960) on what I hoped would be some sort of exorcism, even if I told them it was a holiday. I'd had to borrow the money. We went to Cornwall, of course, and Brighton, where his parents still lived and where the youngest was now being spoiled by Granny and Grandpa.

"Unhappy differences have arisen:" that's what it said on the separation agreement. I was still hoping we'd get back together and couldn't imagine living my life with anyone else. I was thirty-five years old.

Stephen had come from someplace near Troy, New York. Lydia wondered if you are born in a place with a name like that you are influenced in some subtle way.

"You mean he became a travel-writer because he'd lived near Troy, wanted to see 'the topless towers of Illium,' something like that? Do you think more people become doctors from Medicine Hat? You're being silly. I do think it's interesting that you went up to Emma Willard and he grew up in Troy . . ."

"Near Troy."

". . . near Troy, and you meet in a chop-bar in northern Nigeria. But I guess that sort of thing happens all the time. Look at you and me just now."

She showed me a picture of him taken in Syria. He was wearing an Arab head-dress and leaning against the doorway of a seedy-looking hotel. "Ramses Hotel," it said on the faded sign above him. He was tall, with dark eyebrows and a dark beard flecked with grey.

"He has beautiful eyes." I couldn't use the past tense.

"Half Irish, half French-Canadian. He looks like an *A-rab* in that picture, doesn't he? Yet he could look like an old Africa hand or a Frenchman or even Li'l Abner if he chose. I think that's what made him such a good travel-writer. I have a feeling he's blending in somewhere, maybe Angola, who knows. But I haven't heard from him. *A-tall*, as the

West Africans say. I just hope —" she swallowed hard — "that if he's dead it was quick."

" 'If it were done when 'tis done, then 'twere well/it were done quickly.' "

"Shakespeare with Miss Dunn," Lydia said, and smiled. "I loved that class, but Larry seemed more important than dead poets at the time." She made wet rings, each overlapping the next, on the wooden table.

"If I seem calm about all this, Charlotte, it's because I'm cried out. I think he probably would have got word to me by now or someone would have approached me. I offered a huge reward, put ads in every paper I could think of — nothing."

"What about the waiters, or the tuna-fish kings?"

"The waiter said those men were not Ivorians, maybe from another part of Africa, he didn't know where. The tuna-fish men had never looked up. Nobody else remembers seeing them *at all*."

"What about the hotel room?"

"I don't think they went up there. When Steve didn't return after half an hour I excused myself and went to the room. It was exactly as we had left it when we came down for dinner."

After a few minutes the kids had left us at the pub (bored with our talk — had they stayed they probably would have pricked up their ears at the mystery) and decided to walk back to the hotel. It was a long way from South Kensington, but I still told Lydia I felt I should be getting back.

"But what about you?" Lydia said. "I've gone on and on about myself but you haven't said a word. Are you well? Are you happy? Are you perfectly swell?"

So that I was the one who put her head down and wept.

"How strange," Lydia wrote later, "you so much wanted *in* in that Smith world and you were the one who ended up in a home-made cabin, no running water except the creek below and no light except oil-lamps. How you must have laughed when Smith sent you information on 'matching gifts' and the like. No doubt you used them to light your fire."

We began an exchange of letters after that meeting on the steps of the Victoria and Albert. Stephen's publisher had wanted her to take on his old job and she tried, but it wasn't working. I moved in to Vancouver, still desperately unhappy but learning quite quickly to enjoy life without chopping wood or hauling water. I became a research assistant to an English professor with bad eyes.

Two children were in college and the third was in junior high. Soon I would be free. I didn't want to be free — I spent sleepless nights trying to figure out where to go from there, what to do with this freedom. I forced myself to make attractive meals for myself when I was home alone for supper. I set the table nicely, with Great-grandma's silver; I bought flowers. I sat and stared at my plate and when enough time had elapsed I got up and threw the food in the garbage. If I forced myself to eat, I threw up. All I really ate was crackers and cheese or crackers and peanut butter. I ate like a bird. A seed bell would have done me for a month.

And then a letter came from Lydia, marked URGENT. She couldn't do Stephen's job; she kept hearing his voice — the pieces sounded as though she were speaking through an interpreter. Could I

please please please help out? The pay was good, I'd
get to travel and if it didn't suit me I could always
quit. She was going back to Africa for a while —
Stephen had two foster children in Nigeria — and
then she'd see.

On the fridge my youngest had pasted postcards
she was receiving from her father, who was down in
Mexico with his lady love. HAVING A WONDER-
FUL TIME. SAY HELLO TO EVERYBODY.
"EVERYBODY" was me.

"Yes," I telegraphed to Lydia, "yes, I'll do it.
Can I start right away?" That night she telephoned,
paid for a housekeeper for my youngest and said my
ticket would be waiting at the airport.

"Just like that? Doesn't the editor want to see
samples of my writing?"

"Just go to the airport, Charlotte, and don't be
difficult. Your ticket is there and a photographer
will meet you once you get there."

"Get *where*? Would it be too much to ask you
where I'm going?"

"Mycenae," she said, "to look upon the face of
Agamemnon."

She never heard from Stephen again. It was
exactly five years later that Lydia, restless, fleeing
America yet again, met Søren Sørenson at a reception in London. They married and settled in Paris
and then outside Ottawa, on a small farm.

When she wrote me about Søren I was suddenly
back in grade four, self-pitying and furious: why
should Lydia have all the luck?

❧

On the third day there is a letter from my mother.
We talk about someone writing in a spidery hand,

but now, after nearly two weeks without a letter, and in another country, I see that my mother's handwriting is truly spidery — exactly as a spider might write if she could. (A mad spider; like the spiders I heard about, in Australia, the funnelwebs, who weave bizarre, schizophrenic nets, nothing like the fearful symmetry of other arthropods. Their bite is fatal.) The words are made of bits of web — they will lift off and stick to my face as I read them. "Confidential," she writes in the bottom left-hand corner. She knows that is the scent that will lure me in. What new tidbit does she have to offer me?

Years ago I was terrified of her letters and often put them away for weeks before I dared to slit the envelope. Curses, accusations. Ingrate. Slut. The past dragged up and flung at me; the thankless child, but she had the serpent's tongue.

Now she has lost the power to wound — just a little old lady frightened of the shadows on the wall. I worry about her — the fact that she can't sleep, that she has no friends, that she sits all day in her small apartment thinking about the past. Perhaps she will never die, just grow smaller and smaller like the Delphi sybil to whom was granted eternal life but not eternal youth. I seem to recall she was shut up in a bottle.

As I slit the envelope I picture her in her pink duster, hair newly waved, sitting at my father's old desk, writing letters. She mostly does this when she is upset, as she is today (or last Monday, when she mailed this). The woman in the next apartment has drowned. Apparently she got into the tub with the water running, slipped and hit her head and drowned. Nobody knew it until water ran under her door and out into the corridor. This was the woman on her right, the one who thumped on the wall when Mother, who does not like to wear her hearing-aid, turned up the TV too loud.

Now she is afraid. She is taking only sponge baths until she figures out what to do. She needs to be in a place with more supervision, where the money doesn't all go on fancy carpets and a fountain near the front door. Maybe it's time for a nursing home. Can't you girls get it through your head that I am *old*? When you finish gallivanting we should all three sit down and discuss this. You'll have to figure it out — this old brain is too tired.

And then a P.S., a by-the-way. She has changed her mind about willing her body to Harvard. She has, in effect, taken her body back.

"One reason I've changed my mind re: Harvard Medical donation is the new bone graft joy-ride hospitals are on at the present — and I can't see my old bones grafted on a half-wit African or Cuban etc. or my eyes looking out of some Puerto-Rican face. It's bad enough to have fresh medical students poking around one's muscles and bones so I decided to pay now for cremation. Do you mind? It's nice to think the problem has been going on for ages for everyone."

❖

In the pizza parlour, where we went that night to have dinner and listen to a string quartet, I said to Robert:

"My first marriage took place in the middle of the Susquehanna River."

"I didn't know you had been married more than once."

"Oh yes. I was ten years old at the time, at Scout Camp. Another girl was Mr. H_2 and I was Miss O. Our wedding ring was a lifebuoy.

" 'Mr. H_2, wilt thou take this woman to be your good ole buddy. . . ? Wilt thou protect her as long as thou both shalt swim?' "

"God."

"God indeed. I suppose they meant well. Water safety was really important at those camps. But a marriage. . . ? There were a lot of bridesmaids as well."

"The Susquehanna can't have been very deep if you were ten years old and in the middle of it."

"Well, I guess it's deep in places, though the saying back home was that the river was a foot deep and a mile wide." I took two flat, grey stones from my bag.

"These are from Snake Creek; they've been touched by the waters of the Susquehanna. Or the waters that flow into it at least."

He took them in his long, fine fingers.

"You brought these all the way to London?"

"Don't smile at me that way. Perhaps it's simply due to all those years of living in my hippie paradise, or perhaps it's due to the other side of the family, the Irish side, but I believe things, objects, like these stones, give off some kind of — well, vibrations — energy, call it what you will. My mother waded in that creek. She walked across stones like that. I've brought other things as well. Just to keep me going."

"Like a dog on the scent?"

"Not exactly. Or only metaphorically. But I do have one thing that's a mystery." I handed him the slug or button or whatever it was from the old button box. "Have you ever seen anything like that before?"

"It could almost be a cog for a piece of machinery. Except it hasn't got a hole." He handed it back. "Is this from Snake Creek as well?"

"No." I was telling him about the buttons in my mother's button box when a thin, bearded, middle-aged man put his hand on Robert's shoulder.

"Well, well," he said — an American with a New England voice — "I thought you'd be holed up with your bone project and here you are eating pizza with an attractive lady." He was drunk, could hardly stand, and Robert, although vaguely friendly, did not introduce us or ask him to sit down.

After he had moved away to a large table near the door, I said, "Who was that? I've seen him someplace before."

"I met him at the Cambridge Poetry Festival. One of those minor American poets who write one good book and then become a burnt-out case. They hang around festivals reading stuff they wrote thirty years ago to unsuspecting foreigners. Perhaps it's a bit like your stones; they hope they'll pick up the muse's vibrations."

"L. Carradale Carter," I said. Soon everybody I'd ever known or heard of would turn up in London. If it had been Lydia, sitting here, what would she have done?

"You know him? He didn't seem to recognize you."

"I knew of him long ago," I said, "when he was promising."

I put the stones and the brass object back in my purse and looked over to where Larry sat laughing too loudly and waving his hands. A minor poet who appeared on the outskirts of festivals. I remembered a book we had in a poetry class at Smith: *Silver Poets of the Sixteenth Century*. At the time I wondered what it would be like to be classified as silver, not gold. But those poets were good, most of them. "The Burning Babe" was in that anthology. Poets like Larry wouldn't be classified as silver, if they were noted at all. The Leaden Poets of the Twentieth Century. The Plastic Poets.

"He's a shit," I said. "Let's go."

On our walk back to Mecklenburgh Square we saw a great stump still smouldering in Coram's Fields. The rail lines to the south were back to normal now so I was off to Hastings and Battle the next day. He was off to Italy. At Goodenough House we shook hands; neither of us is the sort to kiss at greetings or farewells, although we do occasionally hug. I wouldn't see him for a while, a year or more perhaps, and we were nothing special to one another, yet when I went up to my room I felt suddenly bereft. Around Robert I felt that what I was doing was important, serious. He had read some of my early stories and encouraged me. He thought travel-writing — the kind I did — was silly, but did not belabour the point.

I thought of L. Carradale Carter and how he had hurt Lydia. I thought of my mother and of all the notes I have been keeping on her — I spy with my little eye. Bringing her presents of flowers and warm new slippers, suggesting we get out the photographs. I pick at her past as though it were yesterday's turkey. Was I a shit? Am I? Why can't I just celebrate the energy that enables a woman of ninety to sit herself down and write an utterly coherent (usually) letter which is also (usually) completely legible, stick it in an envelope, lick it shut, slap the stamps on and, putting her door on the latch, walk past the scene of last week's drowning, the carpet still water-stained perhaps, and drop the letter in the mail?

She doses herself with Tylenol when she can't sleep and then she suffers from dizzy spells. Two years ago she fell and broke her arm. The woman next door could have been her. What *am* I doing gallivanting around Britain? Shouldn't I leave the dead alone and rush home to help the living?

I should, but I know I won't. Besides, there is my sister Jane; she will cope. She always does. Three cheers for Jane.

❦

I finally got through to Lydia on the Sunday night.

"Where've you been?" she said. "I've called about ten times in the last two days."

"Out and about. At the Maritime Museum today and then out to supper. I bought you a present at Greenwich, you and Søren. I'll give it to you when I see you."

"I bought you a present as well. I'm sending it down."

"I miss you," I said.

"I miss you too. I've been wandering around, listening to the voices, hanging around the Bull Ring, sitting in pubs hoping somebody I'll recognize will come in. Tomorrow I'll be able to go to the Registry Office and they should help."

"Do you remember anything?"

"Just a kind of déjà vu when I walk around Gosta Green. But the city has changed so much anyway. The archivist at the library is getting together old photos from that era, but the street we lived on is gone — the whole neighbourhood is gone, Charlotte. And the school. Sometimes flashes of things come back, but more because of what isn't here than what is. I've called all the Fulfords in the phone book but none of them are related. And the school records are sealed for fifty years."

"Whatever for?"

"I don't know. Maybe somebody famous went there and he — or she — doesn't want to admit to such 'umble beginnings. I'm tempted to write to Prince Charles, I really am — to see if he can't help me. He's so keen on helping the Birmingham youth, why shouldn't he help me?"

"Don't you remember the names of any of the kids you went to school with?"

"I don't *remember* anything, really. All the shrinks I've been to say it's some kind of protective amnesia. I remember a bit about my mother, and I remember the night she was killed." She sighed. "I'm thinking of being hypnotized."

"Go to the school board tomorrow — or whatever they call it."

"Education Authority — I've already thought of that. Of course they're closed this weekend."

"You should have stayed in London over the weekend."

"No. It's good to be here. Something — or somebody — will turn up."

After I hung up I wondered if I should have offered to go up and help in the search. Lydia had sounded discouraged, not the old Lydia at all.

The next day when I talked to her, it was even worse. There had been no record of any child of that name — Heather Fulford — having been born on

Lydia's birthday or in that month or year or the year
before or after.

"So even the name on my original passport was
a fake. How could that be?"

"Did you ever *see* your original passport?"

"Lots of times. My mother took me to Canada
every year so I could keep my British citizenship.
We always carried my passport on those trips."

"Strange that they would be so secretive about
your past and yet want you to keep your citizenship."

"They were strange people."

"I don't see how they could have faked your
passport."

"Nor do I."

"Go back to the Registry Office — there's been
a mistake."

There was a pause. "I called Prince Charles,"
Lydia said.

"You didn't!"

"I did so. Or I called Buckingham Palace and
asked if I could leave an urgent message."

"What did they say?"

"They took down the message and said they'd
see that he got it. But I didn't believe the guy on
the phone. I kept thinking of that Milne rhyme —
'King John/said he was sorry,/so did the Queen and
Prince.'

"Charlotte," she said, "who am I?"

❦

"What's this book at the bottom of the drawer?" I
held it up. *The Water-Babies.*

"I can't see from here, my eyes are so bad. Bring
it over here."

I took the book to my mother, who was sitting in her recliner, surrounded by boxes. That is what we do now, when I visit — we go through things, we "sort." At the top of her cupboard she has layers of dress boxes from stores that no longer exist in my home town, stores that always seem to have been founded by troikas of local families: Hills, McLeans and Haskins (known as McLeans): Fowler, Dick and Walker (known as Fowler's). Boxes full of mementoes and documents. And in the bottom bureau drawer, photos, dozens of photos. This was the first time I had seen a book.

"It was my mother's book," she said. "Betty and I read it over and over when we were children."

I opened it up ("To Grace, with love" on the flyleaf) and flipped through.

"Someone must have read it to you. This isn't a book young children could read — too many big words."

"Maybe she read it to us — I don't remember."

"Did she read to you a lot?"

"Oh yes. And gave us elocution lessons. Once, in Corbettsville, we recited for somebody — the Fish sisters maybe — and they said we were good enough to go on the stage."

"How come you never read this book to us? How come we never saw it?"

She began turning the pages. "My eyes are too bad — I can't see the words."

"May I have it — if you've no use for it any more?"

"No!" She practically shouted. "No, you can't."

"Of course: it was your mother's book. It doesn't matter. I can read it sometime when I'm here."

"You never stay long enough to read a book. I told the lady in the store that I had to stay alive because my girls are too busy to come to a funeral."

I did not point out to her that she had said, had written even, that she did not want a funeral. I looked at her. When she is upset she pulls on the fingers of her left hand, as though she were pulling off gloves. Pull Pull Pull Pull Pull. Her skin is so thin now that I'm afraid she'll pull it right off. The veins in her wrists and at her right temple are like swollen blue rivers, blue worms.

"I mustn't get upset," she says. Pull Pull/Pull Pull. "I might have a shock."

"I'm sorry I asked about the book. I was just curious; you've kept it all these years, taken it with you when you moved, and yet I've never seen it before. At one time it must have been very important to you."

She doesn't answer, just keeps pulling at her fingers. I start to tidy the boxes we have already looked through, tying them up with faded blue ribbon where they are crammed too full.

"Here, take it," she finally says, throwing it on the floor. "You might as well. You'll get it anyway when I kick the bucket."

"Thank you," I say, but leave it where it has fallen. I only retrieve it as I'm saying goodbye.

Once I'm on the airplane and we're actually up in the air, I begin:

"Once upon a time there was a little chimney sweep, and his name was Tom."

❧

The earliest work tending to a real settlement was the first cutting through of the

Great Bend and Locheton Road, in 1791. Quite a number of sturdy pioneers were engaged in this work for a considerable time, chopping and clearing out the old logs by day and camping in the thick woods at night.... Robert Corbin was then living in the present limits of the borough and his family was probably the only one in this section. Rough and uneven though this pathway was, and full of knolls and roots, it formed a primitive passage-way for those who had the courage to brave the trials of frontier life, and who did not mind the slow pace of the ox team or the jolting and sliding of the cumbersome sled, and it may be said to be the advance work of civilization in the wilderness.

— "New Milford" in *The Centennial History of Susquehanna County, Pennsylvania*

Elizabeth Corbett hadn't wanted to go. Her family lived in Holliston, and northern Pennsylvania seemed like the ends of the earth. And at the last minute she refused, sitting on a chair by the front door, nursing the youngest, Cooper, tears rolling down her cheeks. Robert and Asaph looked at one another, then picked her up, baby and chair and all, and put her in the wagon. It was 1790 and it seemed as though the whole world was on the move.

The baby came loose from his mother's breast and began to howl. "Hush," *she said,* "There, there. Shhh."

Nine days it took them, going west into the wilderness of northern Pennsylvania. In the pocket of her dress she carried twists of seed and a small glass bottle of laudanum, in case the baby became fractious, in case anyone, on the journey, took ill.

They settled in northern Pennsylvania, on a spot where an old trapper had had a cabin. But they were the first settlers; they were the first to truly clear that land.

There was no settlement nearer than Great Bend. Herds of deer were seen almost every day and bears were common; they didn't lack for meat.

Robert Corbett set out to tame the wilderness as though it were an animal. No rest. No rest. Wolves came within a few yards of the house and howled. The youngest children, except for the baby, all slept in one bed, with their heads beneath the covers. In the wet season the mosquitoes were bad. Robert and Asaph built smudge fires to keep the bugs away. Cooper said later he felt as though he had been born with an axe in his hand.

Because of the mists, because of the stump-burnings, the smudge fires, the world of their settlement was like a landscape in a dream. Shapes dissolved into one another, reformed.

Robert built an enormous stone fireplace at the end of their log house. This building of fireplaces, even fireplaces at the ends of tents, became a tradition, something passed down through the male Corbetts even to this day. At the age of seventy-two my grandfather fell from a scaffolding where, with the help of the hired man, he was putting the finishing touches on the big stone chimney. Picked himself up off the sandy ground and said, "What's everybody staring at?"

"Utopia" means "nowhere." Warren Corbett died in 1791 because his mother had knit him a red toque. Accidentally shot to death, mistaken — playing hide-and-seek at the edge of the clearing — for a turkey. Red blood on the white snow.

The children had been warned to stay out of the way of the grown-ups. Papa went out early, with Asaph, to bury the turkey up to its neck in snow and mark out the line behind which the men would fire. Everyone hoped that Asaph would win the shoot but the Hayden brothers, especially the oldest, who was sweet on Edith, were equally determined.

Warren was wearing his new red toque. His sisters were told to keep an eye on him, to get him out of the house and out from under his mother's feet.

It was nobody's fault; there was no blame, then — or ever. The turkey, forgotten, froze to death in the blood-soaked snow.

For years afterwards, they said, Elizabeth could not bear the sight of anything red and refused to make petticoats, shirts and combinations from the new cloth called "turkey red."

Then there were nine.

(Forgetting everything in the fun of the chase, running into the line of fire.)

Land was fifty cents an acre; Robert had one thousand acres of virgin forest. He named the settlement New Milford, after the place they had left behind in Massachusetts.

The house grew; more settlers came. One winter, when the ferries couldn't cross the Susquehanna safely, because of floating ice, Asaph helped the ferrymen at Great Bend make an ice bridge. There was solid ice on each side of the river to a

distance of about five rods, but the middle of the
stream remained open. After measuring the distance from the solid ice on each side of the river
they laid out the length and width and sawed out of
the solid ice a bridge. Then Asaph and Benjamin
Hayden and some of the other young men, lining
themselves up, held fast to one end and swung the
other across the open chasm until it settled on the
solid ice on the other side; then, by dipping water
from the river they formed a safe, strong bridge,
strong enough for teams of horses to pass over.

The night it was finished Asaph went back
home and brought Sewell and Cooper out to see it.
Robert brought out Elizabeth and the girls in a
horse-drawn sleigh. Lanterns and torches lit up the
night; men and horses stamped their feet.

"See," said Edith to her brothers, "it's a fairy
bridge. The fairies will come across tonight."

"If that's a fairy bridge," said Benjamin Hayden,
"then you are the snow queen."

Asaph saw his mother at the edge of the clearing. Her eyes were searching the crowd, looking for
her sons.

Asaph waved and pointed and saw Elizabeth
smile with relief.

The very next day a horse bolted and the team,
sledge and driver went into the river. That did not
prevent people from using the bridge but it made
them careful.

One of the Hayden babies died of putrid sore throat.
It didn't take long for the little cemetery at New
Milford to start filling up.

The older girls married the older sons of the
new people. The house, briefly, became an inn.

Robert, the patriarch as well as (later) postmaster, wore silver buckles on his shoes. He had a special desk made for sorting the mail.

All this in the space of four or five years.

And then something happened. Some say he was cheated out of his property; some say it was not so simple as that. Something happened, and they were all on the move again, over the line to establish themselves near a tributary of the Susquehanna River called Snake Creek. All except Asaph, who refused to go with them and set off for the Lake Country in the Genesee Valley, the country his father had surveyed with Mr. Cooper, now Judge Cooper, years before. Robert and Asaph had quarrelled. A quarrel between father and eldest son cannot be solved by anything as simple as a twelve-foot piece of wood. Later on, it was Robert's grandson Ira who hit upon the idea of solving disputes with a twelve-foot piece of burning rail.

That too became a pattern in our family: stone fireplaces with stone chimneys and quarrels between father and sons, fathers and daughters also.

They all went, except Asaph, except the married daughters who stayed with their men in New Milford. Except Warren, who slept under his stone in the cemetery, the first person to be buried there. Almost two hundred years later I brush away the leaves from his stone as though I am brushing the hair out of his eyes.

More goods this time, fewer people. And by the waters of Snake Creek, they prospered, so much so that in a few years the hamlet took the name of Corbettsville.

— From *A History of Broome County* (with illustrations), 1885:

Corbettsville. — This is a small hamlet in the town [of Conklin] and is situated in the southeastern part and near the line of the Delaware, Lackawanna and Western Railroad and the Susquehanna River. It is picturesquely located amid the surrounding hills. Sewell Corbett was the first postmaster here, and when Ira Corbett built his store in 1845, he took the office and filled it for nearly twenty years. . . .

Ira Corbett built his first sawmill here in 1856 and has operated it ever since. The lumber trade of the town had been vigorously prosecuted, however, since as early as 1815, having been developed largely by Cooper Corbett, and continued since by his son Ira. The business has amounted to from $50,000 to $100,000 annually. Ira Corbett built a second mill on Little Snake Creek, a mile below Corbettsville, in 1865; this was a steam mill and one of the best in the section. It was burned in December of the same year. In 1876 he rebuilt the Conklin mill, it having also been burned. Mr. Corbett also built a mill in Binghamton and one in Pennsylvania, and has been one of the most extensive lumber dealers in the county. . . ."

"Planing-mill, sash and door factory"
"Foundry" (built by Sewell, sold later to Sewell Jr. and Julius Corbett)
"Wagon shop" (built by Sewell)
"Carding mill" (Sewell Corbett and Cooper, his brother)
"Hotel" (built by Cooper Corbett)

It will be correctly inferred from the preceding pages of the records of this town that the Corbett families must be given much credit for the energy and enterprise that has enabled them to accomplish so much for the general welfare and material advancement of the community.

Cooper begat Ira begat Marshall J., begat Lawrence, begat Frances, begat me.

Lawrence Jr., Frances and Betty spent their summers in Corbettsville, sometimes in Ira's old house, sometimes in the big house with a tower room, built by Marshall J. after his retirement. Marshall J.'s wife was named Alice. Lawrence was the eldest and only son. After him four beautiful sisters, famous for their luxurious auburn hair: Clara, Grace, Mabel, Alice. Mabel went to Europe with her parents and danced with the Prince of Wales.

"Before he met Mrs. Simpson, of course," wrote my mother.

Grace ran away down south to marry a man named Mr. Campbell.

"Marshall made her have an elaborate wedding at the Corbettsville house on her return. Then built them two houses and generally made a nuisance of himself. Finally, at Clara and Mabel's insistence, took her away from her husband so she wouldn't have any more children. Put in State Hospital, her sisters claiming she had never been right since Scarlet Fever when young. <u>Nice Pair.</u>

"Grace Corbett Campbell spent the last half of her life in a mental institution . . . father committed her through no fault of her own other than becoming a burden financially, she and her children, to a father who refused to let her lead her own life as best she could. It's fairly easy to commit a helpless person by just getting <u>any two</u> doctors' signatures" (more underlining, in case I miss the point).

"Grace was removed by my Dad (L.B. Corbett) to Windsor farm household. Developed TB and died at our house."

"Can't you just <u>smell</u> the burning of witches," writes my mother, gleefully, "scarlet letters, pillories?"

My mother is invigorated by other people's misfortunes. She herself should have lived in a village all her life and been one of the village gossips. Instead, she has no one to tell but Jane and me, and Jane (who can blame her?) is not interested. Jane believes that one should live in the present. From time to time she threatens to put Mother in the funny farm.

"More," I write to my mother, "tell me more!" I send bundles of envelopes and American stamps. I tell her, don't stop, don't stop. What was it like when your aunt was dying of TB in the back bedroom? Wasn't your mother afraid that you might catch it?

"She only lasted a month; we were sent to stay in Corbettsville. It must have been very hard on Mother, but Dad loved his sister so that was that. I sometimes wonder if he didn't marry Mother because she had the same name as his favourite sister. Stranger things have happened.

"Grace Campbell had two boys, Donald and Benjamin, and a girl Marian (blonde) — got involved with a dollar-a-year major in Washington and committed suicide — her niece came to Grandpa's Woods, do you remember her? — Donald's oldest daughter — yes, she was very homesick. Cried at the table — long, blonde hair."

Clara married the son of the president of National City Bank. Clara's husband locked himself in the garage and turned on the motor of his fancy car. Alice married Uncle Fred Williams and bled to death. Mabel married the widower of her best friend who died in an early flu epidemic. Mother is not sure what happened to her later on. After Marshall J. died, Grandmother Alice Waldron Corbett went to live with Clara in her big house in Binghamton but she was unhappy. She returned to Corbettsville and died there. The Corbettsville dynasty never materialized — or not in this branch of the family.

Hardly a hamlet now, just a series of rather shabby houses, the creek, the cemetery. The post office is in a trailer. Only a barking dog was home at the house with the tower room. I left a note in the mailbox, disappointed.

There were four men plus the barmaid in the State Line Tavern. "Give me a Genny," I said, feeling suddenly sixteen years old, doing something forbidden. Only bad girls went to taverns, bad girls and *dee-vhor-says* looking for pick-ups. My parents didn't drink. I sometimes wonder if Mother would be better — or worse — if she did.

The men at the bar gave me a quick once-over then went on talking about the flash flood which had occurred the week before. This has always been an area of fires, floods and Acts of God.

❧

"We're off like a bride's nightie," said my grandfather, turning on the ignition.

"*Dad,*" said my mother, who was coming along for the ride.

He was a big kidder and a practical joker. In a box labelled "A hammock built for two," with a silhouette of two lovers in a hammock on the cover, we found a miniature brassiere. In a box labelled "Gone with the Wind" and a picture of a southern mansion, we found a pot of beans.

My grandfather, behind a desk eight months of the year and then up to the mountains. Sometimes in April he went in on snowshoes. Always building something, making things. I felt safe there, protected and yet free. Nothing bad could happen to me at Grandpa's Woods. ("You gave it that name," my mother said. "When you were three. You gave it that name and it stuck.")

The minute it was sold he started to go downhill.

"Didn't you think he was *odd*," Lydia said, in one of our midnight confessions. "The glasses with the girls with the disappearing dresses, the cartoons . . . didn't you find it all rather strange? For a grandfather?"

"Well who did I have to measure him against, Heidi's grandfather? Other grandfathers didn't figure very large in literature or movies or my own real life. I thought everything was rather strange — he was just part of it. Later, when I read about Olympus, all those gods with 'sex on the brain,' as Mother would say, always chasing after maidens and punishing those who got in their way, I did think about Grandpa Corbett. Except that he was ascetic in so many other ways. He didn't drink, he didn't carouse, he lived a very abstemious life. The other stuff was just fantasy — I think.

"And he was good to us girls — in a distant kind of way. I loved those summers in the woods; it was the only time I felt really free. There was order, and good manners and plates without cracks or chips. When we went to Speculator to shop he paid cash. Storekeepers greeted him politely — 'Good morning, Mr. Corbett, what can we do for you today?'

"My parents had to behave, up there, and they knew it. We had a rowboat of our own and once we were old enough we spent hours on the water. We went to Scout Camp for two weeks in the summer but I didn't really like it — except the campfires and sing-songs. I didn't really know how to socialize with other kids. Only in the dark, around the campfire.

"You were the best singer in our cabin, the one year my mother let me go to an ordinary camp."

"Was I? I only know I loved to sing."

I was nearly asleep when Lydia said:

"Lotte, are you awake?"

"Not really."

"Let's sing a few rounds — for old times' sake?"

"Lydia, go to sleep."

"Please?"

"Our neighbours will think we're crazy."

"Pretty please, with cream and sugar on it? Start with 'White Coral Bells.'"

And so, in the darkness, gliding smoothly over the cold Atlantic, we sang "White Coral Bells." And "Scotland's Burning." "My Pigeon House I Open Wide." "John Jacob Jingleheimer Smith" and, finally, "Now the Day is Over." We didn't hesitate; we remembered all the words.

"All we need," whispered Lydia, "is some cocoa in tin cups."

"Good night, Lydia," I said.
"Good night Charlotte, good night."

❧

"There was a salmon he had caught on his one trip
west. It was mounted on a plaque and underneath
the salmon it said, 'I wouldn't be here if I had kept
my mouth shut.' "

❧

My dreams of the past year have been filled with
images of travel, anxious images. A conductor calls
out "Toronto, all change." My bags aren't packed; I
stuff them madly and race off the train singing
"There'll be bluebirds over the White Cliffs of
Dover/Tomorrow, just you wait and see." Or I'm in
the back seat of a car, a baby is at the wheel, steer-
ing. We are approaching a hill and I know the baby's
foot can't reach the brake. I try to shove my leg
through, in the space between the front seats, but
my leg isn't long enough. I dream my bedroom has
come loose and is flying around, like Dorothy's
room in *The Wizard of Oz*. The walls of the room
are peach. I have to take a subway and go through a
turnstile, down some stairs. A woman says "Do you
speak English?" and because I'm in a hurry, I say
"No." When I get to my track it's the wrong one —
I wanted a train that stops at Babylon.

I always wake up in time but full of dread. I tell
myself I like to travel, I'm looking forward to my
trip, but something in me says, "You don't know
what you're doing; you've lost your way."

The girl at the reception desk said that my
friend had left a parcel that wouldn't fit into my let-
terbox. It was a second-hand copy of Partridge's

Origins. I took it upstairs to add to my collection.
A present from Robert, who was now on his way to
Rome.

cruise, from crux, cross (a perpendicular sup-
porting a horizontal beam)
L. crux becomes MD cruise, cruyse, D. Kruis,
whence Crusen (crucen), D. Kruisen, to move, especially sail, crosswise, hence to "cruise," whence
cruise and "a cruise."
cruise — 17th C (1651), to sail to and fro over
some part of the sea, on the lookout for ships, for the
protection of commerce, for plunder, or for pleasure.

The second time I went to Greenwich I skipped
the observatory and made a quick visit to the P&O
exhibit, as the firm was celebrating its 150th year.
More possible article material. P&O originated the
idea of cruising; on one of their first voyages (a
Mediterranean cruise) Wm. Thackeray was given a
free ticket. "He published a lively and complimen-
tary account of his voyage." I made a note to look
up Thackeray's account. There was a replica of a
P&O cabin (first class, of course) and samples of
menus from the great days of travel by ship. Eating
is a very important part of life at sea. One is served
morning tea, coffee or bouillon on deck at eleven,
afternoon tea, midnight sandwiches, not to
mention the three main meals of the day. I have
crossed the ocean fourteen times by ship. The
quality of the food varied, but as to quantity, there
was always plenty.
Looking at a menu from the 1920s, with its
multiple choices under each category — appetizers,
soups, eggs, entrée, fish, main dishes, vegetables,

potatoes, cold buffet, salads, cheese, sweets, savouries, dessert, beverages — I thought of Thomas Cooper's advice on crossing the Atlantic (crossing, not cruising) in the 1790s. Thomas Cooper was Joseph Priestley's son-in-law and interested in emigration to America. It is thought that Coleridge either met him (in Bristol) or, at the very least, read his book.

"Take care to provide yourself with lemons, apples and any other fruit that will keep; you will find them very grateful, especially after sickness." He also gives remedies for costiveness ("brought on by sickness and want of exercise"): Sena, Lenitive Electuary, Jalap, Rhubarb, Calomel. "This tendency is increased by much animal food and porter and even the usual quantity of wine. English men are too apt to live in hot weather and southern climates, as they do in the cold and rainy winters of their own country."

"You will soon get tired of ship biscuit," he says; "therefore provide yourself with rusks or slices of bread baked over again, which you will be obliged to Dr. Franklin for having recommended."

Hardly Ice-Bombe Victoria or Little Tongues with Jam. But in the seventeenth century, when the original Robert must have sailed — on a voyage that could have lasted up to five months — the food would have been mainly bread or ship-biscuit, salt meat, peas and cheese. One must have needed a compelling reason to set out on such a voyage. How well-equipped was Robert Corbett for such an ordeal? Was he alone, or did he bring his family with him? What did he think he would find in the New World that he couldn't have in the old? If he were simply fleeing, couldn't he have gone somewhere closer — France, Holland, Italy? When I left America I was "running from" as much as I was "going to." Was this the case with the original Robert? If I could find his name in a passenger list I might know more about him.

But he wasn't there. I sat with all the elderly men ("R.N. Retired") who were writing memoirs or histories of famous naval battles, and I went through the passenger lists. The room was very quiet. I took notes; I examined large folios of maps. I realized that I could go on doing research forever, if I felt like it, never getting down to the hardest part, turning the whole mess into something more than the sum of its parts, something that would make the world shiver and turn the pages. Something that would make the reader say, "You go ahead, I'll be up in just a little while."

I took the last boat of the day, just as the sun was setting, sitting up on deck in my heavy sweater pretending I was a queen in a royal barge, not an idiotic tourist on a metal chair, hands tucked under her armpits because she was so cold.

> The barge she sat in, like a burnished throne
> Burned on the water . . .

We tied up by Tower Bridge and I took the Tube the rest of the way home. The sunset was by Turner ("it beggared all description").

> My country, 'tis of thee
> Sweet land of liberty
> Of thee I sing:
> Land where my fathers died

Land of the pilgrims' pride,
From every mountainside
Let freedom ring.

Heather was excused from pledging allegiance to the flag. She stood stiff-backed at the side of her desk, a new silver barrette keeping her straight brown hair from falling in her eyes, but she did not put her hand across her heart, nor did she sing our patriotic songs. Or not at first. She joined in when wc got to the Lord's Prayer.

She stopped saying "Yes, Miss" and "Please, Miss" when the other children giggled. She learned quickly that a lorry was a truck, in America, a lift an elevator, knickers, underpants.

When the boys asked her to describe the bombs, the dead bodies, she told them to bugger off and was taken, gently but firmly, to the principal's office.

Mrs. Armstrong arranged for Heather to have elocution lessons and she, like the rest of us, was sent to dancing class at the Monday Afternoon Club. When it was my turn to march in and shake hands with the teacher she whispered in my ear, "Would you have your Mother call me, dear, about the bill?" She whispered it so quickly there was no halt in the progression of children in white gloves and polished shoes who marched in two by two to a polonaise. To the other children she said, "Good evening, how lovely to see you here again."

Mats with black feet painted on them took us through the dances. Step together/step together/slide/slide.

I was in the "Five to Six" while my sister was in the "Six to Seven." I sat in the hall, with my coat on, waiting for her, pretending to read *Hans Brinker or the Silver Skates.* I could read almost anything by the time I was in third grade. I was good at memory work and spelling bees.

"You must have liked school," my children say and are surprised when I say "No" with such vehemence, when I say, "I hated it. You have no idea how much."

"I loved going to school," my ancient mother says, "I was very good at it and was pledged to Delta Kappa, but we couldn't afford it so I had to drop out."

"I was good at basketball," she says, "that's where your father first noticed me — on the basketball court.

"I was salutatorian for my class," she says. "I dressed up as a witch and predicted the future."

WHAT HAPPENED TO YOU? I want to shout, WHAT DEFEATED YOU? LIFE? MARRIAGE? CHILDREN? WHAT?

I want to scream at her; I want to shake her till her old blue eyes fall to the back of her head. She won't even try. She hasn't tried for years and years. Always some excuse. No clothes, too tired, how could I return the hospitality. But she has nice clothes now — she orders them from catalogues; she has her wits; she can boil a kettle, make some tea, offer cookies — the residents' store sells cookies, cookies that are soft and chewy enough for old teeth, false teeth and partial plates.

She tells me about a new woman who moved in down the hall, who knocked at her door several times, invited her down, obviously wanted to be friends.

"I finally had to tell her to leave me alone, that we had family problems right now and I just wasn't up to it."

"What family problems, Ma?"

The only family problems she has at the minute are self-created. She has recently written one of her disgusting letters to my sister, one of the classic ones full of accusations and dark hints of perversion and betrayal.

"I'm sure your sister has told you."

She has, but I'm not going to admit it.

"Why don't you tell me?" I sound like the dispassionate psychiatrist again.

"I don't want to talk about it."

"Is the woman down the hall nice? Does she seem nice?"

(*Nice*, by my mother's standards, would mean not an R.C., not "common," not "pushy," "refined" — like white sugar.)

"Nice enough, I guess. I'm just not up to making new friends."

Lately she is "not up to" getting dressed until the middle of the afternoon. She can't sleep, she says, until near morning, and then only if she takes her Extra-strength Tylenol. This of course makes her "woozy." But never too woozy to write letters or tell over past injustices, like a rosary, to herself.

"Maybe the woman down the hall is lonely," I say, setting out muffins and fruit, arranging my bouquet of daffodils in a vase.

"That's *her* problem," says my mother.

One day, Mrs. Armstrong arranged for our Brownie troop to take a tour of the bread factory. Huge vats of dough being turned round and round, a sweet rather pleasant smell of yeast and flour and sugar. Everyone (except Mrs. Armstrong and Heather) ate white bread then — everyone on our side of the city. White bread sliced. Even "whole-wheat" was pale and even-textured, nothing peasanty about it, nothing coarse, nothing lumpy, nothing one might use to sop up cabbage soup or eat with cheese that smelled like dirty socks.

After we had seen through the factory we were treated to doughnuts and milk and given a box of assorted doughnuts to take home. The doughnut machine made a sound like underwater farts as it pushed out yet another doughnut from the long cylinder of dough. *Puuuhh.*

I think I was the only one who knew the Armstrongs never ate this stuff, but Heather was sure I wouldn't tell. The week before the visit she'd invited me to stay overnight, and after her nanny, who slept in an adjoining room, had said "Goodnight dears" and left us in the dark, Heather suddenly put her pillow over my face and sat on it. "Hold up your right hand," she ordered, as I kicked and twisted to get free. "Swear you'll never tell about the bread we eat or anything else we do in this house. Swear!"

She didn't need to do that; I would not have told. Heather was the only person who ever invited me to stay overnight. A night at Heather's, whatever minor cruelties she might practise on me (once she locked me in the clothes closet and pretended to go out; often she gave me a brush burn on my arm or pulled my hair) meant a night away from home.

I took the doughnuts home to my father. His favourite snack was doughnuts and Canada Dry ginger ale. He had a joke about "Drink Canada Dry" and a drunk.

Mrs. Armstrong baked their bread herself — something called a Cornell loaf. She said a family could live on bread like that if they also drank a glass or two of milk a day and had a few fresh vegetables. She was a disciple of Bernarr MacFayden. I liked that bread and wondered why she didn't have it made in quantity at the factory.

"It's really for poor people," Heather said. "Nobody on the West Side would buy it."

"She could sell it on the East Side."

"Don't be so stupid. The people on the East Side make their own bread — at home. There's no market for our bread over there."

We were never allowed to go over to the East Side, never. Over there the people were different from us: first- or second-generation immigrants from eastern Europe who ate black bread and worshipped at churches with onion-shaped domes. Their last names were full of consonants. Ukrainians, Czechs, Polacks, Greeks. Heather said the domes of their churches looked like that because they ate so many onions.

I was seventeen years old before I ever crossed to the other side of the city — and that was without my parents' knowledge. I went with a boy I'd met at the hospital where I was working. John's Tavern, that was the name of the place.

Nobody seemed to care that I was under age. I drank rye and ginger ale. It was also the first time I'd ever had a drink. He had to stop the car on the way home so that I could be sick.

❧

I held the little Charlotte doll against a ruler I had taken from my father's desk after he died. It came from the Coca-Cola Bottling Co. in our town and said on one side: "A GOOD RULE." On the other: "DO UNTO OTHERS AS YOU WOULD HAVE OTHERS DO UNTO YOU."

Charlotte was five and one-half inches exactly. She had black painted hair in a puffy bob and a perfect little rosebud mouth. Blue eyes, elegant eyebrows (a single stroke of black paint with a fine, fine brush). Blue ribbons tied just above her knees, gilt slippers. Or one gilt slipper; her left leg was broken off above the ankle. Her arms were bent at the elbows with the hands flat, palms downward, as though she might have been leaning slightly on a lectern, giving a talk on hygiene to all the little boys and girls.

Her belly was rather plump — in fact she was sturdy all round. A head girl perhaps, good at games as well as studies, *mens sana* and so on.

On her backside she had a hole between her buttocks. I used to be married to a potter — I knew that the hole was so she wouldn't blow up in the firing, it wasn't supposed to represent her anus.

There were Frozen Charlies, too, Dulcie told me, although they didn't have any at present.

"They give me the shudders," her sister said.

I once had a rubber dolly with a little hole in her bum — could she have been called a Didee-Doll? I fed her from her baby bottle and she wet on her little white diaper. What fun! We had no baby brothers or sisters — we had never held (had we even *seen*?) a new baby in our lives. The first time I babysat for an infant it was for a doctor's family on Riverside Drive. The mother left a stack of spotless diapers and said the baby might need changing if he began to cry. The nursery was painted a primrose yellow with a blue border. All of the furniture was white. It was like a nursery in a magazine.

When the baby cried and I went to change him I was disgusted and terrified; I thought the baby was sick — all that mustard-coloured stinking mess. I called the emergency number by the phone and asked for the doctor's wife; she came to the phone right away and I explained what had happened to the baby. They were at a dinner party; I could hear talk and laughter in the background.

When I described the baby's symptoms the doctor's wife laughed. Then she said, not unkindly:

"Charlotte, haven't you ever taken care of a baby before?"

Later I thought of the doctor's wife going back to the elegant table, set with flowers and candles and silverplate, like the ads in *The Woman's Home Companion*, telling the amusing story of the baby-sitter who had never changed a baby before and thought the baby was ill. It would be all over the West Side, how stupid I was. But I never heard another word and was asked to sit again.

I turned the Frozen Charlotte on her back and put her next to *The Water-Babies*. It seemed appropriate. Poor Tom had to drown to get that clean.

"Mother Carey's chickens, that's about all I remember," my mother said as I was leaving, with the book tucked into my handbag. "That's about all I remember from that book."

❧

"Remember Slam Books?" I said to Lydia one night.

"Of course I do. That was the year before I went away to school."

"I don't know why I started one around," I said,

"budding masochist I guess. You had very distinctive handwriting then — it was more like printing."

"That's the way we were taught in England. Over and over on our slates:

'The north wind doth blow
And we shall have snow
And what will the robin do then, poor thing.'

"There was another verse but I can't remember it."

" 'She has dirty fingernails,' you wrote, and 'bog Irish.' "

"Oh Charlotte, did I really? I must have, as you've remembered it all these years."

"It was true — but it was also unfair. My mother thought we were delicate and there was no heat in the bathroom — she didn't like us to take too many baths. We took sponge baths in the winter, that's all." We had to show our hands and fingernails in Health Lesson. No matter how hard I tried, with orange sticks, bobby pins, even with straight pins, my fingernails were never clean.

Sometimes on Sundays we went to look at houses for sale. Mother always hoped we could move. My father waited in the car, smoking Luckies.

We always looked at the bathrooms first, lovely bathrooms with tiled walls and tiled floors, mirrored medicine cabinets, heat, new cakes of soap, Camay or Palmolive, in soap dishes. Sinks without cracks.

After one of these excursions Mother would lock herself in her room and weep. Our father always made the Sunday night supper: home-made vegetable soup, pear and cream-cheese salad, cocoa with a marshmallow on top. It was always the same

in the wintertime. On the Sundays when we went
to see bathrooms Mother did not come down to
supper. We ate in silence and then we went to bed.

"You were a real sad sack," Lydia said in the
darkness. "It's amazing to me, how you've changed."

"It was a long time ago," I said.

"And in another country," she said, "and
besides, the wench is dead."

"Shakespeare? The Bible?"

"Webster, I think, although I can't remember
which wench or what she died of."

"I think my mother is afraid to die," I said.

"Well, aren't we all?"

"Yes — most of us I guess. But I think she is a
believer. I think she believes she will be judged."

"By God the Father?"

"Exactly. Last year she asked me if I believed in
forgiveness."

"And —?"

"And I said yes, I did. I thought if one were truly
sorry for something, then one would be forgiven.
But she said, 'Well, I don't. I don't believe we're forgiven.' "

৫

I look at the copy of a photograph in the Book of Begats. Mother is in the front row, straight-haired and
solemn, wearing a big bow at the back of her head.
1906. She has just turned nine. My grandmother,
Grace Corbett, my great-grandmother, Alice Corbett, and my great-great-grandmother, Juliet
Corbett, are all there, in shirtwaist dresses and
rather elaborate rolled hairdos. Great-grandfather
Marshall J. is sitting on the ground, cross-legged,
with the children. ("He wanted to start a *die-nasty*.")

My mother stares straight ahead at the camera, or at my grandfather, who may be taking the picture. Was this before or after? — I'm not sure. I get out my magnifying glass and study the faces of my grandmother and her eldest daughter, like an old-fashioned detective looking for clues. The picture is very fuzzy, but Mother's lips look tightly closed whereas Grandma, her head tilted to one side, is smiling slightly.

The fact that the hired girl is not in the picture proves nothing. There are thirteen women posing and no doubt all of them had hired help. This is a *family* picture. The servants might not be in the picture because they were making pies and salads for the picnic. Or standing in the garden hanging up the clothes. ("Along came a blackbird and snipped . . .")

— From the Book of Begats

Marshall Joseph Corbett was educated in the common schools, and afterward attended a commercial college in preparation for a business career. On June 18, 1862, he enlisted as a private in the 137th Regiment of New York Volunteer Infantry, and when that regiment was mustered into United States service on September 3, 1862, he was elected 2nd lieutenant. He was promoted to 1st lieutenant May 30, 1863, and to captain December 30, 1863, and was brevetted major for meritorious service and honorably discharged June 9, 1865, at the close of the war. He participated in many of the important battles, including Gettysburg, where he fired the first shot on the 3rd day of battle.

In April 1870, he was appointed a clerk in the United States Appraiser's Department, where he was advanced to become examiner and assistant appraiser of merchandise of the Port of New York. After 22 years in the customs office, he established his own business as a Customshouse broker. He retired to his ancestral village of Corbettsville, New York.

The children of Marshall Joseph and Alice Waldron Corbett were:

907. Lawrence Bowes Corbett, born in 1870 in Brooklyn, New York.

908. Alice

909. Grace

910. Clara

911. Mabel (who danced with the Prince of Wales. Who travelled all the way back across the continent with her grieving mother, Papa in the freight car in a wooden coffin.)

A handsome man, my mother says, a tyrant, who built churches and kept a horsewhip just inside the kitchen door.

The cemetery was the same as I remembered it, although back then I hadn't known its name: Stillwater. Someone was keeping it up and there were

bearded irises, pale-yellow and mahogany, bloom-
ing to one side of my grandparents' grave.

| Laurence B. | † | Grace Albertyn |

I wondered if Aunt Betty would be buried here. Not
Mother. No way Ho-Say.

No angels with blind eyes in this small place.
No crosses, no mausoleums. One urn, atop the Fish
family monument ("We are the Fish sisters." My
young grandmother, sheltered city girl, staying for
the summer with her in-laws. Never mind Granny,
I asked what kind of snakes there were in the creek,
not even thinking about its shape, even after I saw
it on the map).

The only verses are the ones written to Anne
and Amelia, a dialogue.

Anne   Amanda
d. 1830   d. 1835
6 yrs. 1 mo.   9 yrs. 16 da
21 da

To the dark and solemn tomb
Soon we hasten from the womb
Scarce the dawn of life began
Ere we measured out our span
We no smiling pleasures knew
We no gay delight could view
Joyless sojourners was we
Only born to weep and die

Happy infants early bless'd
Rest, in peaceful slumbers, rest;
Early rescued from the cares
Which increase with growing years
No delights are worth thy stay
Smiling, as they seem, and gay
Lasting only, and divine
Is an innocence like thine.

Memorial Day had just been and gone. There was a marker and a small, new flag by Robert Corbett's grave; he fought at Lexington and Concord. There was a flag and marker by the grave of Waples Hance.

My uncle is buried in Massachusetts; who knows what my aunt will do. She is probably the only one left who truly believes in God, in Heaven and Hell, all the old, grim fairy-tales. I would like my mother to be buried there, beside her father and mother, near to the other small brothers and sisters, near to Baby Grace, 1901–2.

I have brought winter crocuses and a small trowel. My hands are dirty so I walk down and wash them in the creek. I imagine my mother in her pinafore and bare feet, her little sister always by her side, the big boys, Laurence and Cousin Marshall, off somewhere being naughty. Frances and Betty have been playing in the cemetery, making posies for the babies.

It's very still, almost noon, almost dinnertime. Darning-needles zoom above the water and a hawk flies low, looking for signs of movement in the corn-field. The church bell in Conklin begins to ring. One. Two. Three. Four. Five. And then it stops,

*begins again. One. Two. Three. Four. Five. Six.
Seven. Eight. Nine, and on to Seventeen. She can
almost see the notes — large, round — as they float
down to earth. A man, a young man. Probably an
accident, a hired hand. She wonders who it is. Edna
will know — she always knows everything. Frances
grabs Betty's hand and they hurry down the dirt
road to Grandpa's house. For a minute she had
hoped that the dead man was Father.*

❧

cemetery: from a Gk. word for "to put to sleep," "I
lull to sleep," Κολμάω: a dormitory.

— From *A History of Broome County* (with illustrations), 1885:

> The first settlers came from Massachu-
> setts or Connecticut or up from Pennsyl-
> vania. The Wyoming Massacre and the
> great flood of the Susquehanna ice freshet
> (which carried away many dwellings and
> was actually referred to as "The Deluge")
> persuaded those who had settled in north-
> ern Pennsylvania to try their luck else-
> where. Indians were still living along the
> shores of the river but they did not seem
> hostile.

(*Après le déluge, moi,* with my notebooks and
box of pens.)

By the time I grew up there were no Indians,
except on reservations, although my grandfather
had a quart jar full to the top with flint arrowheads
and we slept under cotton Indian blankets at his

camp. Our town was run by Catholics taking orders from Tammany Hall. My mother was hostile to Catholics; I secretly yearned to be one. Confession: to unburden oneself to a dim shape behind a grating. Novenas. First Fridays. The Virgin Mary. Bless me Father, for I have sinned.

At Scout Camp we sang "Red Wing," we learned to paddle a canoe, we wore moccasins. We listened to the Lone Ranger. We told jokes.

Q. Why did they bury the Indian on a hill?
A. Because he was dead.
Q. What do you call a Mother Indian?
A. A Squaw.
Q. What do you call a Baby Indian?
A. A Squawker.

We read the *LeatherStocking Tales*; we memorized long sections of *Hiawatha*.

As unto the bow the cord is
So unto the man is woman
Though she bends him, she obeys him,
Though she draws him, yet she follows,
Useless each without the other.

I asked my teacher, once, why the Indians were all on reservations.

A. "Because they are happier there."

The earliest printed use of the word Susquehanna occurs (four times) on John Smith's map of 1608: Sasqusahanough flu; Sasqueshannoug (twice); in a phrase accompanying an illustration, in colour, of a warrior.

"The Sasqueshanougs are a gyant like people and thus attired."

Indian mothers carried their babies on their backs. Their babies were called papooses. I cried in the movie *Broken Arrow*.

For years my grandfather's Christmas gift to my parents was a subscription to the *National Geographic*. There were issues of *Life* we were not allowed to see but we could always look at the *National Geographic*. Any time. I saw the world beyond my state, my country, as endlessly interesting and always under a clear blue sky. No disease, no leprosy or yaws or elephantiasis, no bottle babies with fly-bedecked eyelids, no hostile natives or district commissioners who had gone mad from heat or boredom. Never a slum in the exciting cities of the world; never a scared child crying.

And always in the back of the magazine the ads for passenger liners: Cunard, Shaw-Savill, Canadian-Pacific. Slim women in dinner dresses stood at the rail looking up at tall, masterful, successful men in dinner jackets. I wanted both, the elegance of crossing the ocean by liner plus the adventure of "Copra-ship Voyage to Fiji's Outlying islands" or "Down the Susquehanna by Canoe."

The *National Geographic* taught me something else, as well. Like strangers (the strangers my mother warned me about), those who adventured abroad were usually men.

In school we learned the names of the world's longest rivers: the Nile, the Amazon, the Mississippi (Missouri, Redrock — it changes its name as it just keeps rolling along), the Ob-Irtysk, the Yangtze, the Hwang Ho, the Congo.

The Susquehanna is just a rivulet compared to

these; it's only four hundred and fifty miles long. However, that's only slightly shorter than the Seine (482) and much longer than the Hudson, the Tiber or the Thames (210). It enters our county in the town of Colesville and flows in graceful sweeps and curves towards the south, towards Pennsylvania. But just after crossing the state line it seems to have a change of heart, makes a great bend and re-enters New York, flowing northwest to our town. Then it goes back to Pennsylvania and flows south-south-east into Maryland, where it finally enters the northern part of Chesapeake Bay at Havre de Grace. John Smith, of Jamestown, in 1608, was the first white man to see — and travel on — the Susquehanna. He explored the river's mouth. It is a broad and shallow river; the shad runs, in the old days, were so heavy that a man could walk across the river on snowshoes. And eels. At the zig-zag weirs, made of loose stones, the men would pitchfork eels by the dozen into their boats.

"We had an eel-weir up Snake Creek," my mother said.

The water was pure and sparkling when the first settlers arrived — and well into the late nineteenth century — except during the spring freshets, or floods.

This is the river where Coleridge and Southey hoped to start their pantisocracy. In later life Coleridge told Dr. Gilman that he chose that river because he liked the mellifluous sound of the name.

PANTISOCRACY

No more my visionary soul shall dwell
On joys that were; no more endure to
      weigh

The shame and anguish of the evil day,
Wisely forgetful! O'er the ocean swell

Sublime of Hope, I seek the cottag'd dell
Where Virtue calm with careless step may
    stray,
And dancing to the moonlight roundelay,
The wizard Passions weave an holy spell.
Eyes that have ach'd with Sorrow! Ye shall
    weep
Tears of doubt-mingled joy, like theirs who
    start
From Precipices of distemper'd sleep,
On which the fierce-eyed Fiends their
    revels keep,
And see the rising Sun, and feel it dart
New rays of pleasance trembling to the
    heart.

                        (1794)

Joseph Priestley, the discoverer of oxygen, moved to Northumberland, Pennsylvania, in 1794. "I do not think," he wrote, "there can be in any part of the world a situation more beautiful . . . when I compare the perturbed state of Europe with the quiet of this place I wish all my friends were here." His son-in-law, Thomas Cooper, came out to see, went home, came back to settle, wrote a book.

Thomas Poole, a prosperous farmer friend of Coleridge's, wrote a letter about the Pantisocrats: "Twelve gentlemen of good education and liberal principles are to embark with twelve ladies on April next . . ." They would settle at — "I do not recollect the place but somewhere in a delightful part of the new back settlement." Although they had never farmed in their life, they would be able to clear the land, plant thriving crops, read, write poetry and educate their children. If you substitute "play music" for poetry it sounds very like the Utopian dreams of the sixties. Even Coleridge's views on love seem strangely modern and self-serving.

"That we can love but one person is a mistake," writes Coleridge to Sara, "and the cause of abundant unhappiness. I can and do love many people dearly — so dearly that I really scarce know which I love the best . . ."

I like to imagine Samuel, "Sam," living in some commune on the West Coast, smoking up with the rest of us. Or taking a bottle from his back pocket.

"I'll give you something I'll wager you never had before."

I imagine Coleridge on the west coast of Canada, circa 1968.

Christabels are all around him, lovely, long-haired ladies easily manipulated, maidens barefoot, smiling, wearing no knickers, like the girls in dreams.

"Oh wow," they say, "oh wow." The blonde one, who has changed her name to Seedpod, touches his cheek with her smoky fingers.

"Say it again, Sam. For me?"

They love the bit about the mastiff bitch.

"Far out," they say, offering around another joint, *hnnh, hnnh, hnnh* — "Far *out*."

Sam takes a bottle from his back pocket. He smiles at the blonde. "I wonder if you'd like to try some of this . . ."

Michael said to me: "Why can't we all just love one another?"

❧

I remember the mists rising off the rivers and the smell of burning leaves. The purple hills were truly purple during our Indian Summer. With newspapers underneath to catch the mess and warnings to be careful, be careful, we carved jack-o'-lanterns with our Girl Scout knives (be careful! be careful!) and carefully carefully set the candle ends inside.

No possibility of razors in apples, no UNICEF cans, we went from house to house along Chestnut Street, down Johnson Avenue, around and up Bennett, then home. Sometimes we were invited in and given cider and doughnuts (always Armstrong doughnuts; nobody ate any other kind) if we recited a poem or sang a song. I was never afraid of the dark (be careful, be careful) but steered clear of the big boys, who raced through the streets like wolves, setting off firecrackers, putting dog poo on the steps of the high school principal, uprooting FOR SALE signs and relocating them on the lawns of the mansions on Riverside Drive.

I was born in November just before Thanskgiving. In Primary School we cut pumpkins out of orange construction paper (replacing black bats and cats), turkeys (the teacher gave us a stencil). If we did good work that month there were colourful stickers at the top of our papers. We learned about the *Mayflower* and Plymouth Rock, about the first Thanksgiving. We sang songs.

> We gather together to ask the Lord's blessing,
> He hastens and chastens His will to make known.

The wicked oppressing now cease in
distressing . . .

We went to Grandpa's for Thanksgiving dinner.
Starched white linen and silver cutlery. "For what
we are about to receive . . ." The housekeeper cooked
the turkey. Grandpa offered around the pope's nose.
Mother always said "Dad!" and turned red.

("Which was I," I asked my mother once, "trick
or treat?")

❦

We were driving past the Rexall drug-store when he
suddenly pulled over and stopped the car. "You girls
wait here."

When he came out he was smiling and carrying
the cardboard woman who'd been sitting in the
window offering something on a plate. It was Jane's
turn to sit up front so I had to endure the drive home
with the cardboard woman across my lap, her
tanned legs in their white, open-toed shoes sticking
out the window.

Later, when we arrived up at the woods (he
always went up first), there she was, sitting in
Grandma's old rocking chair on one side of the big
stone fireplace. He was sitting in his regular place
on the opposite side.

"How do you like my new girlfriend?" he said.

I could hear my parents talking in low voices
after they went to bed.

"Just leave it alone," my father said, "don't
start any trouble." He always called Grandpa "Mr.
Corbett."

"In *Mother's chair*," our mother said. "In my
mother's *chair*."

"Just leave it alone," my father said, "for God's sake go to sleep."

During those first few days in London I found myself talking to God, or to the Norns or whatever was responsible for the power failures, the uprooted trees, the DANGER signs everywhere. "All right, that's enough! Knock it off." I had a fixed ticket and very little extra money. I wouldn't be paid for my *Batory* article until it was written and accepted. I needed to get down to the coast as soon as possible; there were just so many times I could leaf through the Book of Begats. The jolly old British were out there in their green wellies "getting on with it," "coping," all those things the British do so well (and seem to have such fun in the doing — "Oh yes," says Lady Somebody on the radio, "it's dreadful what's happened to our park, dreadful. But we're coping, you know, the children have made a super playhouse out of some of the trees and we won't lack for Yule logs this year, har har har") while I sat around, walked around, killing time.

There is a story about Great-great-grandfather Ira Corbett and a log. Whenever there was a dispute between him and his wife, he went to the back of the woodpile where he kept his longest logs. One of the children would be called upon to carry one end of the log, and when they arrived back at the house it was stood endwise into the fire so that it extended out a few feet into the room.

"Now then," he would say, "those that agree with your mother sit over there, and those that agree with me shall sit over here."

They sat in silence, and as the log burned down,

Great-great-grandfather kicked it further into the
fire. No one was allowed to speak — there was no
discussion.

By the time the last of the log was in the fire the
quarrel would be over. Ira Corbett lied and said his
father had done this and his father before him and
he believed his father as well.

"And your father?" I asked my mother. "Your
grandfather, Marshall J.?"

"Never. Maybe he was afraid the house might
burn down. Anyway, that's a countryman's story, a
countryman's way of doing things. Marshall
Corbett wasn't really a countryman like his father.
He lived in New York and was a businessman until
the Civil War broke out. Afterwards he had this
pipe-dream about starting a dairy farm, about
running one of the acid factories. And besides, I
don't think his wife ever quarrelled with him; she
wouldn't dare."

His wife, Alice, who produced one boy and then
four girls all noted for their lovely hair.

The insane asylum, known to the citizens of our
town as "the Hill," started out as the first Inebriate
Asylum in the world.

— From *A History of Broome County* (with illustrations), 1885:

> The site selected for the inebriate asylum
> is a delightful one, comprising over two
> hundred and fifty-two acres of land, pre-
> sented by the citizens of Binghamton for
> the purpose to which it is devoted. It is sit-

uated about two miles eastward from the courthouse, on the summit of a gently-sloping eminence, some two hundred and forty feet above the water, and commanding a view of the Susquehanna and Chenango Rivers and valleys for eight or nine miles each way, while to the north-west every part of the city can be seen. The grounds surrounding the edifice are devoted to suitable walks and lawns, and the remainder to farming purposes for the use of the institution.

The corner-stone was laid by the Grand Master of the Free and Accepted Masons. Rev. Henry Bellows, D.D. paid tribute to Dr. J. Edward Turner, whose project this had been. There had been a comet in the sky the night before the ceremony and this promoted the following remarks:

"As I looked last night at the flaming comet in our sky, and saw it inclined and plumed like a pen, fit and ready for the Almighty's own hand, I could not but feel that if He should seize it and inscribe with its diamond-point upon the sky the chief event of this *annus mirabilis* it would be the foundation of a policy and a usage such as that we now celebrate — of an institution, the first of its kind in the world, which proclaims that mercy is better than justice; nay, that mercy is an exacter justice."

Dr. Bellows was warmly applauded for his remarks. However, the Almighty, in the person of the New York State legislature, declared the experiment a failure and turned it into the Binghamton Asylum for the Chronic Insane.

It was here that Marshall J. sent his daughter Grace Corbett Campbell on the advice of two of her sisters and here that she remained until the last months of her life.

It was here that his son Lawrence B., through the agency of his daughter Frances, while he and his wife stayed in the bedroom, behind closed doors, sent his daughter, Elizabeth Corbett, when she drank iodine at Thanksgiving dinner. When she came out she left for Massachusetts and worked in a women's reformatory. Somewhere along the line she got religion and was saved.

It was here, in 1953, 1954 and 1955, that I spent my summers, moving from ward to ward as I was needed — shock ward, ambulatory wards, the O.R., where I saw clever men drill holes in the skulls of recalcitrant patients — but ending up, more and more, on female geriatric, Ward 88, "The Shit Ward."

Coming home on the bus I sat at the very back, convinced, in spite of the shower I took before I left the grounds, that my skin reeked of pee and shit.

No one enjoyed the extensive grounds or the view of the Chenango and the Susquehanna and the valleys in between. When I led a group of insulin-shock patients to the commissary for milk shakes and ice-cream sodas they could barely put one foot in front of the other. When nurses and staff finished their shifts they hurried away down the hill to the real world of city and home.

My parents never asked me any questions about my work. Years later my mother said, "I never would have let you work there if I'd known."

"What did you think I was doing? Arranging flowers in vases?"

But she must have known. Did she never visit her sister? She'd certainly gone to Bellevue, but maybe that was different.

"Poor Betty," she always says, "poor Betty." But smiles her little smile. "When she came out of Bellevue Father came to New York, dressed up in a tuxedo, and took her dancing, just as though he were her beau."

"Did he ever take you dancing?"

"I wasn't crazy, was I?"

"How was your summer?" said the girls at Smith, tanned and fit from their weeks at the lake, the ocean.

"Interesting," I always said. Lydia, who could have told, kept quiet.

&

The one thing that has never rung true to me in *Jane Eyre* is the description of Mrs. Rochester as a large, vicious, snuffling, hairy beast. The translation from beauty into beast is too complete. It may justify Rochester's actions but it does not, to this reader, make sense. I have seen madness of all sorts, en masse, en mess. I have seen those we used to call cretins, idiots, retarded, nuts — "out to lunch" as well as out to breakfast and dinner.

Mrs. Rochester's bestiality seems like a throwback to Elizabethan times, when the crooked back of a king would indicate his twisted soul. *Jane Eyre* is much earlier than *Dr. Jekyll and Mr. Hyde*. Where did she get her ideas of madness and the dissolution of personality from? It has always made me suspicious of Rochester, such a cold, judgmental man. He does his duty; he never (until he falls in love with Jane) deserts his wife. He keeps her in the attic, locked up and guarded by a woman who likes her drink.

That she had feelings, we know. Why else attack the wedding veil? No doubt scholars have argued over her in learned journals; I wonder what, if anything, psychiatrists have had to say.

(The smell of the wards — medicine and urine and shit. The noise. The things said, the objects thrown. And at the end of each summer a haircut, new clothes — my clothes from the Hill put out with the week's garbage — never a thought, then, to those I left behind.)

For Christmas I'm going to give my mother an eight-by-ten enlargement of the photograph I took on my last visit to Corbettsville. It shows the house with the tower room quite clearly. She had drawn me a sketch one day and cut a picture out of a magazine.

"It looked a lot like this," she wrote. "The railroad tracks were across the way. Betty and I used to go up in the tower room on rainy days. I'm sure it's still there."

I don't know why, exactly, I haven't told her that I found it, why I haven't given her the photograph before this. Maybe I was afraid that if she saw the picture she would stop remembering. Now — with the latest development, I think I, like her great-grandma (my great-great-grandma), must be something of a "mystic." I have the photo with me. "That's the house where it happened," I say to myself, "that's the very place." And I hear my mother's voice:

"I mustn't get a shock."

❀

"She had several children that died when they were a few months old and one that was born dead. Still life, is that what you call it? And Baby Grace, her namesake, who only lived six months. That's what caused her breakdown, that and the fact that her mother died shortly after.

"That's when she went to the Ladies Hospital for a while. I think they told Father that she mustn't have any more babies — the doctors at the hospital. She had developed a weak heart . . ."

❀

Mama was cooking hotcakes on the griddle. Frances and Betty had to be especially good as Mama wasn't well. Lawrence had been sent to Cousin Marshall's for a while.

Frances saw her mother's tears bounce and sizzle on the griddle.

"Mama," she said, frightened. "What's the matter?"

Her mother turned, the ladle full of batter in her hand. The children watched as she turned the ladle over and let the batter dribble on the floor.

That's when Father took her to the Ladies Hospital for a rest. A week later Frances went as well.

"They cut me down there," my mother said, "because I was too high-strung."

❀

Even if it were true that we are descended from Norman nobility, how much Norman blood would be in my veins, a thousand years later? Is a blood-line like sourdough starter? You use a small bit to start a new batch of dough but the original is always there? The sourdough pail of the mountain-men was self-perpetuating, and many felt it actually improved with age. You can use commercial yeast to make the starter but that's like impregnating yourself with a turkey-baster. The results may seem the same but the mystery and excitement are missing. Who "started" our branch of the Corbetts? And is it merely a coincidence that the French for bread is "pain"? Give us this day our daily pain. The prayer of the masochist, my mother.

Are there Viking cells in me, even one or two? Reduced from raider to writer, swooping down and taking what I want, then leaving.

"When is a raven like a writing-desk?"

❀

The present from Lydia arrived on Monday after-noon. *The Companion Letter-Writer: A Guide to Correspondence on all Subjects Relating to Friend-ship, Love and Business, with Commercial Forms B&C.* She had post-it notes at two of the entries.

From a little girl to a friend, asking her to come and assist in dressing the doll

Gothic Villa, Monday

My dear Julia,
   Mamma has bought me such a large doll, and such a pretty one, too, and as I should like it to have nice clothes, I write to ask if you will be so kind as to come here on Wednesday afternoon, and help me to

dress it? Your own doll is so well dressed that I should very much like mine to look as well as yours does.

> Your loving friend,
> Elizabeth

From a little boy to a gentleman who saved him from drowning

Sir,

It is with feelings of the deepest gratitude that I address you to return my thanks for your noble, generous, and devoted efforts by which I was snatched from a watery grave. I feel certain that, had your hand not been stretched forth at that awful moment, I should not now be alive to pen these lines.

Although I am but a boy, I trust that I am properly impressed with a sense of the heavy obligation under which I lie to you; and it is my sincere hope that I may hereafter convince you that the life you have saved is not altogether a worthless one; and also that I may have opportunities of repaying, to some extent, the heavy debt which I do not repine at having incurred but which I feel I shall never be able wholly to discharge.

My parents join me in these acknowledgements, and that every blessing may attend you, in their prayer as well as that of

> Your grateful and respectful servant

He was probably a naughty boy, like the boys in my mother's McGuffy Readers, boys who played along the river when they should have been in school (presumably learning to read from McGuffy Readers).

Five years ago my mother handed me an object wrapped in blue tissue paper. It was a doll, a young-lady doll with a beautiful face. She had come unstrung, so that although head and cloth body were all of a piece, the limbs were all separate. The only bits of clothing left were her black leather high-topped shoes. Even her hair was missing. Mother wanted to have the doll restrung to give to my eldest daughter.

"Where did you get this doll?" I had never seen it before.

"I've had it nearly all my life; a great-aunt gave it to me when I was eight. Betty got one as well."

"What's her name?"

"I don't remember. Maybe she didn't have a name?"

My mother is a woman who tells everybody her life story, a compulsive talker to bank managers, teachers, salesgirls. When I first read *The Ancient Mariner* I thought immediately of my mother who also has to tell her tale. I thought I knew just about everything there was to know about my mother. And yet she had carried this doll around with her for over eighty years, hiding it God knows where. Every time I visit there is a new surprise.

"Was this a very special doll?"

"I suppose so. We didn't have a lot of toys so it must have been. I remember they came from some shop in New York. She had a smart outfit, skirt and coat and hat, forest-green trimmed in black braid, but I don't know what happened to that. I'll have to get her a wig and find somebody to restring her. If I weren't so old I'd make her some clothes."

"Do you remember the doll hospital back home, where we used to take our dollies to be mended?"

She didn't remember.

"Past the orphanage, on the other side of the street."

"I don't remember."

Now the doll, named Frances after my mother, sits in my daughter's bedroom. She has luxurious brown curls and a hat with a curling feather. My daughter sent her grandma a picture of the doll but my mother does not display it. The doll is German — I have not told my mother that. Did my mother and her sister dress and undress their young-lady dolls — did they speak for them, in elegant young-lady voices? There was not much money in the house; did my grandmother set her lips in a stern line when the girls unwrapped their presents? My mother told me nothing about the doll except who gave it to her and when. I had a nice doll (not so nice as this, but nice) with real hair and china eyes. I gave it to my eldest when she was five. Why did my mother keep quiet about this doll? I've asked her, but she says she doesn't know, she was afraid it would get broken, she was afraid we'd fight over it, she didn't know which one to give it to.

And so she kept it hidden in a bottom drawer, unstrung, wrapped tight against prying eyes. It was like a secret child, always there in the bottom drawer. Did she take it out after she had locked herself in her room?

Now Lydia sends me a book she has found on a market stall. She marks two letters out of dozens. I can understand why she marked the watery grave, but why the doll? Just a coincidence, but it made me reflect again on how, if one is already in a heightened state of awareness for whatever reason (love, hate, grief, drugs), certain things become numinous. It was as though I were receiving messages — or one message in bits, like a treasure hunt. Go to the hollow tree and there a message you will see.

("I saw something," my mother said.

"What did you see?"

"I don't want to talk about it. Ever. I'm not supposed to get upset.")

Once on a working holiday in north Cornwall I decided to get up early and walk to a neighbouring village that had a romantic history. I would take the coast path along the cliffs and be there and back before breakfast. In the nineteenth century all the inhabitants of the village had disappeared: some say they drowned, some say they simply moved away when the fishing died out in that area, others say it was foul play. I wanted to see the village for my own (romantic) sake, and I also thought there might be an interesting article in it.

I set off just after dawn and followed a footpath map I'd bought at the newsagent's: *A Walk to Port Quin*. There was no one about but me as I walked out of the village and up onto the cliffs. The sea was down below, a sea so treacherous that in the old days each village had a particular knitting pattern that was knitted into the navy "ganseys," or pullovers, the fishermen wore. Then, if a man drowned and his body washed up along the coast weeks later, the folk who found it would know which village the man had belonged to. Even today the lifeboat is kept in readiness and people (summer sailors mostly) are plucked from a watery grave. Sometimes people fell off the cliffs; I kept well away from the edge.

Following the map I crossed fields and went around boulders until finally I started down a narrow path between a hedge and a fenced field full of black-and-white cows. Soon I could see the chimney-pots on houses and as I came into the village itself I was surprised, not only by the number of houses, but by the fact that the place seemed to be inhabited. As well, the village was an exact twin of Port Isaac, the village in which I was staying. Then I realized it was Port Isaac, that somehow I had gone up and down and around and about and arrived right back where I had started from, only the final descent had been along a different path. I was too embarrassed to tell anyone, so I crept back to the house where I was staying, got out the frying pan and started breakfast. A few days later we drove to Port Quin, which was more or less as I had imagined it.

There were times, and receiving the book was one of them, the Frozen Charlotte another, when the quest I was on reminded me of my abortive walk to the deserted village. No matter how much I tried to follow the itinerary I had set for myself, Fate — in the form of hurricanes or dolls or whatever — was going to bring me right back to where I started.

Even the play Robert and I chose to attend one evening: Anthony Hopkins in *King Lear*.

Cordelia: Nothing, my lord.
Lear: Nothing!
Cordelia: Nothing.
Lear: Nothing will come of nothing, speak again.

"Where was Queen Lear?" I asked Robert as we walked across Waterloo Bridge and along the Strand.

"Perhaps she died in childbirth?"

Robert had objected to the way Shakespeare ends his scenes in rhymed couplets. "You just object to anything in couples," I said, and he laughed. I would like to be as self-sufficient as he is but I still long for what we nowadays call a "partner." I read the ads in the local papers, in the *New York Review of Books*. "DWF" — it sounds like "Dwarf," as one of my daughters pointed out one day.

"Then there are a lot of dwarfs in New York City," I replied.

I write out ads but I never send them in. I have read *Looking for Mr. Goodbar*. I have read *Loves Music, Loves to Dance*. If the ones you know aren't safe, what about the ones you don't know? Has "permanent relationship" been reduced to an oxymoron?

At breakfast in London House that morning I sat next to an Australian historian and his wife. They said they came from "Cans." They were eating identical breakfasts: porridge, two sausages, fruit juice, egg and tomato, toast, tea. A full English breakfast — the kind that might keep you going if you were going out to plough your fields or clear a few acres of trees. The kind that makes you feel, if you are not a farmer, as though you have breakfasted on stones.

I say I am going to Hastings.

"Why do you want to go *there*?" he said, forking up a tiny stack of toast, sausage, egg and tomato. He was very tidy and precise in all his movements. "There's really nothing to see."

"I suppose I just want to smell it, walk around, close my eyes and imagine things."

"Smell it," he says, and gives me an odd look. I can feel the men in the portraits pinching their nostrils together at my idea of research.

The professor cuts up another little package of breakfast and pops it in his mouth. His wife does exactly the same thing at the same time. Dickens could have made use of them, or Lewis Carroll. They are like synchronized swimmers. I think of Richard ("My job is all lies"). This man looks like such an earnest seeker after the truth. Cut this up, pierce that, be precise. Chew each mouthful one hundred times. How would he — how can I — measure the pain of the battle, the horror of the losing side (who were so sure they would win), even the boredom of the men in Normandy, waiting weeks until the weather was just right and they could set sail. Duke William rode up and down with the relics of St. Valéry in order to keep their spirits up.

"——— book?" says the Australian wife. (It sounds like "berk.")

"Couldn't you git what you need from a berk?"

"Not really. Or I don't think so."

"Right-o, Mother," says the professor. "Are we ready then?" They are at the end of his sabbatical and will be going home on Friday, his research on the Poor Laws neatly stored on index cards, to be written up in book form later on. The book will be dedicated to her, "without whose help and support . . ." She drops her shopping list and I go after them. "Reject China Shop," it says, "Mothercare," "Nivea Creme for Mrs. Avis."

Sevenoaks was still called Sevenoaks but all the way down to the coast I could see the damage the storm had done. Trees lay along both sides of the track, like giant skittles.

It was Wednesday when I finally got to buy my cheap day-return from Charing Cross Station. Everyone in the world seemed to be going in the opposite direction — businessmen in dark suits carrying umbrellas and rolled up copies of the *Times*; housewives with empty carrier bags, up for a day of shopping. I had to wait until 9:30 to take advantage of the lower fare, so I bought a coffee in a styrofoam cup and stood and watched. The pink-and-white English, but also the black English, the English the colour of my coffee. It still surprises me to hear two black schoolgirls speaking in Cockney accents. The Commonwealth: now *there's* an oxymoron if there ever was one. The pink-and-whites the true English, of course — the rest just let in because of the Empire's short-sightedness, granting all those wogs British passports. They were meant to be honorary citizens, not to pack up all their bundles and babies and actually move here. The Empire strikes back.

Wednesday, Woden's-day, or Othin's day, the Norse god whose familiars were two ravens, Huggin and Muggin, Mind and Memory. Each day they circled the world and then came back to perch on his shoulders and tell him what they had seen.

When I was a child my father took me to the Brooklyn Zoo, where I saw an electric eel light up a light bulb. Since then I have avoided eel even dead, even embalmed in jelly, in case an electric eel might have got in by mistake. Even dead it might have the power to shock. I have eaten cockles and winkles off the end of a pin in London; I have eaten crocodile and goat in West Africa; frogs' legs in Massachusetts, sea snails in Greece; sea urchins and sea cucumbers on the coast of British Columbia. But I have never eaten eel.

My parents both ate eel as children — or it looks as though they did. On my bureau back home is a picture of my father, aged seven or eight, holding an eel at the end of a fishing line, very pleased with himself (my father, not the eel). And my mother, when I asked her about Snake Creek, didn't remember any snakes, "but there was an eel-weir." Did *she* eat eel? Did her mother or her grandma cut it into slices and fry it up, like eggplant? It is no doubt very good, but the Eel Bar in Hastings is closed, as is a fish-and-chips stand which says:

> We are open 7
> Days a week with
> Time off at Christmas
> for Good Behaviour

Perhaps now that it is the end of the season, or maybe because of the bad weather last week, the Bad Behaviour of the wind and the sea, the owners have decided to take time off now. Or it is too early in the day? There is no cardboard sign saying "FRYING TODAY" with a clock whose hands point to the hour of opening.

I walk past the Shipwreck Heritage Centre: ONLY MUSEUM IN BRITAIN WITH RADAR/ DAILY LIVE PICTURES OF BRITAIN FROM SPACE. It too is closed, but there is a garish picture of "the *Amsterdam* in the Gale, 1749" on the side of the building. I wish I had a picture of what the *Stefan Batory* looked like, from the shore, in the early hours of October 16. I pass the NETSHOPS, forty-three very tall, black, wooden buildings, back

to back in double rows, used for storing and
mending nets. When you are up in the new part of
town you could never imagine that Hastings is still,
at the bottom, a fishing village.

> A fisherman was reported dead after being
> hit by a beach hut, which was hurled along
> the shore at Hastings by a gust.

> Also at Hastings guests were rescued from
> the Queens Hotel after it collapsed, killing
> one person.

> As emergency workers strived to keep up
> with record numbers of calls, the question
> many were asking was: Why did we get no
> warning?

I was told by the tourist office in the town that
Hastings has its own "Bayeux Tapestry," a 243 ft.
embroidery that "colourfully depicts 81 great
events that took place in Britain between 1066 and
1966." But I can't find it. I wonder if the ladies of
the various altar guilds have done the embroidery
and if any of the events, other than the coronations
of queens, have anything to do with women.

On Harold Street I see a man in big gumboots
and a sailor's cap, and a beard like a great bird's
nest. He wears an earring in one ear. My grandfather had a library of the world's classics, bound in
dark blue, with thin, crisp pages and print that was
very hard to read. *Treasure Island* was my
favourite, even though it gave me bad dreams. For
a long time I thought the fifteen men were all
sitting on top of the dead man and not on his

treasure-chest, sitting on him to make sure he was dead, the way the fat boy Leo Cassella knocked me down in the playground and sat on me until the teacher pulled him off. He wanted a bite of my candy apple and I said no.

I smiled at the man in the gumboots and he smiled back but neither of us stopped. I wanted to ask if he knew of any fish shops that were open but felt too shy. I was an idler, a tourist, whereas he was obviously heading down to his boat.

I passed a sweet shop with jars of English sweets in the salt-frosted window:

SHERBET PIPS
FIZZY FRUITS
TOM THUMB DROPS
LEMON CRYSTALS
FRUITY CHEWS

and dozens more besides. So much more fun to buy than a package of "assorted" somethings, the assortment already chosen by someone else, or a machine. I went in and bought some jelly-babies and asked about fish and chips. I was directed to a café in the oldest part of town, but in the end, seeing a wholefood restaurant, I went in and had an enormous bowl of leek-and-potato soup, then asked to see the telephone directory.

In the ancient church of All Saints I saw a memorial brass to Thomas Goodenough and Margaret, his wife. He was bailiff of Hastings in 1520. A rubbing from this brass hangs in William Goodenough House where I am staying. There are times, I thought, when I seem to be doing several jigsaw puzzles at once.

What interested me more was a Doom painting over the chancel arch. I had heard about them but never seen one before. Christ is sitting on a rainbow, wrapped in an ermine-lined cloak. I went back to the stall by the church door and put 10p. in the wooden box so that I could buy the information pamphlet. Thou shalt not steal.

The painting looked as though it had been done by someone high on drugs. From Christ's wounds sprang stems of flowers. Only the stalks remained but the pamphlet said "one can only guess that they were lilies." There was an angel in a red mantle, with red wings ending in peacock's feathers. Mary is in red and green with long yellow hair.

The stars look like starfish. In the background are the towers and mansions of the New Jerusalem.

Far down on the right are the Torments of the Damned, here not torment by fire but by hanging.

Is this how my mother sees what lies beyond the grave? Is she afraid she will be judged and damned? I would like to ask her but I'm afraid she will become frightened or accuse me of wanting her out of the way. Last year my sister sent her minister, a woman, to see Mother. The next day she wrote me a letter:

"She asked me what my answer would be at the 'Pearly Gates' and I said I didn't believe in 'Pearly Gates' which was really a *knock-out blow* to a *minister*, wasn't it?" BAM. BAM. BAM.

Or does she simply see a void, nothingness, unbeing? Is the pain she is in, appears to have been in all her life, preferable to nothing? The grandmother of a friend of mine died recently; there are two versions of her last words:

  (1) The daughter's version: "How lovely, how lovely," as though, at the end, she saw beauty and peace and a fair field of folk.

(2) The nurse's version (told in confidence to the granddaughter): "Get me out of here!"

Outside the church a poster assures me, apropos of AIDS, that it's perfectly all right to drink from the chalice at communion. If I wish to know more there is a number I can ring.

(Our grandfather took us to see a Danny Kaye film, *The Court Jester*. The vessel with the pestle had the pellet with the poison but the chalice from the palace held the brew that was true. Take this — in remembrance of me.)

Coventry Patmore lived in Hastings, although he didn't worship at All Saints. Patmore's friend Rossetti was a reluctant bridegroom here, marrying his beautiful, consumptive Lizzie at St. Clement's, lower down in the valley, in 1860.

Lizzie had a still-born child ("still life, is that what you call it?") and was dead of a laudanum overdose by 1862. I have been to see her grave in Highgate Cemetery. When she posed for drowned Ophelia she had to lie in a bathtub full of water.

Still-born. Not exactly an oxymoron, like bittersweet. But a curious compound just the same. What do the French call it, I wonder, since what we call "still life" they term, much more accurately, *nature morte*. Did she name her child? Did she take laudanum for her physical pain — the consumption — or the mental anguish? "Still" can also mean it's not over, yet. "I am Duchesse of Malfy, still."

Grandmother Corbett took laudanum, I am sure of it; she always smelt of liquorice.

The hired girl said, "Shh, shh, don't bother your poor Mama, she's lying down." The hired girl put on Mama's big straw hat and suggested they all pick berries down by the creek. When they returned their buckets were full and their lips and the tips of their fingers were stained with purple. The hired girl made three pies and set them in the larder to cool.

❀

Twilight Sleep: "a form of anaesthesia used during childbirth, to obliterate the pain and memory of childbirth while the muscular power for successful delivery is retained."

It is made of morphine and scopolamine (hyoscine obtained from henbane) and is now considered too dangerous to use. Formerly it was used not just in childbirth but also for "agitation" (D.T.s, mania, psychosis). It may have been used, therefore, on people who were too high-strung. It may have been used on my Aunt Betty.

Poultry are often killed by eating the seeds of henbane, hence its name. Another name is deadly nightshade.

Other members of the nightshade family are tobacco, eggplant, potato, cayenne pepper and belladonna. When Mother was young, she said, women put belladonna in their eyes to make the pupils bigger.

❀

Neighbours never phoned or arrived at the door but they must have heard. These were city lots — the houses close together. At least in the summer we went away to Grandpa's Woods; in the summer we weren't there, windows wide open to catch any breeze.

Perhaps they didn't hear; the storm windows

were on from November until the end of March. Mother calmed down in April, May and June. Only now do I realize it must have been connected to removal of the storm windows, that calm. And the day after school was out we took off for the mountains. No fighting up there, no arguments about breadwinners or mama's-boys. The smell of pines, the frogs in the creek below, the clean sand and the water. She smeared us with Coppertone but left us pretty much alone. She had to; she was in her father's house. For two months of every year he paid all the bills.

"Are we there yet are we there yet are we there?"

Had she been happy in her winter rages — dramatic, excessive in an operatic sense — had there been even a hint that she was enjoying this we might have felt differently.

Once, on rue St. Denis in Montreal, I witnessed a terrible argument between a young woman and her boyfriend. I don't know what set it off but there they were, screaming at one another while all the world and his brother stopped to stare. Finally she yelled at him, "Do you think I am your *chien de poche*, your lap dog," and walked away. He stood there for a moment, then gave a great whoop of laughter, set out after her, caught her up and they embraced.

I had been afraid; I had thought there would be violence.

I still tremble at the sound of broken glass.

❧

"The hail will never come any more," said the strange lady to Peter Grimes. "I have told you

before what it was. It was your mother's tears."

🙰

mother — female parent. f. *Mater*, para. 5. The basic mā, which with var. mē or mĕ, represents that most fundamental of all sounds, the cry or murmur of a babe at the breast. (redup. Ma Ma)

🙰

The Corbet(t) coat of arms, says the Book of Begats, is a raven sable on a gold (or) background. Sometimes the background is argent.

    corbet — OFr. corbet, crow, raven. dim. of Ofr. *corp* — L. *corvus*.

    corbie (1450) Sc. a raven; also the carrion — crow.

    "And the ravens brought him bread and flesh in the morning and bread and flesh in the evening: and he drank of the brook." (And so Elijah is fed.)
    "Who provideth for the raven his food? When his young ones cry unto God, they wonder for lack of meat." (God convinces Job of his ignorance.)
    "He giveth to the beast his food and to the young ravens who cry." (Psalm 147)
    "Consider the ravens: for they neither sow nor reap; which neither have storehouse nor barn; and God feedeth them: how much more are ye better than the fowls?" (I knew we had to consider the lilies but I didn't know about the ravens.)
    Noah sent forth a raven after forty days, before he sent the dove, and the Lord told Moses, the ex-foundling, and Aaron which beasts they might eat and which not.

Ye shall have in abomination among the
 fowls . . .
The eagle and the ossifrage and the osprey,
And the vulture, and the kite after his
 kind;
Every raven after his kind . . .

. . . UNCLEAN

Ravens are not crows although they are of the
same family; crows and ravens are cousins. Ravens
are much bigger than crows: they have a four-foot
wing span and they do not "caw," they "croak."

In France, people who live in hotels are said to
be *sur la branche*.

An informer, during the War, was *un corbeau* (a
word which cropped up again during *l'affaire
Gregoire*).

A raven appears on the Danish flag of the
Vikings and their flag was called The Raven Standard. Hugo's family came to France (now Normandy) with Rollo. I think Hugo must have been
Hugo the Raven; crows irritate and annoy us, but
ravens signal death.

Hugo's son Roger de Corbeau built a castle in the
marches between Wales and Shropshire. He named
it Caux, from the area in Normandy where he came
from. This was eventually corrupted to "Caws." The
pays de Caux is Emma Bovary country, another
woman who thought she was too high-class for those
around her. Hoity-toity, as Ma would say. Whose author declared his heroine to be himself.

The *raven*, say the bird books, is a non-migra-
tory bird.

At one time, *raven* was used as a verb, at the

end of the fifteenth century (from OFr. *raviner*, to
rush, ravage). It came to mean to take goods away
by force, to rush, to ravage. (Flaubert's parrot;
Corbet's crow.)

raven, a small bit of bread and cheese (tavern-
talk, now obsolete. Ex. the story of Elijah and the
ravens or possibly also ex. Aesop?)

Add some pickle and you have a Ploughman's
Lunch.

There were twenty-two Corbetts in the Hastings telephone directory. It's a pity, I thought, that
there weren't twenty-four. I thanked the woman at
the wholefood shop.

"Would you care to use our telephone?" she
said. "A local call is 10p."

"No," I said, "but thank you very much."

❧

The sun set, on the night of the battle, at 17:50
(5:50 p.m.). This was nautical twilight: that is, dark
enough to see the stars but light enough to see the
horizon at 6:59 p.m. William, with his knights, rode
away; the priest blessed the dying; the wounded
horses whinnied and groaned; the earth sucked up
the blood.

The next day the sun came over the horizon at
5:57, shining dimly in the fog that covered everything for miles around.

The news spread north: the King is dead long
live the King. The sons of Hugo the Raven would be
rewarded before the year was out.

"Well done, lads, jolly good show" or the
French equivalent. The Crow brothers, soon to be
landed gentry.

"I'm the King of the Castle," my children

played. "Get down you dirty rascal."

"We come from good yeoman stock," said Michael's father. Just think, if I had known, I could have mentioned, casually of course, the Corbeaus and William of Hastings.

They didn't like Americans very much, my in-laws. "To be perfectly honest," they said, "to be perfectly frank with you, love, we're *not* very fond of Americans."

❧

Before my mother snatched the paper away I saw the headline: CHILD MOLESTER NOT YET APPREHENDED. "What is 'apprehended,' " I asked at dinner.

"Caught," my father said. He hadn't read the evening paper yet.

I thought the other big word was mole-taster. I had a small brown mole on my neck and there was somebody out there looking for children with moles. I had heard about vampires who sucked your blood; this person probably bit the end off the mole and sucked up your blood through the hole.

I was afraid to go outside and told my mother I had a stomach-ache. It was easy for me to throw up. On the third day my mother called the doctor, who came with his little black bag. He was a friend of the family and wouldn't send the bill-collectors after us.

He called me "young lady."

"What seems to be the trouble here, young lady?"

He reassured Mother there was nothing much wrong and I began to cry. I didn't want to go to school, not until they caught him.

"Caught who, caught who? What has he done to you? Who is it?"

"The mole-taster," I said, "the one who sucks moles."

Mother still laughs about that one, over forty years later.

"Well I wasn't far off," I say, not laughing.

❧

In the *Batory* gift shop I bought an amber ring and a pen which contains a ship. Against a backdrop which is meant to be Gdynia, the ship, if the pen is tilted, goes back/forth/back/forth/back/forth. The ring is an oval of Polish amber set in silver. The amber looks like the yolk of a fertilized egg, even to a small fleck or speck embedded in the yellow.

Double yolks were lucky, my mother said, and no doubt her mother before her. But a fertilized egg wasn't nice. She tried to get out the little bloody dot with a teaspoon, chasing it around the bowl. "Your father will never eat it if he sees this."

"What is it?"

"Just a speck of blood. Where a chick started."

"How? How *started*?" I was a city girl.

"Go and set the table."

Blood in the egg. Sometimes I saw something in the moon, after that, on nights when the moon was round and yellow. I saw the specks in the moon as blood. Not the man in the moon but the woman in the moon, her doing.

Female blood was disgusting. You called your period "the Curse." Mother called it "falling off the roof."

What tempts men into battle? I spread my jacket on

the damp sand and sat on the beach at Hastings, facing France. I could see where the idea of battle in the abstract might appeal: you get to dress up, live in proximity with other men, drinking, shooting, whoring, all for a noble cause (CAWS, CAWS). But when reality strikes, when the man riding next to you has his head lopped off or his warm guts come spilling out over his saddle, steaming like a Full English Breakfast in the October morning air. What then? What keeps you going? The thought that because he's dead you won't be? Is it sexual? Do you get to a point where you *can't stop*? To a child, the sounds of adults making love can be terrifying — someone is being hurt, someone is hurting Mommy. Don't stop don't stop don't stop.

Do the groans of those dying in battle resemble the groans and cries of sex?

Are you afraid of being laughed at, court-martialled, dishonourably discharged? Did they drum you out in those days, like they did in the Civil War?

Were you high on something? Drugged? Coward, from *coda*, means quite literally "with tail between legs." In Old French, *couard*. You dog! You cur!

On a bench in a *plazuelo* in Mexico I met a woman who had been a nurse in the Second World War. She told me about S.I.F., self-inflicted wounds. You could always spot them, she said, because the men invariably shot themselves between the first and second toes. Nothing disfiguring or life-threatening, but enough to keep them out of battle.

Were there cowards at the Battle of Hastings? Did the Normans do it with lances?

"What did you nurses think of those guys?" I asked the woman on the bench.

"Oh, we dressed their wounds but we didn't have any respect for them."

Ralph Waldo Emerson didn't like the Normans. "Twenty thousand thieves landed at Hastings," he said. "These founders of the House of Lords were greedy and ferocious dragons, sons of greedy and ferocious pirates. They were all alike: they took everything they could carry, they burned houses, harried, violated, tortured and killed, until everything English was brought to the verge of ruin."

In the Bayeux Tapestry Dukc William's horse has a fully erect penis — obviously going into battle excited *him*. The Normans were clean-shaven but the English wore moustaches. "Well, think of all those movie colonels and RAF types," Lydia said.

Under the altar at Battle:

REX INTERFEC
TVS: EST

This was the spot where Harold had fallen.

Bones are still being dug up, and arrowheads. I bought the souvenir booklets; I always do. I walked the battle site, following the plan. It was like a treasure hunt: through stiles, around a pond, watch for the bridge across the stream, up and down, another bridge, up and down. Out on the High Street the inhabitants of Battle were hurrying about their business. Women with shopping baskets on their arms, women pushing prams. The butcher, in his straw hat and blue apron, stood in the doorway of his shop, picking his teeth.

Up and down, around and about, I go the whole distance. It was a lovely October day, a slight chill in the air, but sunny.

"One side attacking with all mobility, the other withstanding, as though rooted to the soil."

Even here the sound of chainsaws, the smell of burning.

After a battle, I read somewhere, the land recovers first, almost while the widows are still weeping.

❧

On the Sunday I went to Greenwich I first had breakfast with Dorothy Moore.

"I'm only here for a few days," I told her. "I'm doing a little research and having a holiday at the same time."

The woman's eyes lit up at the word "research."

"Not academic research I'm afraid, just family history, just for fun."

The woman in brown, her prayer book set carefully beside her tray, seemed puzzled by the idea of research being fun. She frowned.

"Don't you enjoy doing research?" I asked. "If not, why would you do it?"

I waited for her to crumple, to say, "What else am I supposed to do with my life, how else am I to get through the minutes and the hours?" but she didn't.

"Of course I enjoy it — but it's my life, my vocation." She leaned forward. "I really only teach so that I can get the money to do research."

"What is your field?" I asked.

She sat back in triumph. "My magnum opus will be a book on the great god Pan." So there. So much for distressed gentlewomen.

She gathered up her prayer book and her handbag, glanced at her watch and said she must be off.

"The great god Pan is dead," I murmured.

"Don't be so sure," she said.

All my life I have been haunted by the idea of the Woman in Brown, the women in brown or black or dusty purple, chalk marks on their clothes, sensible haircuts, sensible shoes. My father's sister Ethel in her gabardine dresses — her black lace-ups, her folding umbrella and Anglican prayer book, her fat, facetted glass bottle of pink nasal spray, her nervous gestures and determined air. My aunt the mathematician; my aunt the old maid. We learned early: how could a woman be truly happy without a man, without children?

"A man, without a woman," we sang at Camp Amahami, "is like a ship without a sail . . ."

(is like a boat without a rudder, is like a kite without a tail)

How we belted out the ending:

> But if there's one thing worse in this
> un-i-verse
> It's a woman
> I said a woman
> I mean a woman with-out a *Man*. (Yeah)

"Poor Ethel," my mother said with satisfaction, "poor Betty." To be an old maid teacher was a Fate Worse Than Death, worse even than being married to a Mama's-boy, a Milquetoast, a Fool.

It is a hard lesson to unlearn, perhaps impossible.

Yet think of the two sisters at the stall on Portobello Road. They may have been widows but maybe not. They looked content, well-fed, cheerful. I imagined the house they might live in, filled with a wonderful clutter, antimacassars on the backs and arms of Mother's chairs. The telly. A good fry-up for Sunday morning breakfast. Each knowing the other so well, the thoughts passing unspoken between them. Friends to the end.

Why did our family so furiously rage with one another, fathers with sons, sisters with sisters, brothers with brothers? My mother hasn't seen her sister in over twenty years. ("Frances," said the old woman, "you know Frances?")

"Would you like to see Aunt Betty again?" I said to Mother. I did not add, "one last time?"

"Oh no," she said, "not really. There's been too much water under the bridge."

We lived in a valley where people suffered from coughs and sinus problems. There were often fogs. I imagined young women detaching themselves from the fog, young women in white dresses, fog dresses, putting their wrapped bundles carefully on the steps of St. Mary's Orphan Asylum. Catholic girls in white dresses with Pre-Raphaelite hair. Gold crosses on gold chains. "Please look after my baby."

"Are you my daughter?" said my old mother, in a rare moment of confusion.

"You ought to know," I said.

Out come the dress boxes of forty years ago. She is looking for something to show me, some material she wants to give one of my daughters, two exquisite lace fans, one red, one black, carried by my great-grandmother to some grand affair a hundred years ago.

"These will be yours when I'm gone. That is, if you're interested."

I hardly hear her. The names on the boxes still

have the power to humiliate, to make me feel sick at my stomach. I see myself walking up and down in a pretty dress while my father sits uncomfortably on a chair and the saleslady smirks. This was the dress or jacket that was going to turn me into a girl who gets invited to all the parties and dances. Who needed a fairy godmother when there was Hills, MacLeans and Haskins; Fowler, Dick and Walker; Sissons; Drazens House of Fashion.

It is shame I feel now — that I went along with this, that I believed her even as I knew it wouldn't work. That I despised her even as I coveted the dress.

The power of names on the tops of boxes long after the stores have been boarded up and their founders' bones rotting in mausoleum drawers.

"You're not listening to me," she says. We are surrounded by boxes.

"Yes," I say, "yes. I'd like the fans." I have never seen them before and she has forgotten their history.

If I was over town I always put a dime in the blind man's cup. Because he couldn't see me, because he had no idea who it was.

In a kitchen drawer I find box after box of spices. Some of the tops are rusty, they are so old.

"Let's clean out some of these drawers," I say. PAPRIKA. CINNAMON. ALLSPICE. SAGE. WHITE PEPPER. "When was the last time you used any of these?"

"I won't have the money to replace them," she says, whining. "If we throw them out, that's that."

"Just tell me, when was the last time you used any of this?"

NUTMEG. CELERY SALT. CREAM OF TARTAR.

"They are all so old they won't be any good if you do use them. Let's chuck them out and I'll get you some more."

"No. Don't get me any more." Her eyes are full of tears. "I just don't have the energy to cook much."

"It doesn't take much energy to scramble eggs."

"I'm not supposed to eat eggs; they're full of *colsterol*, is that how you say it?"

"Close enough: I think these dinners you buy in a box are worse for you than scrambled eggs or a nice salad." There was a dinner in the fridge containing such mysteries as carrageenin and tetra-sodium pyrophosphate. I start to throw things into the waste-paper basket, which is lined with a plastic shopping bag. Down the hall is a closet enclosing the chute to the incinerator. Instant oblivion, the *oubliette* of *oubliettes*. Mother sits there, tying old bits of ribbon around the bulging dress boxes. Her hands are shaky. She is afraid of me. Will she be next, an old useless container filled with stuff that has "gone off"? A quick trip down the hall and wham, bam, thank you ma'am, she's disposed of. I know that I am being mean; what difference does it make whether she keeps the spices? Someplace in the back of her mind a small voice must be saying, "See, Frances, you'll never bake another cake, never roast a chicken. It's no good pretending." Another fantasy over; one more baby-step towards death.

When I am finished I make us tea from a selection I gave her five years ago. I have brought cookies, large, chewy chocolate-chip cookies from a delicatessen. She gives me a shopping list and her chequebook and I go down to the residents' store.

"We haven't seen your Mother this week," the owner says. "Is she all right?"

"Right as rain," I say, "hunky-dory."

I take the groceries back and then get in the elevator to go down to the library. Two old women are talking about the christening of a great-grandchild, who wore a dress blessed by the Pope.

❧

The Pope came to Canada once. Some enlightened nun got herself in trouble for saying that this time she hoped he'd kiss the women and step on the ground.

I was walking home from somewhere when I saw the Papal helicopter overhead. Noisier than the Holy Ghost.

The Pope was on his way to Empire Stadium to bless the children waiting there, fruit of their mothers' wombs, apples of their fathers' eyes.

When I took the lessons for Confirmation in the First Presbyterian Church I had to learn a series of questions and answers.

Q. What is the Bible?
A. The Bible is a series of books written by men to glorify God.

In Sunday School we poured plaster of Paris into rubber moulds of Mary, Joseph, the baby, the three Wise Men; then we painted the dead-white figures and brought them to brilliant life.

After the immaculate conception, the maculate delivery, Matthew, Mark, Luke, John, bless the bed that I lie on. How would anyone ever know, from myths and legends, from fairy-tales, that women *bleed*?

"Bloodshed" refers to war, to carnage of one

sort or another, not to what women do.

It always amuses me, on airplanes, to hear men ask so casually for a Bloody Mary or a Bloody Caesar. I want to say, "Have you ever stopped to think about the name of the drink you are holding?" Maybe I'll do it one day. That should bring out the barf bags pretty quick.

Did one of the lowing cattle eat up the Holy Placenta? Among all the various relics of Europe (heart, bone, bits of the True Cross, which must, judging by the number of surviving splinters, have been as tall as the Christmas tree set up each year in Rockefeller Center) I have never seen or even heard of a bit of the One True Placenta.

But of course, Mary would say, we didn't know He was the Christ then; He was just a little baby. We gave it to the cow, as was the custom.

Very good. I'll accept that. But what then of the True Foreskin, or the True Baby Teeth? Didn't you save *anything*, after all those visitors, after the herald angels?

He was my son. And besides, I soon had other children; he was just one among many. You know how it is. We just thought he was a gifted child, might make a name for himself and look after us in our old age.

The little boys in the class fought to be the black king because their faces and hands would be blacked with burnt cork. The little girls fought to be Mary. On the night of the Christmas pageant, which was also the night of the White Gift Service, there was real incense, pungent and foreign-smelling, so unlike the perfumes of the mothers, the aftershave of the smooth-cheeked fathers. I couldn't get enough of it. Years later, at Christmas

time in Athens, an old man in the market weighed
me out fifty drachmas' worth of frankincense on a
finger-scale. Then he poured it carefully into a twist
of yellow paper. *"Epharisto,"* I said. "Thank you."
"Epharisto poli." In the meat market wild boars,
still tusked, unskinned, hung upside-down in front
of stalls. At the place where I was staying we
plucked a turkey in the big kitchen, singeing the pin
feathers.

"I remember my mother doing this," I said.

Two young Greeks, army officers and friends of
the landlord, peered in from time to time but would
not stay — this was women's work. The night
before, drunk on ouzo, the oldest said he had slept
in his mother's bed until he went off to do his
national service, slept in her bed and with his arms
around her.

"Where was your *father*?" I said, "while all this
was going on?"

"Fadder dead," he said simply, "fadder dead
long time."

Could the afterlife be like the afterbirth? Only
not thick and red as ox-blood cherries; not slippery
and viscous like liver but white and light and fluffy,
like marshmallows or meringues. They give it to
the angels to eat, yum yum.

In the vestry before the service, some of the
boys were being very naughty, singing silly verses
to the carols.

> We three Kings of Orient are,
> Puffing on a lighted cigar;
> It was loaded and exploded
> — BANG! —
> We two Kings of Orient are . . .

"Boys," hissed our Sunday School teacher, "stop it. Stop it right now. This is the House of God."

I still believed then; I was scared and moved as far away as possible. If God was going to strike them dead I wanted to see it but I didn't want to be too close when it happened.

I was passing through Rome in International Women's Year. I went to all the important places and then, just as I was about to leave, I remembered a friend who was collecting stamps for this year. In the Vatican shop I asked in my phrase-book Italian for some stamps for the year of the women. The nun smiled and nodded.

The stamps I bought showed Jesus, standing, preaching to a group of adoring women.

❧

How our father loved to jaw with everybody. "Yep, we're on our way up to camp for the summer. Fill 'er up, will you — and check the oil 'n' water?" Ask about the fishing, whether there was a free map or a postcard, while his wife, the missus, out in the loaded-down car with the kids and the dog, honks furiously on the horn.

Frances Corbett, descended from gentlemen, reduced to sitting in a car as hot as an oven while her husband made a fool of himself — as usual — at the Esso station.

When I threw up she'd say, "There, I knew this would happen!" (I travelled with an old saucepan on my lap.)

He stands on my bureau, aged seven, in an old straw hat and oversized white shirt, grinning, holding up, on the end of his fishing line, an eel.

❧

"The Norman legend did not entertain the possibility of a Norman peasant."

❧

We hear of "an unkindness of ravens," "a murder of crows."

The Entertainments Officer wrote his Master's thesis on Edgar Allan Poe.

The Sunday morning breakfast with Dorothy Moore turned out to be more than worthwhile. Yes, she was lonely and wanted me to be her buddy in all sorts of excursions and adventures, from mass at St. Paul's to "hopping over to France for a few days." She had what used to be called "pluck." But I knew that she would do these things anyway, without me. I did not feel guilty about saying no — no — no.

On impulse I asked her about a book I wanted to look at, Thomas Cooper's letters concerning immigration to America. Robert had mentioned them. On Monday there was a note in my box. "The book you are looking for is in Goldsmith's Library at the University of London." She had drawn a map and added a P.S. "Would you like to meet for a meal tonight — my treat?" I scribbled my thank-yous and regrets and stuck them in her box. If she'd been smart she would have arranged it so I had to go to dinner in order to get the information. I admired her for not being devious but I have a horror of being beholden. And I needed to concentrate on what I was doing — or so I told myself. I didn't have much time.

Lydia had assured me she was all right, that I wasn't to come up to Birmingham for any reason whatsoever, but she still had no clue as to who she was — who she had been. She sounded cheerful in a fake way and I was worried about her. What if she couldn't find out, or, conversely, what if everything came back at once? Was it okay for her to be alone?

"But what are you doing with yourself?" I said.

"Looking at stuff in the archives, walking around, sitting in pubs listening to people talk. What comes back, Charlotte, is nothing specific but it's like a familiar smell from your childhood, like that iodine on the *Batory* — a general sense of recognition. The archivist at the library is incredibly kind; he's become very interested in what he calls my 'case.'

"What I probably need is another blow on the head. Isn't that how it always worked in the movies?"

"Don't do anything stupid."

"I won't.

"Ter-ra, luv," she said, in a Birmingham accent. "Ter-ra."

❧

Although I do a lot of sitting in libraries, I feel very North American when I go into places like Goldsmith's Library. Just getting in required a Reader's Ticket and after that a trip back downstairs to leave my jacket and briefcase in the cloakroom. I waited for them to ask to see my fingernails and hanky. No doubt Dorothy Moore, with her Ph.D. and academic letters of reference, shines in a place like this, but I shrivel. However, they had the book and after I had filled out a request it was brought to my table very quickly, a small book covered in grey cloth with an orange-red binding and gold trim. On the inside, in ink, the original owner had written "5th Nov. 1794, Thos. Gregory." Had Thomas Gregory gone to America, I wondered, or had he decided to stop at home? Gregory is an Irish name and the book was printed in Dublin. How did it end up in Goldsmith's Library?

"I quitted England in August, 1793 and embarked at New York, for Europe, in February, 1794. I left this kingdom expressly to determine whether America, and what part of it, was eligible for a person like myself with a small fortune, and a large family, to settle in."

The book is laid out as a series of four letters discussing where to settle and what sort of differences one might expect to find if one decided to emigrate. Of particular interest to me were Cooper's descriptions of Pennsylvania, as they are nearly contemporaneous with Robert Corbett's settlement there. Cooper thinks that Pennsylvania is an ideal choice, not just because of the climate ("avoiding the seven months' winter of New Hampshire and Massachusetts and the parching summers of Georgia and the Carolinas") but also because one would encounter excellent soil, less fever and ague and fewer Indians.

"Pennsylvania may fairly be regarded as the most flourishing state in the Union." The land went for three half-crowns to half a guinea an acre, and if one settled close to the branches of Susquehanna (Suʃquehannah — the small s is written like the ʃ — holes on a violin) "it will convey produce to Philadelphia and Baltimore. . . ."

Cooper has a lot to say about the word "farmer," and as I read I begin to see how Robert Corbett could be both a farmer and a man who wore silver buckles on his shoes.

"The term farmer is not the same in England as in America. Here a farmer is a land-owner, paying no rent, no tythes and few taxes, equal in rank to any other rank in the state, having a voice in the appointment of his legislators, and a fair chance, if he deserves it, of becoming one himself. In fact, nine-tenths of the legislators of America are farmers."

Cooper settled farther down than Robert Corbett, in Northumberland County, between the east and west branches of the Susquehanna, a little over one hundred and sixty miles from Philadelphia. Joseph Priestley had already settled there.

"It is the only English settlement I know of in America, and although American manners and society approach nearer to English than any other, they are not quite English. . . ." And it is here, I am sure, that Coleridge intended to create his utopia. This sounds very like the beginnings of a pantisocracy:

> If indeed, a *number* of people, personally, or by reputation, acquainted with each other, with similar habits of life and general pursuits, were to quit your country, they would naturally endeavour to pitch upon a settlement where they need not be so divided as to renounce the society they have been accustomed to enjoy; or to accommodate themselves suddenly to a change of habits, and manners, and friends, and associates [afociates]. With many of them in middle life, or advanced in years, this would be a circumstance of the utmost importance to their

future comfort. . . . It would in such a case, therefore, be desirable to fix upon some part of the continent where a large body of contiguous land could readily be procured at a reasonable price.

❀

"— criticize poetry when hunting a buffalo and write sonnets while following the plow."

— Coleridge

"Hunt in the morning, fish in the afternoon, breed cattle in the evening, criticize after dinner, just as I like, without ever becoming a hunter, a fisherman, a herdsman or a critic."

— Karl Marx

❀

Suſquehannah

ſavages

And when I had asked the name of the river . . . and heard that it was called the Susquehanna, the beauty of the name seemed to be part and parcel of the beauty of the land. As when Adam with divine fitness named the creatures, so this word Susquehanna was at once accepted by the fancy. This was the name, as no other could be, for that shining river and desirable valley.

— Robert Louis Stevenson in
Across the Plains

We have passed, both in the mountains and else-where, a great number of new settlements, and detached log-houses. Their utter forlorn and miserable appearance baffles all description. I have not seen six cabins out of six hundred where the windows have been whole. Old hats, old clothes, old fragments of blanket and paper are stuffed into the broken glass; and their air is misery and desolation. It pains the eye to see the stumps of great trees thickly strewn in every field of wheat, and hundreds of rotten trunks, of elm and pine and sycamore and log wood steeped in . . . unwholesome water.

> — Charles Dickens, letter to
> John Forster, March 1842.

It was natural for settlers of the 1780s and 1790s to locate along rivers that had been used as Indian settlements. The seasonal runs of shad and herring in the rivers and the abundant deer, bear and bobcats provided supplemental food and skins for the new settlers as they had for the Indians.

> — *A History of Broome County*

In one three-day period in February, 1795, 1,200 sleighs carrying New Englanders and their household goods passed through upper New York State to settlements in the Genesee country and farther below.

> — *A History of Broome County*

"They came," said my mother, "because the Irish were taking over Massachusetts — Boston anyway."

"They *came*," I tell her, "because land was opening up to the west. And I don't think they left because of the Irish."

"Why did they leave then, Mrs. Smarty-pants?"

"A new beginning maybe? Robert was forty-three; the family had already been here for over a hundred years. Restless, wanting to be a pioneer himself?"

"Like you."

"Oh yes — your daughter the pioneer."

In the early days of the New Milford settlement there was a stump-mortar where the people pounded their corn. The story goes that Asaph Corbett, Robert's oldest son, who took grain to that stump to pound it, was asked how long it took to pound a half-bushel of corn. He looked the stranger up and down. "Not half so long as it would take to starve to death," he said.

❧

— *From a History of Conklin, N.Y.*

> The largest industry at this point is the American Acetate of Lime Works, established 1844 by John H. Turnbull. . . . Mr. Turnbull was lost at sea and the works were managed by a man named Saxton until he sold out.

Robert Corbett had started with one thousand acres in what became New Milford, PA. His son Cooper, at his death, owned two thousand, four hundred. *His* son, Ira, quite literally followed in their footsteps.

> Mr. Corbett has for many years conducted the business of lumbering on an extensive scale in the town of Conklin. As many as eighty men and their teams have been

employed by him at one time, and some of his lumber dealings have amounted to thirty thousand dollars a sale.

When Ira Corbett was twenty-three he married Miss Juliet Bowes, of Great Bend, Susquehanna County, Pa. The family of Mr. and Mrs. Corbett consist of eight children, as follows: Marshall J., who is in business in New York City . . .

I thought my great-grandfather, Marshall J., had disinherited his son Lawrence because he blew up an acid factory somewhere in New York State. I thought he'd done it out of mischief.

"Where'd you get that idea?" my mother said. "The acid factories were another branch of the family — we only came in on them at the end. The government took the tariff off and the whole thing collapsed.

"Not before making some of the Corbetts millionaires," she said.

"What kind of acid was it? What was it used for?"

"I don't know. Maybe I knew once but I don't know now. But I remember the factory near Shinhopple — that was the one Dad was sent down to manage — and the men stoking the furnaces, covered in sweat. I think somebody, some institute or other, is trying to buy up that place — make it a kind of museum. Your aunt sent me a clipping a few years ago. I'll see if I can find it." (Which of course she did.)

The first acid factory in the United States was in Conklin, just up the creek from the area they carved out as their own. A group of Scotsmen arrived in America, built a small plant surrounded by a high wooden fence. The locals called it "the Scotch Works" or "the Secret Process" as nobody knew quite what was going on behind that fence. Something called "Destructive Distillation," whatever that was. It involved cutting down a lot of trees and the hiring of husky local men who were sworn to silence.

What they were making was acetate of lime which they sent back to Scotland to be used as a mordant in the textile industry.

What they were also making was money.

Cooper Corbett's brother Sewell had a son named Julius, a real go-getter, unlike Cooper's own son, Cooper Jr., who ran the local hotel for a while before he succumbed to the demon rum and had to be chastised by his father, even from beyond the grave.

When John Turnbull, who owned the Scotch Works, was lost at sea, on his way to a visit in Scotland, it was Julius Corbett who was in the right place at the right time and who, with Thomas and Abraham Keery, plus a man named Ferguson, purchased the rights to the Secret Process.

The Scotch Works now became known as the Brookdale Chemical Company, and soon they were expanding, looking for more wood, more rivers. The East Branch of the Delaware River proved ideal. Soon, in the western part of Sullivan County and all of Delaware County, chemical plants sprang up, and company towns with eponymous names like Woodbourne, Methal, Acidalia, or with the names of their founders: Keeryville, Corbett, N.Y. They used only hardwoods such as beech and maple; they could extract two hundred pounds of acetate of lime per cord of wood. They stripped hills and polluted streams and gave jobs to hundreds of men before the bottom fell out of the market after World War I. Julius's son and daughter (second cousins to Marshall J.) owned the factory at Corbett.

"They made a lot of money."

"I know, you told me that already."

Marshall J. sent his son and his family down to manage a plant that had folded and was due to start up again. Lawrence was at loose ends. He'd been invited to teach at Stevens Institute, where he had trained to be a mechanical engineer, but for some reason he turned them down. Then he had started a soap-making business with his father-in-law but it hadn't come to anything.

His own father had retired and built a house in Corbettsville, close by *his* father's place. He had started a dairy farm and wanted Lawrence to manage that, but Lawrence said I'm damned if I'll spend my life milking cows.

The offer for a job to do with an acid factory seemed much more attractive. There was money to be made in acid — his uncle was on his way to being a millionaire. His wife left all decisions up to him. And it would be a healthy life for the children. (She didn't add that the thought of being away from her in-laws was also an attractive proposition.)

❧

We didn't really travel very far when I was a child. Back and forth to the Adirondacks every summer, of course, and once to New York, where a waiter followed us out of the restaurant and threw his tip at our feet. Once to Niagara Falls. Crossing the Peace Bridge at Buffalo my mother became flustered and

couldn't remember where she was born. Once to
New England, where a fat lady got stuck going up
the secret staircase in the House of the Seven
Gables and my mother quarrelled with her brother
when we stayed overnight in Worcester. We had to
leave in a hurry and didn't have the money for a
decent hotel. It is strange the things that children
remember. At the motel mother made us push a
bureau against the door.

On the New York trip the radiator overheated
in the Catskills — my father cursing and swearing
in his usual manner, we children in the back seat
afraid the whole thing would blow up. My father
said Jews came for their holidays to the Catskills
and at a lookout point we saw a family of Jews
eating ice-cream cones. My father said, "Do cats
kill rats? No, cats kill mountains." I was glad when
we finally got back home even though we'd seen the
Rockettes and sat in the audience of "The Archie
Andrews Show" and "Our Miss Brooks."

If we came along Route 17 — and we must have
— why did my mother not say, "I used to live at
Shinhopple; we lived at Corbett, New York, and in
the summers at a place we called Treasure Island. I
was happy there, happier than I've ever been since."

"Here," wrote my mother, enclosing the clipping about Corbett, New York. "Betty sent me this
years ago. I don't know if the institute bought it or
not; you could go down there and find out."

The clipping was from a column in the Binghamton paper: SOLD: MOUNTAIN VILLAGE.
Friday, Nov. 26, 1976. There were photographs of
the ruins of an old factory, of a tall, Italianate
chimney attached to nothing, of a grim-faced man
in front of a wood stove, of Beulah Stuart, "the last

of a fabulous generation," sitting in a rocking-chair.

"Remember Shinhopple?" Aunt Betty had written underneath and, "She was a pretty girl, but like most of us age does its job on us."

A long article: I copied it and the next time I saw her I returned it.

"You can have it," my mother said, "since you're so interested in all this Corbett business."

"Aren't you interested? You're the one who really got me started on all this."

"I wouldn't give you two cents for the Corbetts," my mother said.

"You're a Corbett."

"Well I wouldn't give two cents for me, that's for sure. Nor would anyone else. Anyway, it's all water under the bridge, you're welcome to it."

Under a Roebling bridge, as it turned out, a narrow iron bridge across the Delaware, just wide enough for one car at a time. It was another Memorial Day weekend, flags everywhere. We stopped at the general store in Shinhopple to buy some cold beer and picnic supplies and to ask directions.

"Just around the corner," the storekeeper said, "you can't miss it. Are you a Corbett?"

"Sort of," I said, "my mother is a Corbett."

"They're having a barbecue tomorrow," he said, "you ought to go."

Were there a lot of people still living there? Was Beulah Stuart there?

Oh no, she was dead, but there were enough people, with family and friends and people from around and about.

On the wall behind the counter a book was advertised. I copied down the name and where to order. *The Acid Factories of Yesteryear*. "There'll be lots of stuff about the Corbetts in *there*," the store-keeper said.

The old post office was over in one corner, with its bank of glass-fronted oak cubbyholes. You'd be able to see if you had any mail before the post-mistress told you. Which box had been for the Corbetts who lived on Treasure Island, the Johnny-come-latelies, Marshall's son and his family? A strange lot — the father always building stone fire-places at the back of the tents, the girls never allowed to play with the company kids, kept them-selves to themselves.

I bought my mother a bumper sticker for her nonexistent car: I L♥VE SHINHOPPLE, it said. Where did all this I ♥ nonsense start? Myself, I have a bumper sticker that says LOVE YOUR MOTHER and a picture of the Earth. Once a man came up to me in a Safeway parking lot and said, "Why?"

"Why what?" I said.

He pointed to the sticker. "Why should I love my mother? I hated the old bitch."

I pointed to the picture. "Mother Earth," I said. "It's sort of a pun."

"Some joke," he said, and walked away.

I sat in the car with the windows rolled up, trembling. The man's anger had frightened me.

Since then it has happened several times. Always an old, or older, man. Always "I hated my mother." I am thinking of replacing the sticker with something else, something more acceptable like I ♥ NEW YORK or I ♥ Rottweilers.

❦

Recently I suggested to Lydia a revisionist fairy-tale: "Snow White and the Seven DWFS."

But in the good old days when Snow White opened up her pretty little painted mouth and sang "Some Day My Prince Will Come," we believed it. Not just for her but for all of us.

Now I'm too old for the Prince, or even King Charming or his cousin the Archduke Charming. "DWM, a fit 52, wishes to meet slim attractive woman 19-35."

Shall I send in a similar ad to one I saw recently in a neighbourhood paper?: "Over fifty and still nifty." (Fifty-One, still loads of fun, Fifty-Two and loves to screw. One has a better chance with "widowed millionairess," or "Siamese twins — we're twice the fun.")

❧

I was too shy to go to the barbeque, I knew that. I couldn't just walk up and say, "Hello, I'm a Corbett, could I have a plate of them spare-ribs and some of that there potato salad?" Even if someone might show up who remembered my mother and her family, I couldn't do it. I wished Lydia were with me but she was off in Europe someplace, Paris I think, being diplomatic. I was with a friend, a photographer, who was almost as shy as I was.

We went and stayed at a fishing lodge in Trout Brook instead and the next day took in the Memorial Day Parade at Downsville. Even babies in strollers were waving flags, and one woman wore a sweater knitted in the Stars and Stripes. The Prom Queen came by on her float, waving.

A man so bent and ancient he seemed more marionette than man was lifted out of the back of a van and wheeled up to the grandstand to be presented with a lifetime membership in the Legion. I listened to the Assemblyman's speech; he kept his head slightly on one side and tried to sound like Jack Kennedy. "This is a nation founded on rhetoric," I said to my friend, a born-and-bred Canadian.

His parents were immigrants from Ireland.

Focussing in on the faces in the crowd, he said, "All nations are founded on rhetoric."

"Except maybe Canada," he added, after a minute. "Except maybe your home, my native land. That seems to me to have been a deal among businessmen — the only country in the world founded by a department store. So we have to think up 'days' to celebrate — like Victoria Day, which is really just an excuse for a long weekend at the right time for people in Ontario to open up the summer cabin or put the garden in."

We stood still for the salute to the flag, the singing of "The Star-Spangled Banner."

"Whoever set that to music," he said, "must have been a castrato."

The trees had all grown back and the river ran cold and clear.

"What does 'posted' mean exactly?" he said, looking at signs along the road.

"It means NO TRESPASSING. My grandfather used to have NO TRESPASSING signs around his camp. Underneath it said TRESPASSERS WILL BE PROSECUTED, but nobody ever came. I waited for trespassers, so that I could forgive them and win a gold star in Heaven."

"Is this trip, all these trips you are making at such an expense of time and money, an attempt to forgive your mother?"

"Why do you say that?"

"Because I say it, Charlotte. Because you are so angry with your mother."

"Not any more," I said, beginning to move back to the car.

"Oh yes you are," he said to my back, "and you're looking for something that will give you a reason to forgive."

"I'm looking for material."

"Okay," he said, "I'm looking for a washroom. I'll meet you back at the car."

At Shinhopple, Lawrence and the other boys made a deep cave out of clay and sticks and they built a fire way at the end of it. Frances and Betty were told to stay away, it was a secret place for boys.

On the island a schoolgirl helped; she made good bread and the boys, Lawrence, Cousin Marshall and their friend Bob Trusdall, would eat a whole loaf at one sitting, each wearing the straw hat he put on before even getting dressed.

Once her brother, down on the river, casting for black bass, flung his line backward and cast into her face. The hook stuck in her eyelid and her mother had to cut it out. That night she heard her mother weeping in the tent but didn't go to her and ask her what the matter was.

Father came down and put the boys to work cleaning bricks, for the time when the acid factory would reopen.

I held the brick I own, the one I picked up in the tangle of weeds and blackberry bushes at Corbett, New York. It's an ordinary brick, a dull red-brown except where a corner has chipped off, showing the flower-pot colour beneath. "D B Co.," it says, in relief: Delaware Brick Company. The tall chimney rose above me (" 'Look on my works, ye Mighty, and despair' ") and I tried to imagine this place as it must have been. A world of men — fallers, drivers, stokers, engineers: a world of sweat and swearing. The men hid bottles of the tarry residue from the distillation process under their jackets, took it home to cure their hams. They called it "oil of smoke."

"Wherever we were," Mother said, "we were never allowed to play with the factory children."

❦

> Dad's own girls, who can either long for
> city life or otherwise for country, ready to
> row, paddle, swim, drive a nail, cook, sew
> or any other sport.

— from a postcard in Grace Corbett's collection, Mother and Aunt Betty on the shore of Treasure Island, their canoe pulled up alongside.

❦

— From *The Binghamton Times*
   April 11, 1876

> None of our veterans have been so long
> identified with the early settlement of the
> Valley of the Susquehanna, in this vicinity,
> or have been more familiar with its, in
> many places, torturous courses, as well as
> the progress of civilization along its banks
> from city to tidewater; as Mr. Cooper
> Corbett.

Robert named his seventh child Cooper after his
friend William Cooper, one of the great developers of
Pennsylvania and the Genesee tract in New York
State. I like to imagine Robert, a thin man with a
large nose and an unsmiling mouth, writing to
William Cooper and asking to name his newborn son
after the Cooper family. Perhaps he thought some
money would come out of it. Was something sent, a
christening mug or a spoon, along with remarks
about his own son, Fenimore, "a thriving lad"?

We were taken to Cooperstown by our grandfather, but no mention was made of his great-grandfather's connection with the Cooper family or of how
Robert and William had surveyed vast areas of land
together when they were young. Perhaps he didn't
know. My grandfather never talked about his personal history, not ever. But he showed us the plaque
marking the place where Clinton dammed the waters of the Susquehanna so that it flooded its banks
and hundreds of "bateaux" swept down the river,
frightening the Indians and securing victory for the
whites. He bought us the *LeatherStocking Tales*.

I remember the lake was very still that day, as
though it were truly made of glass. My grandfather,
my mother, my sister and I took a ride in a motor-
launch up to the end of the lake and back. I trailed
my hand in the water, which was cold, but not icy.
I would rather have been in a birch-bark canoe, paddling silently and swiftly close to shore. "My paddle
keen and bright/flashing with silver": We were
learning that song in music class at school.

My mother did not pipe up and say "I know how
to paddle a canoe." That came out as a by-the-way,
over forty years later, last spring. She was showing
me photo postcards that her mother, Grace, had

sent back to her parents in Brooklyn.

Some of the postcards, or the photos on them, are blue, as though they've been done on blueprint paper. Grandma has written on one of them, "going for the milk." My mother and her sister are tying up a canoe at the bank of a river and there are some wooden steps, looking more like a ladder than a permanent construction, ahead of them.

"The new luxury," my grandmother writes underneath, "the steps up to the road. We now have a bridge over this side of the river, giving us use of rowboat and canoe on other side of island."

On the back she has written, "The kind of life we had with our children for nine summers. We have worn out about three tents and fly."

"So where is this?" I ask my mother.

"An island on the East Branch of the Delaware, near Shinhopple."

"Did you like it there?"

"Oh yes. We called it Treasure Island."

She hands me another. She is in a bathing suit and cap in the back of a canoe. Her sister is in the water, up to her shoulders, and her brother and some friends are posed on a makeshift diving-board secured with large flat stones. The island is in the background.

"It must have dropped off very quickly, if the boys are going to dive off that board and Aunt Betty is only standing in the water."

"Oh it did."

"Why were you on an island near Shinhopple?"

"Because of the acid factory down the road in Corbett."

"The acid factory?"

"Of course."

GRAVEN IMAGES / 219

Another piece of the jigsaw puzzle, only there is no box with a picture on the cover to show me what the finished product will look like. (And my mother has an enormous number of the pieces tucked away in drawers and in her head.)

"Here," she says, and hands me another photo-card, not blue this time. I see white clapboard buildings, piles of brush, some railway cars and an enormous chimney belching smoke.

"That's Corbett, New York," she says. "Dad managed the plant there, or maybe the one at Fish's Eddy."

Feb. 26, 190-something, Shinhopple, NY.
To Mr. F.B. Cleary
101 Walnut Street
Binghamton, NY

(By this time Grace Cleary Corbett's parents had moved to Binghamton to be near their only child.)

> Every day I know how anxious you are for the cold to let up as much for Mamma's sake as your own. I am thinking of both of you constantly. The old groundhog's six weeks of winter is nearly gone. But it's a beautiful day. The sunshine just dances in our windows minus shades — and the fireplace is crackling away in a different sort of joyousness. Hope you're feeling better and Mamma too.
>
>   Much love
>   GAC

(If not too much trouble keep this for me.)

Windows? Fireplace? "You didn't live in the tents in the wintertime?"

"Good heavens no, we lived in a house."

"I didn't know you could paddle a canoe."

"Of course I could. And row a boat. There's lots of things you don't know."

"Regular outdoor girl."

She smiles. My mother, in her tiny overheated apartment, has not been outside the senior citizens' complex for three months. The winter has been particularly severe and she is afraid she will slip and fall. She reads (a biography of the John Adams family is on her bed table) and watches TV.

I see the little girl with the straight brown hair scraped back from her forehead and tied with a bow. She and her sister are paddling across the river to go and get the mail and the milk. Aunt Betty jumps out first and leans over to pull the canoe up on the bank. They are barefoot, although they are wearing clean dresses. They feel very important and *trusted* to be sent on this errand every other day. Betty is younger but she is the bold one; she chats with the storekeeper while Frances hangs back, waiting for the mail.

"I'll carry the letters," she says to Betty, "you can carry the milk." She knows already that to her mother letters are more important than spilled milk. The letters must not be dropped, must not get wet. Or the small parcel which comes every few weeks from a chemist. Something to help Mama get to sleep.

"We called the island Treasure Island," my mother says, again.

❦

"They carried the sleeping girl to a pretty spot beside the river, far enough from the poppy to prevent her breathing any more of the flowers, and here they lay her gently on the soft grass and waited for the fresh breeze to awaken her."

"They followed the bend of the river."

" 'Didn't you know water would be the end of me?' asked the witch in a wailing, despairing voice."

The Wizard of Oz

❦

Acetone, formaldehyde, pure methyl alcohol, as well as acetate of lime. With his brother-in-law John Leonard Stuart, Julius Corbett built an empire of acid. Once Julius knew about "the Secret Process" he saw new possibilities in wood. "Destructive Distillation": there may even have been something in the sound of that phrase that appealed to the Corbett soul.

"When they finished with one forest," Mother said, "they just moved on and built another town."

Julius's sister Nettie, married to John Leonard Stuart, had a son named Merritt Corbett Stuart. He lived in our town. I went to school with his stepsons and never knew it. Julius's son Merritt Corbett was a millionaire. In the library of the State Historical Association, Cooperstown, New York, there are seventy-two boxes of Corbett and Stuart material, everything from bills of lading and new designs for retorts to a letter from Mrs. J. Edgar Hoover asking for donations to the Girl Scouts. No mention of my great-grandfather, Marshall J., or his son Lawrence Bowes. By the time I was born my grandfather was head of a department at IBM. He had a little plaque on his desk that read Think!

After I had my appendix out in Lourdes Hospital, not knowing the place had once been a Corbett mansion, my mother brought me home-made chicken noodle soup in a mason jar; my grandfather sent me yellow roses. The beautiful camp in the mountains had been sold — I had to recuperate in the sticky August heat of town. I've only been back once.

The present owner said to me, "I felt so sorry for your grandfather. He was sitting on the porch, looking out at the lake, and he said, 'I always intended to die here.' I think your uncle needed his inheritance, right then; I got the feeling your uncle had some kind of hold over him."

"Only son, I guess." I thanked him for letting me walk around the property.

They were very nice, the new owners of the land. Not so new, really, owners now for a quarter of a century.

The wife made dolls from moulds she kept in her basement workshop. There were bisque heads waiting to be painted, and boxes labelled SHIRLEY TEMPLE DOLL, CRYING BABY HANDS, AMERICAN SCHOOLBOY LEGS, small baskets full of assorted eyes. In an old fridge there were racks of ceramic candy dishes shaped like turkeys, ready for Thanksgiving. They had both been married before, and when the families got together at Christmas and Thanksgiving there were always at least twenty people, of various ages, sitting down to dinner. WELCOME said the door mat.

I went outside and stood looking down at the lake. Why had my grandfather not asked to have his ashes scattered here, instead of being buried at Corbettsville? I suppose he wanted to be buried beside his wife, across from his parents, his grandparents, his great-grandparents and so on. As a child I never thought of him as a lover of tradition, although there were certain rituals: the raising and lowering of the flag each day, grace before meals, chicken every Sunday, the weekly trip to Speculator to get the groceries.

I took away a pine cone and in Speculator I stopped to buy a pillow almost identical to one I had bought in the forties. It was filled with fragrant needles and said I PINE FOR YOU AND BALSAM.

I wondered if my grandfather, who could make anything, fix anything, could have unfixed that furnace in some way, so that the house would catch on fire. My mother has always felt that the people who bought the place set it on fire for the insurance, because the wife had asthma and found she couldn't breathe up there. I have not told her that the original buyers are still there. I have not told her that I returned to the lake and came away knowing I would never go back again. The grandfather I knew there must remain separate from this other man. He was the god of my childhood and I can't let him go, not just yet. He — or his camp — kept me sane. When things got too bad at home or at school I would get out the calendar I kept hidden under my mattress. On it I kept track of good days, GD, and bad days, BD and VBD. I also crossed off each day, after Easter, that drew us closer to the lake.

"He named it Journey's End," my mother said. "I guess he didn't stop and think. Mother must have seen it as a cruel joke."

"Did she ever say so?"

"No — but it wasn't a very nice name, considering the circumstances."

"Did she know she was going to die?"

"Oh I think so. She had her first heart attack before the place was even thought of. And she was never very well after her breakdown. And then there was Betty to contend with — her shenanigans."

"I thought she didn't deal with Betty's shenanigans, that was left to you." (I try to imagine the first time, in New York, Mother typing away when the superintendent comes to fetch her:

"Miss Corbett, I'm afraid your sister's on a window-ledge up at Barnard College, threatening to jump.")

"Well Betty was *her* daughter; she must have asked herself a lot of questions about what went wrong."

("Frances," said my Aunt Betty, drying her hands on a grey dishtowel. "You know Frances?" She tilted her head to one side, like a bird.)

"Poor Betty," my mother said, "when she had her second breakdown they had to break down the bathroom door."

I began to laugh.

"What's so funny about that?"

"Oh, breakdown, break down, it just struck me as funny."

"Well it wasn't." Her mouth is set in a thin, grim line. "I don't think Betty ever forgave me. Getting me to do their dirty work."

"You could have said no; you could have said 'Do it yourselves.'"

"You didn't say no to L.B. Corbett. Besides, Mother wasn't well."

I wondered if they went back and finished the turkey, the cold drifts of mashed potato, the gravy cold as mud.

"I don't remember," my mother says. "I only remember that they stayed behind the bedroom door until the men had come and taken her away."

GIRL SCOUTS

[INCORPORATED]

NATIONAL HEADQUARTERS

189 LEXINGTON AVENUE
NEW YORK CITY

October 22, 1923.

My dear Mr. Corbett:

Are you seriously concerned over the tendencies of present-day young people?

Have you wondered what kind of mothers our girls will become if their ideals and boundless energy are not directed?

The Girl Scout movement is working to develop healthful mothers of tomorrow. And because Girl Scout work is fun in doing, more then 7,000 girls come to us each month for our program of home-making, child-care, outdoor living — of group loyalty and service to others.

We believe that Girl Scout work builds morally, spiritually and bodily our future mothers of men.

We need money — we want your help.

Sincerely yours,

Mrs. Herbert Hoover
President

Make checks payable to
Girl Scouts, Inc.

❧

I realize that I have said more about Lydia than I
have about myself — in the husband department I
mean. If I could be as economical as Shakespeare:
"My father had a daughter loved a man" . . . that
about sums it up. I met him — Michael — when I
was on holiday in St. Ives with a girlfriend. We had
decided to walk the coast path and met Michael
coming the other way. He was a potter, he said,
studying with Bernard Leach. He talked a lot about
"centring," about what happens to you — inside —
when you pull that shape up and out from the lump
of clay.

He gave me a salt-glazed box the colour of slate,
of pigeons. Inside was a fortune from a fortune
cookie: EXPECT CHANGES. One day he drew a
circle around me in the sand.

I went back to America, to finish my degree, but
we began a correspondence. I loved his letters and
have them still; he was a man who noticed things.
He wasn't at all like the boys from Yale or Harvard
or Amherst that I met on blind dates. He was gentle
and loving and not afraid to discuss his weaknesses.
His hands were rough and later, after I went back
and we made love, I told him that his hands were
like cats' tongues, raspy.

His granny had a budgie who played football on
the dining table. She would give it a nut, which the
bird batted to the other side of the table; then it flew
over and batted it back.

He came from Brighton, of good yeoman stock.
When his father was sixteen he was given a guinea
and told to go out into the world and make something of himself. Which he did. None of this UB40

then, love, you had to make something of yourself or you starved.

After our first child was born we emigrated to Canada on the old *Empress of France*; we had the cheapest cabin, on D Deck, but the baby smiled and slept the whole way across.

Fifteen years later he left me. What can I say?

Those books and magazines that tell you to write about what you know lead neophytes to think that means you should write about yourself. But who ever knows oneself in any distanced, objective way? I think I am nothing like my sister and am amazed to discover we have recently bought the same coffee mug — a very expensive, English coffee mug — thousands of miles apart. I think I am *nothing like* my mother, and yet the hounds of hell are inside me too and on a bad day I can hear them howling. Those studies of twins have given the lie to the shaping power of environment. The twins, who haven't seen each other for years, often since birth, who live in different parts of the country, show up wearing the same colour ties, or the same hairstyles, have married mates with the same first names. We are all Maruska dolls, carrying within us another Maruska, then another, then another. Macbeth says to the witches: "What! Will the line stretch out to the crack of doom?" And the answer, of course, is yes. Yes it will.

So if I say I do not know myself perhaps that is the biggest lie of all. I am my mother's daughter. Or, as she would say, a chip off the old block.

People who turn state's witness in big mob trials are given new identities, sometimes new faces even. It may help them avoid being gunned down as they step outside to get the morning paper, or blown up when they turn the key in the ignition. But surely they give themselves away to the sharp observer? Their mothers would know them I think.

Michael encouraged me to write — when I wasn't chopping wood or hauling water. When I wasn't playing with the babies. It wasn't just his fault that I didn't — it was more fun baking bread or feeling in the nests for eggs, more fun playing with the babies. I wasn't like Jane Austen, who could write in the corner with family life going on around her. Writing was something lonely and private — perhaps shameful and self-indulgent?

One summer, however, I managed to finish two stories. "Write about what you know." I won a contest. I built myself a writing shed.

He never forgave me.

❧

There are societies for every kind of sadness now — if your parents have been alcoholics, if your child has committed suicide, if you have been left a widow or a widower, talk with a stammer or walk with a limp. Once I boarded an airplane in Vancouver that seemed to be filled with children missing limbs. Then I realized there were many adults, elderly men mostly, also missing limbs. I wondered if I were on some sort of charter plane by mistake but the flight attendant said no, this was an excursion of CHAMPS and AMPS. I shook my head. I knew what AMPS was, WAR AMPS the signs always said, and the solicitations, as though even the proper word — *amputee* — had to be lopped off. But I had never heard of CHAMPS.

The woman sitting next to me filled me in. The WAR AMPS were gradually dying out in Canada, she said. A few men had been in Korea, a few in Vietnam, but Canada itself had not been at war for almost fifty years. So the Society had looked around and decided to help child amputees. "Sort of like the Big Brothers," the woman said.

I tried to concentrate on my book but it was hard. The little champs were lively and naughty, just like any children in a confined space. They raced — if they were able — up and down the aisles, screamed, wanted to be taken to see the pilot. The AMPS and the chaperones were kept busy; the flight attendants lost their indulgent smiles. "Please," they said, "coming through, please." These children were young. At puberty the real pain would begin. For the girls especially, I thought. Was there ever a woman in a Hathaway shirt ad?

You didn't say handicapped any more; you said Physically Challenged. You said Differently Abled.

There are signs in front windows now, NEIGHBOURHOOD WATCH. A frightened child can run up the steps and bang on the door and be taken in. Would I have done that if such signs had been in the windows of the houses of my childhood? It was neighbourhood watch all right — from behind the curtains as our mother ran up the street in her nightgown shouting after our father's car. It was neighbourhood watch as we stood on the front porch, begging to be let in. We had not yet said we were sorry.

The front windows of my childhood displayed small silk flags with stars — a blue star if your husband or son were away fighting the Axis, a gold star if he was dead. It was like grade school: when you were really good at something you got a gold star and your work was pinned up for all to see. Gold star mothers raised heroes — never mind that they were dead. Lydia, lacking a (known) father, invented an RAF pilot. That was about as glamorously dead as you could be. I was ashamed that my father was too old and had flat feet.

An editor said to me once — a man who had lied about his age and joined up at seventeen: "I think that will be the last war where young men line up to enlist."

❧

Lydia, Søren and I went to visit the Bayeux Tapestry. I looked for the Corbett/Corbet nose but all the noses looked alike — largish but straight, no humps or hooks or bumps.

They were like the two angles opposite the hypotenuse in my old geometry texts, or like the rudders on small boats. Women had embroidered the tapestry, gossiping, telling stories.

The scenes were lively and the borders, top and bottom, were filled with animals, including crows, and various lopped-off parts of the body. (ENGLISH SOLDIER LEGS; NORMAN HORSEMAN HEAD) Suits of mail were being yanked off corpses so that they could be used again.

The English could be recognized by their moustaches, the Normans by their *nuques rasées*.

Lydia thought the suits of armour being carried on poles looked like long johns frozen on the line. We explained what long johns were to Søren. "Also called combinations," I said. "Children wore a similar thing in cold weather, at night. They were called Doctor Dentons and had a sort of flap at the back, which buttoned."

"They also had feet," Lydia said, "so the dear little things could keep their tootsies warm. But they only came in one colour — porridge — and were very thick. They must have taken ages to dry." She was looking closely at the tapestry. "Charlotte," she said, "take a gander at William's horse."

En route to St. Valéry, we stopped to see the relics of St. Theresa of Liseux. Her little finger was encased in a gold reliquary and that, in turn, in a glass box.

Søren was taken aback at our laughter and crude remarks. At Chartres a clochard, hearing us talk, had followed us into the church. "Pitie de moi, pitie de moi." Søren told him, in perfect French, that he must not beg inside. We were surprised at his firmness, his distaste, for Søren is a generous man.

"I didn't know you were religious," Lydia said later.

"I'm not, but there are things you must not do in churches."

We stared at him.

"What did you do," said Lydia, "in a church when you were small?" She turned to me, holding up an oyster on her fork. "I have a feeling that was the voice of his mother speaking, don't you?"

Søren smiled and said nothing.

"My sister brought a Jewish boy to church once," I offered, "and my mother walked out. *That* was certainly something you didn't do in church, not our church, bring in a Jew."

And now Søren was looking at us in distress as we cackled and made fun. Lydia paid no attention.

"Poor Theresa. She must have worked her fingers to the bone."

Nowhere in Normandy did we see people who looked anything like our idea of Vikings. Søren looked more like a Viking than these guys, Lydia said, looking at the waiters, the petrol attendants, the farmers who gave us directions.

"What does *pré-salé* mean?" Lydia said. "We can have lamb pré-salé should we so choose. Pre-salted?"

Feeding on the salt marshes, the waiter told us, the most best lamb in the world.

"Do you think they feed on young men's bones as well? Metaphorically speaking, I mean. All that calcium leaching into the landscape."

Søren shook his head at her.

"Sometimes you go too far, Lydia."

"What about the oysters, the apple trees? Remember Rupert Brooke."

I knew she was showing off for me, not for him. That if I hadn't been there she wouldn't be doing this. Søren had tried to persuade her to cross the Channel and find out about her family and she'd refused, but it had made her jumpy and slightly cross. My role was to try and ignore this, but in fact I thought she was very funny. We egged each other on.

At Liseux, when Lydia discovered Theresa had been a Discalced Carmelite, she suggested the relic should have been a joint from her big toe, not her little finger.

We took turns sitting up front with Søren, but at night, in the pensions and hotels, they disappeared into their room and I into mine.

"Are you lonely, Charlotte?" Lydia said to me one morning, bringing me an early cup of coffee that she had charmed out of someone.

"Of course. Not when I'm travelling by myself, not usually, but in a situation like this one, yes. At night I'm lonely."

"We talk about you sometimes. Søren thinks you're wonderful."

"That's nice."

"Sex isn't that terrible desperate thing it used to be when I was young; sometimes I really think I could do without it altogether."

"Yes," I said, "food isn't the terrible desperate thing it used to be either; sometimes I think I could do without it altogether . . . Say that to a starving man — or woman."

"*Are* you starving, Lottie? Or is it just the idea of it that makes you think you are?"

"I want to be loved," I said, "loved, loved, loved. I'll bet you haven't given up on *love*. Go back to your room, Lydia, and don't bring this subject up again, okay?" I got out of bed, put on my kimono and headed down the hall to the lavatory. (Are you having *fun*? I said to myself. Are you having a swell time? And then I began to laugh because truly the answer was yes.)

ॐ

St. Theresa of the Child Jesus had begged to enter the Carmelite convent at Liseux. At the age of fifteen her wish was granted and she spent the remaining nine years of her life behind convent walls.

"After my death," she said, "I will let fall a shower of roses."

Whether this ever happened I do not know. She died the year my mother was born and is the patron saint of aviators and foreign missionaries. She was remarkable for her goodness.

What would it be like to be that good, to see only the best in everything? Boring, unless one were a saint. Lydia says, "When people talk about their mothers being saints, the mother usually died ironing." What would my mother and St. Theresa have to say to one another in Heaven? Are there *foreigners* in my mother's Heaven? Angels with accents? Black angels, Puerto Rican angels, lesbian angels, gay angels, God knows what else, all kinds of heavenly riff-raff? *Roman Catholics*??

Or worse — Hell — an empty place where there is only herself in a long white nightgown, at the top of the stairs, and her father, below, looking up.

hag: 1a.) An evil spirit, daemon, or infernal being, in female form; applied to the Graeco-Latin Furies, Harpies etc.; also to the Teut. 'fairies' 1552. †b.) applied to ghosts, hobgoblins, and other terrors of the night. 2. A witch; sometimes an infernally wicked woman. 3. An ugly, repulsive old woman; often with implication of viciousness or maliciousness. 4†a.) A kind of light said to appear at night on horses' manes and men's hair. b.) *dial*. A white mist usually accompanying frost.

hag. Closed field, pasture. A wooded enclosure, a coppice or copse.

hag. A cutting blow or stroke. A cutting, hewing or felling. The stump of a tree after felling.

hag. v. n. deal ME, to hew.

hag. v. obs. ex dial. To torment or terrify as a hag; to trouble as the nightmare.

hagio-hagi, comb. ff. gr. *āyios*, holy, saintly, as in hagiarchy, the rule, or order, of saints.

A hag was a wild woman of the woods and hedges. "How now, you secret, black and midnight hags." From English, from early German. No one suggests a possible relationship between saints and witches, visions and nightmares. But all of the etymologies I own have been compiled by men, who are most comfortable when women can be categorized as good — or bad; young — or old.

Pretty women say it in the Ladies' room, putting on make-up, exclaiming to one another, "God, I look like such a hag!"

"I think at one point they had to tie me up," said my mother, talking of how she had sleepwalked as a child.

"Tie you up?"

"Tie me to the bed, in some way."

"That would give me nightmares."

"I'm sure they did it for my own good," she said, "so I wouldn't hurt myself."

(In the mental hospital they still used straitjackets. The patient's arms went into sleevelike things that ended in long cotton ties. Sometimes we had to tie them to the chairs, where they sat in a warm pool of their own pee until they calmed down. The chairs were placed up against a wall in the sunroom so they couldn't fall over backwards and hurt themselves. Or they were put in the baths, with warm running water. A grey canvas cover kept them from climbing out; it had a hole for the head so that the head stuck up from the canvas like a piebird out of a pie.

Or they were given shock — insulin or electric.

"I mustn't get a shock," my mother says, when I go
too far.)

❧

SCRAP, I thought. Society for Children Recovering
from Awful Parents
    SCRAM
    SCREAM

❧

    "Boom Boom ain't it great to be crazy?
    Boom Boom ain't it great to be cra-zy?
    Silly and foolish all day long
    Boom Boom ain't it great to be
            — cray-ay-zee."
"What comes next?" Lydia said. "You always
knew the words, Charlotte, to all the songs."
    I was surprised that I remembered. The day
before we sailed I couldn't remember where I
had put the return half of my airline ticket,
London–Montreal–Vancouver.
    "A horse and a flea and three blind mice
    were sitting on a curbstone
            shooting dice —"
    "Anyone passing," said Lydia, "will think we're
mad."
    "No they won't," I said, "they'll think we're
drunks."
    "The horse slipped and fell on the flea."
    "And the flea said 'Oops there's a horse on
me.' "
    "I taught them all to my kids," I said. " 'John
Jacob Jingleheimer Smith,' 'Donkey Riding,' 'My
Hat It Has Three Corners,' 'The Cannibal King With
the Big Nose Ring.' "

"Couldn't sing that one now," she said.

"Certainly not. Strange how we never thought about it."

"Did you call brazil nuts 'niggertoes'?"

"Of course. What did you say with eenee, meenee, minee, moe?"

"How *come* we never thought about it, Charlotte? I never did, not once."

"Me either. Not once. So how come I think I can 'raise the consciousness' of a ninety-year-old woman like my ma?"

"You can't," she said. "Just be thankful she hasn't any power. It's the young ones I worry about, and the ones with power."

One of our table companions had set up a non-smoking section on the Promenade Deck. Most of the Poles smoked. Then at dinner he announced that "the Poles are moving down."

On the flight to Montreal, where we were to embark, the man next to me asked if I was wearing perfume.

"Yes," I said, "are you allergic?"

"Do you know how many animals may have died just so you could smell nice?" he said.

"Jesus," I said, "I hope you ordered the vegetarian menu. I throw up if I see somebody eating anything that died in pain."

❧

In the bottom of a drawer we find a large oval picture frame made of some rich, dark wood, maybe cherry.

"Do you want this?" she said. "I was going to throw it out."

"Sure. It's beautiful. Whose picture was in it?"

"My mother's."

"What happened to the picture?"
"I tore it up."

𝕔

The Corwin Sanitorium offered "hygienic, medical and surgical treatment of chronic diseases."

"The demands have been such as to necessitate extended facilities for aseptic surgical work as well as therapeutic resources of elimination and invigorating baths and massage."

The "comforts and freedoms of home" with "the conveniences of a hospital."

> Elizabeth Corwin, M.D.
> Resident Physician

After a while, when Mama was feeling better, Frances was allowed to curl up on the window seat in her room and look at picture books. She was calmer — for a while — after they did whatever it was they did to her, "down there."

There is a shop off Lamb's Conduit Street that specializes in the medical paraphernalia of yesterday. Skeletons, ceramic feeding-cups, scalpels and forceps, punch-out models of the human skull with all the various sections labelled. I've always been fond of the zygomatic arch — without it we could not be supercilious. Wooden legs, rusty, unidentifiable things that don't bear thinking about.

Years ago, when I worked in the State Hospital, I knew it all. I think now I was partly showing off for the nurses and doctors and partly loving the sound of some of those words. Gluteus maximus sounded like a corpulent Roman Emperor and of course your humerus was your "funny-bone." I worked mostly on the geriatric ward. The old ladies wore coarse white gowns that opened in the back. They cursed or they refused to speak. Some threw balls of shit at one another. They bit and wept. It had nothing to do with me; I might have been a zoo attendant. This was just a way to get the money to further my education.

"You know where she'll go," my sister says, "if she doesn't smarten up? Straight to the funny farm."

"You don't know what you're talking about," I say, seeing again the old ladies with their wild eyes, hearing again the Head Nurse on my first day. "Welcome to the shit ward," she said.

> My father was lost on the deep
> The ship never got to the shore;
> And Mother is sad and will weep,
> To hear the wind blow and sea roar.

— McGuffy's *New Third Eclectic Reader* (For Young Learners)

❦

"I'm lacto-ovo," I said to the man who objected to my perfume. I raised my glass and smiled.

❦

"Did Grandpa ever drink?" I asked my mother. "I remember the day the War ended but that's all."

"When we lived near Shinhopple," my mother said, "at a place called Fish's Eddy, I remember my mother and my brother carrying him in off the front porch. He'd been away up to Binghamton I guess

and fell down drunk at the front door. At least I
assumed he was drunk. It was bitterly cold — the
icicles hung almost to the ground — and there she
was dragging this full-grown man in off the porch,
and she only in her nightgown.

"But that's the only time I remember. I guess
she read him the riot act and that was that. The acid
factory wasn't doing all that well; it probably had
something to do with that."

She gave me her little, twisty smile.

"The Corbetts were very religious — or pretended to be. Marshall J. built a church at Brookdale
— Methodist I think — and we also had prayers
morning and night. On our knees. Anybody in the
kitchen had to come in and pray as well. Nobody
drank — except hard cider when there was company
or raspberry vinegar or lemonade."

She has offered me Lipton's Instant Iced Tea
Mix and I have read the label.

"Would you like me to run to the store and get
some lemons; we could have real lemonade. You
used to make such good lemonade, I remember."

"I used to do a lot of things," she says.

*Baby Grace died of pneumonia, the winter they
lived in Brookdale. Everything had been going
wrong. The house was too cold and for two days
there was no heat at all when they had to replace
the stovepipe, which had rusted out. Betty was
having her nap when they took it apart and great
clouds of soot came down all over her. She woke up
and began to cry. Mama was in the front room with
Baby Grace who wouldn't stop crying; she had the
croup and the doctor in Conklin had been sent for.*

He came too late.

They were allowed to go to the funeral because Mama wouldn't leave them alone, in Brookdale, with the hired girl.

The ground in the cemetery at Corbettsville was very wet; underneath the snow the water rushed into the small grave as soon as it was dug. Papa drew Mama away when they piled stones on the little coffin to keep it down. He took Mama away but he forgot about Frances and Betty, holding hands and staring down at the wooden box that contained their little sister. Lawrence was in Binghamton, at school.

It was a neighbour who took them home and gave them cocoa. When Papa came looking for them he was very polite but Frances could tell he was angry.

I was eight years old; I asked my mother what a gelding was. Heather wouldn't tell me.

"It's a horse that can't have babies."

"But it's a *he*. Boys can't have babies anyway."

Red-faced, the country girl: "Where did you hear that word?" Rolling out pie-crust on her old drawing-board, arms covered with flour — a big splodge of white in the middle of her forehead.

"Heather. Her horse is a gelding."

Very busy with the rolling-pin, pushing out from the centre, push, push this way, push, push that.

"I think it's Dutch," she said, this country girl. "I think it's some sort of Dutch horse. I don't move in those circles."

I said to my grandfather one day — we were on our way to the Ross Park Zoo — sly, "Heather's horse is a gelding."

"Is he now?" said my grandfather, with a little smile.

"It's some sort of Dutch horse," I offered, but he was no more forthcoming than my mother.

He gave a sort of bark.

"Who told you that?"

❧

geld(1) a Crown tax. See **yield**, para. 2.
geld(2) to castrate; **gelding**
castrate related to **castle**, a place cut off. "With L. *castrum* (let) a cutting off, (hence) a place cut off, hence an entrenchment . . . hence a fortified camp."

> What is it men in women do require?
> The lineaments of Gratified Desire.
> What is it women do in men require?
> The lineaments of Gratified Desire.

> — William Blake, "The Question Answer'd"

"Don't forget," said Lydia, "if we were trained to remain Snow White and wait for Prince Charming to break our hymens, *they* were trained to look for "the fairest of them all."

The only difference is nowadays they never talk about shoe size.

I wrote a sort of heartbreak haiku after Michael left:

> I pricked my finger
> I fell down
> But no prince came.

✿

One day I told Michael I had invented a verb for what men do to women — "pedestalize." Where is there to go but down, clunk, breaking off a few pieces as you hit the ground.

"That works both ways," he said. "You women really believe in Happily Ever After. And if you believe in that then you have to believe the man you choose is a prince. Notice he is always a *prince* and never a *king* — in the stories I mean — always young, always with the promise of property and status. In the fairy-tales poor girls marry princes — it's their means of escape from poverty and wicked stepmothers. You married me so you wouldn't have to go back to America. You thought it was romantic to be married to a potter, an Englishman, a 'man of the people,' an artisan.

"*And*," he said, "you wanted babies."

"What did you want, then?"

"I wanted a companion. I wanted someone who would understand."

"Understand what?"

He turned away. "Just by asking that you — never mind."

"*Don't* turn away from me, you asshole," I screamed (fishwife, hag). "What don't I understand? Understand *what*?"

"I'll be in the pottery," he said, heading for the door.

"Right," I said. "That's where you belong. You know what you do out there, don't you?"

He paused in the doorway. "No, what do I do, 'out there'?"

"You try to contain your emptiness, that's all

you do. Empty vessels, that's your specialty. Pots full of nothing at all."

"Thank you very much," he said, and went out.

❦

"All marriages are mixed marriages," Lydia said once.

❦

"I used to lean against the fence and watch you ride," I said. "'Look at her big rear end,' I said to myself, 'that comes from riding horses! Show-off,' I said, but I saw *National Velvet* five times. You never allowed me to even sit on that horse, never once."

"That is simply not true. That's your mother speaking, Charlotte. I offered to let you ride — or at least be up and led around. You were too afraid."

"If you say so, I don't remember."

But it might be true. I was afraid of everything then. Watch out! Be careful! Don't trust anyone! Don't take anything from strangers! Don't kiss me, I might have germs.

Now I move easily among strangers, trust almost everyone, share food on trains, on bush taxis, accept the spoonful of jam and drink the water, shake hands or kiss the offered cheek. It has taken a long time, most of my life, and there are still things I fear; but these are things, not people. Machines of one kind or another, mostly; the sound of breaking glass.

As a matter of fact, I am quite comfortable with strangers. With ships that pass in the night.

My mother called a penis a "tea kettle," and if we put our skirts up over our heads she said, "I don't want my picture taken." It seems to me that only someone as old as my mother would use that last expression. I did not understand, myself, until I was on the Acropolis one day and an old Greek photographer asked if I wanted my picture taken. When I said, "Why not?" he set up his enormous camera and disappeared behind a skirt of material, sticking his head out to say, "Smile."

At the hospital I heard for the first time words like vulva, labia, cunt. Each morning we washed the old women, working in groups of two, rolling them to one side, whisking out from under them the old, sodden bedclothes, rolling them back and whisking on the new. They were a strange colour, these women, creatures who never were exposed to natural light except what came through the high, barred windows.

Their hips and buttocks bloomed with large circles of gentian violet, which we used on bedsores.

"That's right, that's right, you hoor!" they screamed as we tried to cut their yellow toenails. "You'll get used to it," the nurses said.

The last summer I worked at the insane asylum I was sent to the operating theatre for two weeks, so that the Dirty Nurse could take a holiday. My ticket to Europe was nearly paid for, $145 to go cabin class on the RMS *Nova Scotia*. I knew that some of the things I was doing — counting sponges, laying out instruments — I was not qualified to do, but I kept quiet because I wanted the money.

One morning there was a mastectomy and an amputation. The leg was wrapped carefully in bandages and brown paper. The breast was put in a special container. The doctors wrote DO NOT OPEN UNTIL XMAS on the package containing the leg.

I was sent to the pathology lab on my way to lunch, walking in a dreamy fashion across the well-kept grounds, my ring of keys swinging against my skirt. The men who worked here called me "The Princess" because I wouldn't go out with them alone, but I didn't care. In less than a month I'd be on the high seas. Only the money mattered. The day before I'd bought a steamer trunk with brass corners and a big brass lock.

The man at the reception desk signed for the deliveries and then grinned.

"It's lunch time, darlin'," he said. "Which would you like — the drumstick or the breast?"

❧

She cries so easily; she always has. One year Lydia and Søren sent me a postcard from Israel. A large buff boulder rose up out of the sand. "The Dead Sea," it said. "Lot's wife, near Sodom."

"Look what a couple of thousand years of salt will do to a girl," they wrote on the other side.

It's no good looking back, and yet, for the last few years what have I done if not encourage her? When did *this* happen, when *that*? Where were you at that time?

"Your aunt was made to sit in the corner with a dunce cap on. I cried."

"Do you remember why you were crying? Were you sad for her? Ashamed?"

"I guess I cried for all the usual reasons," she says.

"Do you remember what she did?"

"I don't remember. She had a very quick temper. She probably said something the teacher didn't like."

"Did you ever say anything the teacher didn't like?"

"Oh no, I was a goody-goody. Butter wouldn't melt in my mouth."

"You mean butter *would* —"

"What did I say?"

It is hard for me to imagine my mother as a goody-goody. Quarrelsome, sodden with self-pity, broadcasting accusations left and right by telephone and letter. Goody-goody metamorphosed into baddy-baddy. Why?

One Christmas we received a box of Lincoln Logs in a brown paper parcel tied up with red tinsel string. Not proper wrapping paper at all, no fancy tags and matching ribbon. It came from our uncle in Massachusetts.

"Looks like a package from the meat man," Mother said.

We didn't care what it looked like; it was exciting getting something through the mail. It said DO NOT OPEN UNTIL XMAS.

On Christmas morning my mother said, "Well, isn't that the limit! He knows we have girls."

She sent them right back where they came from.

I was sorry, thinking of all the things we could have built together, my sister and I.

Now my uncle is dead. In his will he left her a few hundred dollars, but when one of his sons wrote to tell her she said she didn't want it.

"They were always in cahoots, Betty and Lawrence," she told me, pulling at her fingers. "I suppose it was conscience money; I don't want anything to do with it."

"You could have bought a big ball of wax and

made a voodoo doll or something. Stuck pins in it."

"What good would that do, he's already dead."

"Is Aunt Betty still alive?"

"Why don't you go and find out?"

❧

"Do you think?" I asked Lydia, "that if one said a word often enough, a word like 'love,' for instance, that one might come to — not just believe in it but feel it? It might be a bit like learning a new language, maybe something idiomatic in a new language. Someone says to you, '*revenons à nos moutons*' and you think, what the hell is this person going on about? But then, after a while, when you've heard it often enough and you understand its meaning, it no longer sounds odd at all. You begin using it yourself — this phrase out of a rural past — and it passes into your new vocabulary, can be pulled out at the drop of a hat."

"You are thinking about your mother?"

"Of course."

"But she does use the word 'love,' haven't you told me that? Haven't you shown me letters signed 'Love, Mother.'"

"That's true. But I don't think I've ever heard her say it. 'I hate' is more her style."

"What would happen, Charlotte, if you said it to her, if *you* practised it until it meant something apropos your mother. Have you ever told her you love her?"

"But I don't."

"I'm not so sure of that."

"I'm sure. Remember *Portrait of the Artist* in English 11? Cranley asks Stephen Daedalus, 'Stephen, do you love your mother?' "

"And he says 'I don't know what your words mean.' Yes. Strange, isn't it, how we both remember that. But Stephen has mother and mother country all mixed together, like those guys who objected to your bumper sticker. He comes home fast enough, later on, when his father sends him the telegram."

"That's duty. What I feel for my mother is duty."

"Why do you worry about her then — if all you feel is duty?"

"Because she's so old and so unhappy. I can't bear the idea of her dying in such an unhappy state."

"Then do something about it, Charlotte."

"What?"

"I don't know. You figure it out. Got to sleep."

Mother wants out. And of course, since this place she's in is not a mental hospital, she can leave any time. But leaving one place implies entering another. She has so little money it scares me; I have so little money. For years and years she has paid into Blue Cross, Blue Shield, as though, like the damsels of old, these knights will wear her favours and protect her. She can't cope any longer, she wants to go "someplace else." She must have seen "someplace else" in the four years before my grandfather died. There are no private rooms at "someplace else," at least not on her income.

Could I have her to live with me? No more travelling, no more privacy — how would I support us? She gives me $250, which she can ill afford to do; she says she'll give me another $250 when she's settled in a new place. My sister, who knows more about Massachusetts health care than I do, has told me the state is bankrupt.

Think if I had inherited all Lydia's dough and invested it wisely; I could build my mother a luxurious cottage at the bottom of the garden — "Granny flats" they call them in England — and provide a paid companion, a listener, a hired ear. She could have whatever she wanted to eat, dainty things, not boil-in-a-bag or Sara Lee Frozen Cheesecake. She could have a dog, even; she likes dogs. The one thing she couldn't have — at least for a while — would be her Knights of the Blue Cross and Blue Shield. She would be a foreigner; she is a foreigner, in my country.

I don't really need Lydia's money to do the things I've mentioned, and if I did she'd lend it to me. Why couldn't Mother live at the bottom of the garden? It's not as though she is seventy or even eighty. She is ninety, a nonagenarian. At one hundred she will get her picture in the paper, something that hasn't happened since the announcement of her marriage to my father in 1933. "Mr. and Mrs. Lawrence Bowes Corbett are pleased to announce . . ." She tore up her wedding picture long ago; one of her specialties is the tearing up of pictures. But what about me? All those years of burning her letters in the woodstove, watching them catch fire before I replaced the lid.

Michael and I didn't have a telephone; we didn't have electricity at all. Once a month I walked to the neighbour's and called her; once a week I wrote: "We are all fine and dandy here." She worried about what we ate and so I sent her a list: salmon, oysters, mussel soup with garlic and wine, baked beans, eggs, chickens, vegetables from the garden, apples and raspberries. I invited her out to see for herself but she wouldn't come. My sister introduced me as her hippie sister.

"When are you going to realize that someone has invented the wheel?" my mother said. "Your hair smells of woodsmoke," she told me when I went to visit.

(In this version of the myth only Eve is driven out of Paradise, Eve and her children. Adam has fallen in love. Eve and the children, hand in hand, with wandering steps and slow.)

❧

We stand by the front door, keeping an eye out for the taxi. The fountain, with its coloured lights, falls gracefully into a small pool.

Mother looks at the other old people in the lounge, sitting or walking slowly, some with canes, some with walkers. "Well it sure isn't the Fountain of Youth," she says. I have persuaded her to come out for a meal to the Red Robin diner at the end of the road. She has not been out of doors for a month.

"Mother," I said, "let's bundle you up and go down to the diner for lunch."

"Oh, I couldn't walk that far." (Dad's own girls.)

"We'll take a taxi."

"Take a taxi for one block?"

"It's a long block; we'll give him a big fat tip."

"That's crazy."

"So let's be crazy. Let's go right now; we can come back and clear up later." Photos and tissue paper everywhere.

We call the taxi and I begin to get her ready. I am the mother now, wrapping up the ancient child against the chill of an April day. She holds tightly to my arm as we leave the building. Her sight is going, she says. Soon she won't be able to read even the large-print books.

I've always loved soda fountains and diners, their booths, their inevitable "specials" of liver and onions, meat loaf, shepherd's pie. The sandwiches: club, tuna-fish, egg salad, hot roast beef, sliced chicken or turkey.

Mother decides on shepherd's pie and creamed corn and a small salad. I order a club sandwich.

"Dressing?" says the waitress, a kindly looking middle-aged woman. She stands there patiently, obviously used to the old people from the complex. "We have Thousand Island, Roquefort, French, Italian."

"You choose," Mother says to me.

"Thousand Island," I say, "I've always liked the name." I choose a club sandwich.

"We used to go to the Thousand Islands," my mother says. "We camped up there several summers."

"Do you remember where?"

She is buttering a roll. I think about my childhood dinners. How there was always white bread and butter on the table, even if we were having mashed potatoes and cake or pie for dessert.

"No," she says. "Maybe it will come to me."

The waitress comes with our orders. My sandwich is stuck together with toothpicks decorated with blue cellophane frills. That's really why I ordered it.

"Am I talking too loud?" my mother says to the waitress, as she changes her mind and decides she'll have coffee instead of tea if it's not too much trouble. "Is everyone looking at me?"

"Not at all," says the kindly waitress.

Then my mother smiles and does something so endearing I want to reach over and give her a big hug. She conquers her anxiety and makes a joke.

"Well, if they are," she says, "maybe it's because I'm so good-looking."

🙬

My Aunt Betty got married at fifty-five to a reformed alcoholic who had tried, while inebriated, to carry his horse across a field. He'd been kicked in the head and saw lights and the One True Light simultaneously. My mother sniffed when she heard the news and said "It doesn't really count." Didn't really count to whom? Mother? God? Aunt B.? Mr. Harris, her latter-day mate? I met Mr. Harris only twice, once when I was briefly home from college, and he told me the story of his horse and the epiphany, and once very recently, when I went back to my home town on the way to Corbettsville.

After a certain number of missed turnings I found the house, a very simple, run-down, clapboard house in a run-down neighbourhood.

I went up and knocked, and although I was sure I could hear someone moving around inside no one answered the bell or my repeated knocking. I went right round the house and in the back found a small building, crammed with benches and chairs and a piano I recognized as *the* piano — my grandmother's piano — which once sat in my grandfather's house. A sign, which must once have been illuminated, lay propped next to the locked door. A large cross on the diagonal, with a crown slipped over it, like a successful ring toss, a celestial quoit, and the words "Mission." The mission or Sunday School or whatever it was looked like it had been given up some time ago.

I couldn't see into the house but I was sure now

that I could hear someone moving about inside, slowly, heavily. Mother said that she thought one or both of them might have had a stroke. I went back to the rented car and began a note which I thought I could slip between the screen door and the front door.

I would leave the telephone number of the Holiday Inn and also greetings from my mother, her sister, in Massachusetts. DEAR AUNT BETTY — printing large and clear in case her eyes were failing or she was having difficulty reading.

DEAR AUNT BETTY,
I HAPPENED TO BE IN YOUR NECK OF THE WOO —

I was just completing the D when a young man got out of a big old American car (I was going to say a Chevy, for verisimilitude, but I have no idea what kind of car it was — big, dusty, with fins) and went up the front steps of my aunt's house.

"Excuse me," I called, getting out of the car. "Excuse me, do you know the people who live in that house?"

He looked me up and down, a middle-aged woman in a rented car. Perhaps he thought I was a social worker or someone about an unpaid bill.

"I'm looking for my Aunt B., my Aunt Betty," I said. "Betty Corbett. I thought she lived here. There's somebody moving around inside."

"There's nobody named Betty lives here," he said.

I wasn't at all sure he was telling the truth. He stood on the porch, looking down at me, a lanky young man of twenty-five or so, his cigarettes tucked into the sleeve of his tee-shirt. I was afraid of boys like this when I was young.

"Perhaps she's died, but this is the address I was given. Betty Corbett."

"There's no Betty Corbett lives here." He turned away from me and opened the screen door.

"Wait!" I called, much too loudly. I sounded operatic. "She married a man named Harris, Roy Harris. I'm *sure* this is the place." Was he a kidnapper or criminal of some sort — was he holding those two old people captive inside, drugged maybe, or gagged?

"There's no Betty here. But Mr. Harris, he's my grandpa, and Elizabeth."

"Betty is short for Elizabeth," I said, pushing past him into the house. Was he really that stupid?

The front room was dim and full of furniture and boxes piled on furniture. Ditto the dining room, but in the kitchen an old man sat at the table in his undershirt. Mr. Harris. The whole place smelled musty, as though it was never aired — no window opened, no door.

"Mr. Harris," I said, "I'm your wife's niece, you've met me before. Charlotte," I said, "Frances's daughter."

"He's deaf," the young man said in triumph. "Deaf as a post."

I was about to go round to the other side of the table and repeat the whole thing when my aunt came out of a small room which must have been the bathroom, although I didn't hear any toilet flush. She was drying her hands on a towel.

"Hello Aunt B.," I said, "do you remember me? Charlotte? Your niece?"

She didn't look very different, perhaps because I never met her until she was in her late forties. Late forties in those days was over the hill — late forties

was old. Her hair was grey then and it was whitey-
grey now. She had on the same kind of red-checked
housedress she had always worn. She used to buy
them at Montgomery Ward. But she stared at me in
complete puzzlement.

"Charlotte," I said. "Your niece. Remember
Jane and Charlotte?"

Smiled at this. "You know Jane?"

"I'm her sister. Charlotte. Frances's daughter.
Your sister." I could feel the young man standing in
the doorway, enjoying all this.

"You know Frances?" she said.

It was no use. We went over it several times, always with the same result: "You know Jane?" "You
know Frances?" She did not remember me at all.

I tried to question her about the family Bible,
about the stereopticon, the albums of photographs
and postcards. No good. A sampler on the kitchen
wall said:

NO PAIN, NO PALM,
NO THORN, NO THRONE,
NO CROSS, NO CROWN.

"I've got to get on," she said, still drying her
hands on the towel. "The breakfast dishes aren't
done. I've got to get on, dear."

As I went down the front steps, I could hear the
grandson lock the door.

❧

"Oh, she had lots of beaux," my mother said, "she
was the pretty one, with hair like Mary Pickford.
But she tried to do too much and look where it got
her. Breakdown after breakdown, poor Betty."

Why did she smile? Was it that so long as Betty was "the crazy one" then Frances could be sane?

❧

Man first employed a flotation device before 6000 B.C. to help him cross small bodies of water, such as rivers and streams. His method consisted first of riding astride a floating log, then of logs bound together with hemp to form rafts.

— Notice in the Greenwich Maritime Museum

From dugout canoes to lighter canoes of frame and hide, or birch bark. From hand paddling to canoe paddles or oars.

By 5000 B.C. there were real boats and ships along the Nile River.

By 3000 B.C. the Egyptians had ventured into the Mediterranean. We have always been on the move. So long as there have been trees — so long as there have been men. My sister and I had a boat at my grandfather's camp. It was called *The Pin-Up Girl*.

When I told Lydia later that I still hadn't found out why the original Robert came from England, she said, "Charlotte, why did the chicken cross the road?"

"Very good," I said, "but why did the chicken *want* to?"

"Perhaps," said Lydia, smiling at the flight attendant and asking if she and her friend could have just a drop more champagne, "simply because it was there?"

❧

When my children were young they were amazed at the number of old songs I knew, how fast I could learn the words to new ones. I took them to church at Christmas — across on the ferry and into the city, then back in time to cook Christmas dinner on the woodstove, get drunk and sentimental on Michael's home-made wine, God bless us every one. We made most of our presents. The children gave me hand-made coil pots, or candles; I gave them stories and gingerbread men. Michael gave me buttons made from juniper wood, a carved bowl, a collage; I gave him poems, a pork pie and English mustard bought in the city, a small transistor radio for his new pottery shed. Friends shared our meal, brought pickles and wine and musical instruments, dope, hash brownies. Huxley had assured us that anyone could have Blake's visions. Large dogs frolicked outside; babies slept in corners (God bless them every one).

❧

The death of a marriage is not like an ordinary death. Is that another oxymoron — "ordinary death"? It's not even like a tragic accident. It's something shameful, a failure. It's like failing an important exam or committing suicide. One does not bury the death of a marriage in consecrated ground. I keep his picture in a silver frame behind a picture of the children. I write travel articles: places to go and things to see. I like crowds now; I used to hate them. I carry a good book with me if I have to go to a restaurant in the evening, although I favour the cheaper restaurants where people sit at long tables, strangers next to strangers. Please pass the salt, *s'il vous plaît, per piacere, parakalo.*

Couples who are fed up talking to one another invite me to join them. I flatter myself that I have saved many a fortnight holiday from ruin, shored up many a marriage.

I genuinely love art galleries and museums. I recommend their cafés for women travelling alone.

For a while I had a cat, two cats. I put tuna-fish on the backs of my hands and let them lick it off.

I am, now, an experienced traveller. I carry in my handbag a wet flannel, a bottle of aspirin, band-aids, masking-tape, a notebook, underpants, both sennacot tablets and extract of wild strawberry. I have a nifty little knife, fork and spoon, very high-tech, in a hard plastic case and — the very latest thing — a drinking cup that is actually a portable filtering system, in case I don't want to wait for the iodine tablets to work. On long trips — or trips by rail and ferry — I carry a thermos of strong coffee. I have a bra with a pocket for a hundred-dollar bill.

"Be prepared": Wasn't that the Scout motto? I am definitely prepared for any emergency. (So perhaps, says a little voice, you are not a real traveller at all, a real adventurer. Doesn't a real adventure consist precisely of the unexpected, the thing for which there is no preparation? Examine the handbag of the Woman in Brown, says the little voice, see if its contents aren't more or less like yours.)

❧

"We talk about fallen angels and fallen women," Lydia said. "Why do we never talk about fallen men?"

❧

"Wherever men *can* be vicious, some *will* be."
— Samuel Taylor Coleridge,
    expounding on his concept of pantisocracy

❧

Could therapy have helped my mother; could it still? I imagine her lying on a couch, the psychiatrist taking her back back back down the long tunnel of time.

"Tell me again what you saw."

I always imagine the psychiatrist as male since my mother says she never liked to work for women and doesn't trust women doctors. A man in a dark business suit; for some strange reason he is holding a cat on his lap. Mother has asked if she can pet the cat and he replies, "Not yet."

"I think now it was really the lightning that woke me up," she says. "I was sleep-walking when the lightning hit the field next door and the flash was what woke me up. I found myself at the top of the staircase, looking down."

Or, under hypnosis, the doctor hands her a baby doll, unclothed, a Didee-Doll. She says, in a small, little-girl voice, "No, this is the wrong one, you're trying to trick me. The other one was all wet." She begins to cry, tiny cries, almost like little mews — mew, mew, mew.

Would a doctor, a "shrink," take on a patient who is ninety years old? Would she go? Would it help? Could someone find a way to let out all the poison inside her so that she can die in peace? "I don't think," I said to Lydia on the boat, "that it is God the Father she is worried about meeting on the other side."

Mother has been in the senior citizens' home for eighteen years, having decided at the age of seventy-two that she couldn't cope on her own. Yet before that, for seven years she had "coped" very well. (Reasonably well.) She moved away from our home town, moved up near my sister in Massachusetts, rented a house with a yard, bought a German Shepherd she named Francie, after herself. Became a live-out companion to an old lady, learned to drive. We thought perhaps her life would take on new richness and at last she would be more or less content.

And then the quarrels began again, the letters, the telephone calls to my neighbour. Her local minister wrote to me and then I phoned him.

"Your mother came to see me; she seems very depressed and says that nobody loves her."

I was harder then, younger then. I had a husband, children, a good life.

"She's probably right," I said, and put the receiver down.

❦

"When the funeral pyre was out and the last valediction over . . ."

Sir Thomas Browne, *Urne Burial*. One of the legacies of my marriage to a potter is an enormous number of pots. None are so large as the burial pots I saw on Crete (the Greeks had an ingenious method of pulling out the brains through the nose) or those at Ras Shamra, outside Latakia, in Syria. There the guide told us, in his valiant English, that (pointing to the pots) "died mans slept here." He also said that the aforesaid mans were always buried in "the fatal position." None of Michael's pots was ever that big, but I have a nice bean pot which might be perfect for Mother, since she has said nothing about scattering. Mélange de Mère, Compôte de Corbet. Gone with the wind. My sister and I could divide them up (someplace I have an old Weight Watchers scale) and each take half, just as we did with the Lifesavers or rolls of Necco Wafers we shared in the back seat of the car on our way to my grandfather's camp. Mother always thought that if I sucked on something I wouldn't throw up.

❧

I send my mother greeting cards that say "Across the miles," with easy rhymes inside, like "smiles," "beguiles."

(How are your piles; do pigs like stiles; your dainty wiles.) I make kisses and hugs.

"Why are kisses crosses?" said one of my children, when young.

(Why are hugs noughts?)

❧

To expire, to kick the bucket, to bite the dust, to croak. To pass on, pass over, meet your Maker, slough off these mortal coils. To breathe your last, to die. To go to your reward.

"I wrote my brother a letter," she said, "when Father began making eyes at that housekeeper from Georgia. Do you remember her?"

"Sure. Bobbie Ann Prew." (Fried chicken, sweet-potato pie, beaten biscuits. A handsome woman, a Christian, who even persuaded my grandfather to go to a revival meeting at Camp of the Woods. Mother sent Jane and me along as chaperones; we loved it.)

"That's right. Well she knew how to sweet-talk him into anything and I was afraid she might take him for all he was worth."

"So you wrote Uncle Lawrence a letter about this?"

"About that and other things; about that night in Corbettsville. Whether he remembered anything about that. Lawrence being Lawrence, of course he sent it on to Father, who called me up and said the letter was now in his safety deposit box and it would stay there until he died. I should've kept my mouth shut."

"Would it have been so awful if he had married Bobbie Ann Prew? Perhaps he was lonely?"

"I was only thinking of you girls. She had a son in the Marines, you know, and a daughter somewhere. She would've had them installed in your grandpa's house quicker than you can say Jack Robinson."

The letter she had written to her brother, about that night in Corbettsville so long ago, was nowhere to be found. He had told her it was in the safety deposit box at the bank but it wasn't there.

"Perhaps it was never there," I suggested. "Perhaps he just said it was there."

Pulling on her fingers, pull pull pull.

"Oh no, it was there all right. Betty or Lawrence probably took it out quick. I wouldn't put it past either of those two."

"What would they do with it?"

"Use it against me."

"How? He was dead."

"Oh — so I wouldn't contest that will. They were always in cahoots."

The pulling on the fingers became more and

more rapid; I decided it was time to change the subject; she mustn't get upset.

❧

Tell-Tale Tit, your tongue shall be slit
And all the dogs in town will have a little bit.
(Only it wasn't her tongue.)
She didn't go to the funeral. When the New York State Historical Association wrote a letter of inquiry she tore it up and threw the pieces in the waste-paper basket. He had left her only a thousand dollars and the right to choose a few mementoes from his house.

❧

Found in a letter from one Eliza Paul to a Corbett:

"It don't do to talk too much."

❧

"Just remember, my sentimental friend, hearts will never be practical until they can be made unbreakable.
"A heart is not judged by how much you love, but by how much you are loved by others."
— *The Wizard of Oz*

❧

In February, my mother sent me a card with two Canada geese on the front, and the words, "I'm glad we're friends." Inside it said,

"all the things
you are
are all the things
I like!"

Underneath she had written, "There. I guess that may surprise you."

❀

Eventually about 1200 A.D. the elder brother, getting tired of living in the hills, came down nearer to Shrewsbury and married a Saxon heiress, from whom he inherited the lands on which my cousin, Sir Gerald Corbet still lives. The place is called Moreton Corbet, and is a lovely ruin, having been burnt by Cromwell's soldiers, this branch of the family being staunch royalists. The house was never rebuilt, but the family erected another a short distance away, some 200 years ago. It was probably owing to the sufferings of the Corbets at that time, which caused your ancestor to go to America.

— part of a letter from Archer M. Corbet(t)
  to Luella Corbet Gault, June 1930.

❀

It was chilly and misty in Shropshire the next morning; I was glad I had brought my heavy Cornish sweater with me. I've had it for years and it never wears out. The Cornish coast, particularly in North Cornwall, is treacherous, as is the sea. My sweater has some interesting zig-zags knitted into it, which the woman who knitted it told me were symbolic of "the marriage lines."

On the map I picked up at the Tourist Information Office in Market Square I could see that Moreton-Corbet was on a side road off the A53 to

Shawbury and Market Drayton. The woman behind the desk gave me several brochures and pointed me in the direction of the bus stop. I wanted another coffee but decided I had better get going. I'd come back in the afternoon and have tea or coffee and sightseeing after I had done the real business I was here for.

The bus was part of the Hotspur line. Henry Percy died near here, and the usurper's cursèd head was displayèd on a pole. I found that out later, in a guide-book. It is not my policy to read up much on a place until after I've been there and made my own jottings. All I knew about Shropshire when I left London was a few lines from Houseman: the bit about the blue remembered hills, and farms and spires; something about the cherry hung with snow.

Women in twos and threes, with baskets on their arms, chatted in twos and threes of the ordinary things of life. One showed a knitting pattern to another. Oh you do not know the yearning I felt to be one of them, out for a day of shopping in a neighbouring town, wondering what to give the family for their tea. The driver showed me where to go after I left the bus and I could see, as he pulled away, the faces of the cheerful women staring down at me, wondering, for a moment, what I was up to in my denim skirt and heavy jumper, my ribbed tights and walking shoes. Across the road and ahead lay a wide dirt track; that was the way to Moreton-Corbet church and castle. Behind me was a large sign that said CRASH LANE/KEEP CLEAR. Helicopters whirred noisily up above what was obviously an RAF base of some sort.

"Season of mists and mellow fruitfulness." I have always liked autumn; I have always liked country roads. The woman at the bed-and-breakfast said that a Corbet still lived there, oh yes; she thought he was married to an Australian.

I hoped the church wasn't locked; I particularly wanted to see the church. My spirits lifted. Forget the women with their shopping baskets and their hesitation between bangers and mash or a nice bit of fish for tea. I was going to meet Corbets, one-t, to be sure, and dead at that, but nevertheless, if the Book of Begats was to be believed — and the letter from Sir Archer Corbett to Mrs. Gault of Ohio — kin, relations, the English side of the family. Perhaps there would even be records that would tell me the truth about the first American Robert. Heigh-ho, heigh-ho. I crossed the road and stepped out smartly.

As I stopped to admire a black-faced ram who stared at me through a fence, a black-and-white collie rushed up, barking, followed more slowly by a man in a blue jacket.

"We've had the ewes to him," he said, leaning on the fence and addressing me as if we were old acquaintances. Then, "Shep, quiet down, there's a good dog." And then, "I suppose you'll be wanting to see Sir Chimes." (Or that's what it sounded like, Sir Chimes. Oi — Oi suppose. I had a sudden stab of memory: listening to "The Archers" during the long final weeks before our first child was born. Were they Shropshire? I had never thought about where they were supposed to be from; just jolly rustics from some other part of England.)

"Why do you suppose that?" I asked him. Was there a Corbett/Corbet gathering on? Were there Corbet/Corbetts behind every hedgerow, ready to pop and shout 'Surprise!'

"Not many strangers come down this road who aren't Corbets."

"Well I guess I am a Corbett," I said, "or my mother is. Her name was Frances Corbett before she was married. Two t's," I added.

"If you wait a few minutes I can take you up to the house," he said.

"I really came to see the church — and the castle ruins," I said. "Do you know if the church is locked? I didn't come to impose upon Sir James."

"He sees lots of folk from overseas," the farmer said, "American, mostly. Americans are very keen to find relatives in England."

"Especially if they have 'Sir' or 'Lady' in front of their name," I said.

He laughed.

It came to me that I should have found out who was the present lord of the manor and written or phoned. I hadn't been thinking in terms of the living at all, only the dead, or some kindly old vicar who might show me the parish records and offer me a cup of tea.

As we bumped along in the van — the man in blue turned out to be Sir James's tenant farmer — I was more and more nervous about an actual meeting with an actual Bart. I assumed this fellow was a Bart, like all the other elder sons who had lived here. It seemed a long way to the house; I wondered if I'd find my way back again, but Jack Pinces, for that was his name, solved that one by saying he was only dropping off some receipts and would run me back down again, if I liked, after I met Sir Chimes.

"She's Australian," he offered, "Lady Anne. No children."

Were all the transatlantic visitors trying to

establish a claim to the title and these obviously thriving farms?

Sir James was just leaving as we drove up. It was not an excuse; he had his car keys in his hand. A middle-aged man in a green suit that looked as though it were made of thistles. Lady Anne was away, he said, and he could only stop for a minute — early closing day. He asked if I were a one-t or two-t Corbet. I told him my mother's name. He asked if I would like to see his pears; pears were his hobby.

Boxes and boxes of pears — bosc, comice, I don't know what all, behind the garage doors. The smell of those pears stayed with me for the rest of the day. Season of mists and mellow fruit. In my Michael days I had a pear tree; I bottled pears each autumn, with a piece of ginger, as Michael's mother had taught me, in the bottom of each jar. The first Christmas of our separation I sent a jar of pears and a tin of Nestle's cream with the children.

He gave Jack a bag of pears for his family, but offered me not a one. If I had written, or been a one-t Corbet, would it have been otherwise? At the bottom of the drive he sped away to the east and Market Drayton. We went back to the road where I had begun.

It turned out that Jack and his wife had been to Canada, had even been to Vancouver and Vancouver Island. Soon he would turn the tenant farm over to his son and he and the wife would maybe travel some more. He wasn't happy about the way the sheep were bred now, for lean; he liked a bit of fat, he did. A bit of fat never hurt anyone.

He told me where the light switch was and asked me to be sure to turn the lights out when I left. He was the sexton of the Moreton-Corbet church, as well as the tenant farmer. We shook hands, then he and Shep went on about their business.

Twenty-four manors, those Corbeau/Corbets had been given. Did the land look so very different then? England's green and pleasant land. By the time of the Domesday Book, only twenty years after Hastings, of the one hundred and fifty-four great lords enumerated only eight were English. From Danish pirates to "Normans" to landed lords in England in 175 years. "He wanted to start a *dienasty*," my mother said of her grandfather, Marshall J. Was that a throwback to the sons of Hugh the Crow? If Robert had been an eldest son, or even a second or a third, would he have stayed in England, on the marches?

"Wayfarers welcome," said a sign on the churchyard gate.

"From an open road to an open church."

The light switch was where Jack said it would be. I turned on the lights and entered the church of my ancestors for the first time.

Richard Corbet, Esq., second son of Robert Corbet of Moreton, Knight, and his wife Margaret, former wife of Thomas Wortley of Wortley in the County of York, Esq. and daughter of John Saville, of Thornhill in the County of York, Knight, were lying on top of their tombs, in their Sunday best, awaiting the last trump.

Richard, d. 16th July, 1567, a Renaissance man. He looks vaguely Spanish, my idea of a grandee. His feet lie on a beast and a crow is whispering into his right ear.

His father Robert is buried in the other elaborate tomb, and here we see the shield with its prominent crows — or ravens? Lengthwise around the tomb are many figures, mostly female, right hand on belly, left hand on heart, although some are carrying books and there is one with an open book. Elizabeth, his wife, is at his side. She has angels at her pillow; he has a crow by his left ear, his feet on a beast who looks almost like an oriental lion. A small dog takes part of Elizabeth's cloak in his mouth. Was this her favourite dog? Did he howl when she died? On both of these figures the thumbs and fingers are broken, but they look peaceful, as though they have decided to have a short nap before the party begins.

Sir James would be buried here, I supposed, and Lady Anne, but in nothing so elaborate. The rest of the Corbets in St. Bartholemew's are commemorated by plaques and urns.

> SACRED to the Memory of Frances,
> The wife of Andrew Corbet of
> Shawbury Park, Esq., in this
> county, only daughter and
> heir of William Prince of
> Shrewsbury, Esq. and whose
> remains were interred in
> the Abby Church of that town
> the 21st day of November 1769,
> aged 59 years.

Also Elizabeth Corbet, the eldest daughter of Frances Corbet. I made a note to tell mother that.

> SACRED to the memory of Robert . . .
> and Dame Mary, his wife.
> Dame Mary died, aged twenty-five,
> in March 1829.

> Richard Corbet, Esq. born
> of the most ancient stock of the Corbets . . .

272 / AUDREY THOMAS

Richard was a soldier during the reign of three
kings, "Charles the Martyr and both his sons." Died
in his 67th year, A.D. 1691.

"Richard Corbet set up this monument to his father, who deserved the very best he could render him."

A bust of Richard the father surmounted the
plaque. Under it an angel's head and wings, flanked
by two very medieval-looking skulls, both looking
towards the angel.

SACRED TO
SACRED TO
SACRED TO

At one point, jotting things down as I walked
around, I made another "sad ghost" sort of mistake.
"Scared" I wrote, instead of "sacred"; scared to the
memory of . . .

The helicopters circled overhead, puh-puh-puh-
puh-puh. There is a Bergman film about a woman
who goes mad and thinks that God is in — or is —
a helicopter. Puh-puh-puh-puh-puh. Could Richard
Corbet, Esq., born of the most ancient stock of
Corbets, be the father of Robert Corbet, Corbett,
possibly Corbin, who sailed away to America?
Think of Banquo — "Fly, good Fleance, fly . . . !"

There was supposed to be a sword hanging on the
wall, used by Roland James Corbet during the retreat
from Mons, but Jack told me it had recently been
stolen. ("Sir Chimes said it wasn't worth much.")
Who took it? Who was running around the country-
side with a hero's sword? A schoolboy? A wayfarer?
How would you conceal such a thing? Mother has
given me my father's sword (used only in Masonic
ceremonies), which was his father's sword before
him. I have left it with a friend in Boston, not sure
I can get it through Customs. Do I declare it an

antique or a dangerous weapon? It's quite beautiful, as swords go; the blade is chased with serpentine patterns and the hilt is inset with ivory. He had a Masonic funeral; why wasn't it buried with him? (Her father's sword she hath girded on.)

My father's middle name was Earle. When Michael and I were married at the Registry Office ("bachelor," "spinster") I gave my father's full name and the clerk looked up with surprise and respect. We laughed. "No, no," I said, "Earle is his middle name. We're just ordinary people." His face fell; as Michael said afterwards, he might have got a few quid from one of the London papers for leaking the story of the secret wedding of the daughter of an earl.

"What's an earl anyway?" I said. "I mean, what's the difference between an earl and a knight or a viscount."

He didn't know.

The helicopters were giving me a headache ("Batter my heart, three-personed God") and the church was cold, even with my heavy sweater on. I decided to sit down a few minutes and think, and then get out of there. I should be out in the sunshine, walking beside the coppery hedgerows, not mooning about with these old bones. I would go outside and look at the castle ruins next door, sit on a bench and eat the orange and biscuits I had brought with me, then head for a village and a pub lunch.

I put my notebook back in my daypack and as I did I touched the thermos of laudanum, mixed with Madeira and spices, that I had made up the day before. I had planned to take it when the right moment came. What could be more right than right now, right here in this old church — "Wayfarers Welcome" — on such a mellow autumn afternoon?

I drank. I drank the whole lot, maybe half a pint.

It was too sweet, not really my cup of tea at all. It made me feel slightly sick.

Nothing happened. It was like the first time I tried to get stoned. I felt nothing except chilly and hungry; time to go.

And then I noticed that the colours in the stained-glass window behind the chancel were glowing like jewels. "A trick of the sunlight," I thought. "The sun has come round to the back of the church."

I had ignored the window because it was modern, late-nineteenth century (1892 it said on the orange sheet I had taken from the pile by the door). Now I went closer. It was a skilful but fairly standard scene of Christ blessing the children. "To the glory of God in loving memory of Vincent Rowland Corbet, 3rd Baron of Moreton Corbet . . ." All of the children were looking up at Christ, waiting to be patted, except for a golden-haired child in a burgundy-coloured dress, barefoot, holding up a posy. She was looking directly out at the viewer, or she would have been if something hadn't happened to her face. Someone — or something — had broken her face and it had been replaced by clear glass. I could see right through it to the landscape beyond. It reminded me of those seaside cutouts of people in Gay Nineties swimsuits, where you stuck your head through and the photographer snapped your picture. I have one of Michael and me at Brighton Pier. So I smiled at first, but then it seemed ominous — what had happened to her face? Was it going to be replaced?

I went back to my pew and took out my notebook again. I had just written — "find out about the child in the"— when I heard a rustling sound, like something moving through dry grass. At first I thought it was mice, or rats, but then I looked up and they were all around me, the dead. Not transparent but substantial, as believable as people on a movie screen.

They took up their places in the old, worn pews: Vikings, Normans, Cavaliers and Roundheads, the Americans — Robert of Weymouth, his children, their children, their children's children. Corbets and Corbetts. Armour and leather, homespun and velvet, some with silver buckles on their shoes. It was all in exquisite detail. I could even see where a suit of chain-mail had been mended and the blackened thumbnail of a farmer.

They did not look at me nor did they speak, but filled up the pews around me, knelt briefly, then picked up *Hymns Ancient and Modern*. They opened their mouths, and sang, but there was no sound except for the sound of the helicopters overhead, *PUH-PUH-PUH-PUH-PUH*.

And then they disappeared, like people in a fog. They melted away.

My grandfather was there, in a dark business suit; he sat well away and did not look at me. "He knows," I thought. "He knows I know," but he did not acknowledge me.

One of my favourite hymns, an "American" hymn: "Once to every man and nation" (comes the moment to decide).

I was angry with myself that I had drunk the whole thing at one go. I knew, without the laudanum, I could not call them back again. The missing Corbett must have been among them.

I left the church, remembering to turn out the lights.

❧

Shep and Jack were nowhere around, so, determining to write to him later, I walked back to the paved road. The ram was still there, staring over the fence, waiting to do his duty once more for Woolmark and the butchers of Shrewsbury. "Have fun," I said to him as I passed, but he didn't speak to me. The drug had worn off, leaving me my ordinary self in the ordinary world, only drowsy. I don't wear a watch but I guessed the time at nearly one or even after. Jack was probably home eating lunch, with pears for dessert.

The next bus wouldn't be along until two so I decided to hitchhike up to the A53. I could ask whoever picked me up the way to the nearest pub.

Two cars drove past with never so much as a glance in my direction; then a farm lorry with an enormous load of carrots. At least he shrugged and smiled. Then a blue Mini slowed down and stopped.

The driver was a no-nonsense farmwoman — or perhaps a district nurse — who drove with both hands on the wheel and eyes straight ahead.

She had told me she would drop me off in Wem, as it was on her way. I could have lunch and catch a Hotspur bus back to Shrewsbury every hour.

I asked her if it bothered her, living so close to such a big RAF base.

Why should it? she said. They were lucky in a way. When the end came they'd be killed in the first flash. They'd be the first to go.

❧

While I was eating my pub lunch I had a look at the local paper. In the "Eating Out Guide" there was an advertisement for the Corbett Arms Hotel, Market Drayton:

This was a two-t place — and so close to home. Perhaps the owners had wanted to make it clear that the hotel's name wasn't French?

I looked at the clipping again. No — they weren't against the French: Christmas Fare dinner included, amongst the starters, Parisienne melon with Cointreau and, listed with the main course, Steak Chasseur. I actually thought the luncheon was better value and would have reserved there and then, were I going to be around. "Crackers, hats and novelties." Did Sir James and Lady Anne host big Christmas dinners at the manor; did Jack and his son get something for their Christmas boxes?

The barmaid was joking with a couple of regulars; they were kidding her because she liked to dust. I paid my bill — one ploughman's lunch, one lager shandy — and asked directions to the bus stop. I should probably go to Market Drayton to interview the proprietors of the Corbett Arms Hotel but I was tired and still feeling the effects of the laudanum, sleepy, somewhat detached. Visually very alert however. All things too bright and beautiful as I went out from the dim pub into the clear November air. The sound of the circling helicopters — CRASH LANE! KEEP CLEAR! — was distant but distinct. Young men up there, practising for war, eager for it. "Who killed Cock Robin?" We used to sing that in high school.

I had left my suitcase in a locker at the station and had a brief moment of panic when I couldn't find the key. But no, there it was, slipped down in the folds of a tourist brochure, *Shrewsbury in a Nutshell*.

When Little Nell died in Shropshire the whole world wept. "The Death of Little Nell" was one of my mother's recitation pieces. People said to my grandmother, those girls are good enough to go on the stage. Nell breathed her last amidst ruins not unlike those at Moreton-Corbet, but the church was another St. Bartholemew's, the one at Tong. Dickens visited Shrewsbury and the surrounding neighbourhood one hundred and forty-nine years to the day that I arrived. He was on a tour of the Midlands and North Wales and came in the coach "by way of Birmingham and Wolverhampton, starting at eight o'clock through a cold wet fog, and travelling when the day had cleared up, through miles of cinder-paths and blazing furnaces and roaring steam-engines, and such a mass of dirt, gloom and misery as I never before witnessed." The heart of the Industrial Revolution.

He put up at the Lion Hotel and addressed the letter to Mrs. Charles Dickens, 48 Doughty Street, London, complaining of a recurring pain in his side that forced him to "take a dose of henbane," the effect of which was "most delicious." "I slept soundly and without feeling the least uneasiness, and am a great deal better this morning." He paid £1/14/0 for lodgings, a shilling to the hostler, £1/12/6 horses & boy, first stage, £1/2/0 horses and boy, second stage, 4/6 in turnpike charges, 2/6 for lunch, a shilling for a "guide up the mountain" near Llangollen. He visited a fort called Castell-Dinas-Bran, northeast of the town and called, on the Ordinance Survey Map, Crow Castle.

❧

Henbane contains scopolamine. As did Twilight Sleep, the narcotic they gave Mother during her two labours. Scopolamine is in the patches worn behind the ears of those who are queasy sailors. "Just in case."

I have often wondered if I escaped the curse of the female Corbetts because I worked in the mental hospital, so long ago. There is another poem of Houseman's that, once again, I remember only vaguely. It has to do with King Mithradites who ate a little bit of poison every day so his enemies couldn't poison him. I remember only the last line: "Mithradites, he died old."

With Dickens the henbane had a salubrious effect and the letter-writer is obviously in good spirits. He signs himself "— your faithful and most affectionate Husband.

Charles Dickens"

Was he already plotting to get rid of her?

❧

— *In a letter from Charlotte to Lydia, sent Express to Birmingham*

Shrewsbury/Shrovesbury November 5 (railway station/dworzec kolejowy)

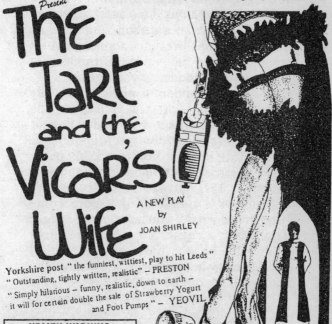

Shrewsbury Music Hall
NOV 9th & 10th ONLY 7·30 PM
BOX OFFICE 0743 50761
TICKETS £3.50 (CONCESSIONS £2.50)

DANNY DAVIES PRODUCTIONS

NOW IN 2ND YEAR
OVER 200 PERFORMANCES
SEEN BY OVER 100,00 PEOPLE

Present
The Tart and the Vicar's Wife

A NEW PLAY by JOAN SHIRLEY

Yorkshire post " the funniest, wittiest, play to hit Leeds "
" Outstanding, tightly written, realistic " – PRESTON
" Simply hilarious – funny, realistic, down to earth –
it will for certain double the sale of Strawberry Yogurt
and Foot Pumps " – YEOVIL

HEALTH WARNING
This comedy could seriously
damage your sex life.

The Subject Matter and Nudity makes it
Unsuitable for Children

I thought you might enjoy this flyer. What is it about the English and "naughtiness"? Also saw that Priestley's play, *When We Are Married*, is coming. We saw that on our wedding day — I think his parents paid for the tickets. This is a town full of famous names: Darwin, Sydney, Hotspur, Cromwell, Clive of India. The tourist brochure also mentions an authoress, Mary Webb (*Amour, Wherein He Trusted, Precious Bane*, etc.). Have you ever heard of such a person? But it turns out the "Shropshire lad" actually comes from Birmingham — or Bromsgrove, which is just outside, as you know.

Back to London tonight, then one more day and we're awa'. Barring the unforeseen, I'll meet you and Søren at Heathrow (airport/dworzec/olejowy) at the Meeting Place around noon. My plane leaves at 3:15, can't remember when yours leaves — 2:15?? but we should have plenty of time for a quick drink before going through Security. If you have any change of plans leave a message at Mecklenburgh Square, I'll be out most of tomorrow. I don't mind going earlier to the airport as I have to check out by 9:30.

"Oh River," as we used to say,
xx Charlotte

PS. Took the laudanum — amazing. Can S. get me some more?
PPS. Do you know anything about the Mormons — in terms of searching for lost

members of the family? Somebody said they will look up anybody's family. Something to do with the Elect. Does that mean they will look up the Damned as well?

PPPS. Overheard at Euston Station: "We drive a HONDA." An American couple, speaking very loudly to a Japanese man who had asked directions to the British Museum. What do they say to Italians? "We eat PIZZA." To the French: "We use GARLIC." My mother says the Japs are taking over the world, why didn't we finish them off when we had the chance? I guess I prefer the Euston Station couple to that; at least they are trying to connect, however clumsily they go about it. ("We love CURRIES!" "We eat RICE three times a week." "We drink WODKA!")

Clickety, clickety back to Lud's town, back to my blue room in the annex but first a look-see in my mailbox. The day after tomorrow someone else's name would be posted above my slot. A card from Robert — a view of the Pitti Palace and a correction about the trees around the square: they were sycamores, not maples. No "having a wonderful time." Poetry was too serious a business to be frivolous. A note from the Woman in Brown. Another letter from Mother. Another old woman has died. The residence held a Talent Night (to which Mother, of course, did not go; couldn't she have recited "The Death of Little Nell"?), and this woman was playing the accordion when she dropped down dead. "At least it was quick," Mother says, and I can't help laughing.

"Good news?" says the receptionist behind the desk.

"Not exactly."

On the train returning to London the conductor's voice, when it came over the loudspeaker, sounded Welsh, but not quite Welsh. Irish? I thought, but no, not Irish either, neither the rushing whisper of the north nor the louder, more lyrical accent of the south. When he finally came through to take our tickets, he was a Sikh.

"Next stop, Calcutta," said one of four men who were sitting nearby, their table littered with beer cans. He laughed uproariously at his joke and the others joined in.

I should have spoken up but I kept silent; drunken men scare me, even one. But Lydia would have said something — something witty and demolishing, something to make them look foolish in the eyes of the other passengers.

When my mother says things I know how to deal with it, through exaggeration of the original premise, through a smile. In public, among strangers, I keep quiet. It was dark, and I turned away, only to be met by my own face in the window.

On a postbox in Vancouver: Keep B.C. Clean: Send a Paki back to India.

In the Métro in Paris: Take one Jew, put him in the microwave, Vive le Pen!

Elsewhere: Yankee Go Home.

On a train in West Africa, a white South African woman says, "You don't know what it's like: we live in fear. We wake up with fear, spend the day with fear, go to bed with it. We have *daughters*," she says, her wide blue eyes staring into mine.

On his reading tour of America in 1867–68, Dickens took laudanum before he went to bed, he became so wound up reading the death of Tiny Tim, and to calm the cough that otherwise kept him awake.

> One of my father's jokes:
>   It's not the cough that carries you off
>   It's the coffin they carry you offin.

Merritt Corbett had one version of "Did Ya Ever Think?" We had another — no moralizing, just the gruesome facts.

> Didja ever think
> When a hearse goes by
> There's comin' a time when you're gonna die?
>
> They'll put you in a great big box
> And cover you over with dirt and rocks
> The worms crawl in
> The worms crawl out
> The worms play pinochle on your snout.

I can't remember the rest of it. We liked songs like that. "Found a Peanut" was another, and this:

> A peanut sat on a railroad track
> Waitin' for his mother.
> Along the line came Engine 9
> TOOT-TOOT
> Peanut Butter.

"I remember you singing," Lydia said. "Once, in the middle of a campfire, I told you there was half a daddy-long-legs in your cup of cocoa, just to shut you up."

"It is so strange and unsettling," I said, "to think that you could have been jealous of me. You knew how to do the crawl; you could do a one and a half gainer off the high dive. Your shorts came from Peck and Peck. You were ten years old and you had a horse."

"What a fool you were, Charlotte; you're not such a fool any more. Are you? Are you? Charlotte, are you awake?"

I would like to give my mother a Viking funeral, make her sleepy then swaddle her like a baby in a pram, set her adrift in a canoe on the Susquehanna River. I hate the idea of the fiery furnace and a bunch of cinders; I would rather see her go out in style.

"I'll be next," she wrote in her letter, "you wait and see."

❀

Elixir paregoricum. Camphorated tincture of opium. For minor ailments and nervous crises.

Laudanum — a reddish-brown liquid, which varied in colour according to its strength.

Godfrey's Cordial, Kendal Black Drop, Kilmer's Swamproot Elixir, made in my home town. Cheaper than beer or gin. Its name in the Fens was "elevation."

In my novel Edna will say, about Grace Corbett:
"Shh, your poor Mama is lyin' down." And under her breath, *"She's taken her little bit of elevation."*

❂

"If a man abide not in me, he is cast forth
as a branch, and is withered; and men
gather them, and cast them into the fire,
and they are burned."

— John 14:18

❂

He took us to the Hope and Crosby "Road" shows
and for a treat at the Ritz Tea-room. The hostess
wore her hair in an upsweep with a peek-a-boo bang
at the front.

"Good afternoon, Mr. Corbett" — and showed
us to our table.

I ordered a French pastry from the trolley. It was
the name I was eating — "French pastry" — as
much as the cake.

"Grandpa," we said. If the pretty waitress was
near he said, "Now I told you to call me Uncle
Larry." He would have been in his seventies at the
time.

Did I love him? Did he love me?

I was afraid of his disapproval.

(Saw a girl sitting on a porch in Brooklyn, a
friend of his sister Alice. He was a young man,
twenty-one, whose father had been a major in the
Civil War, but whose personal gods — although he
himself became a mechanical engineer — were
Telford, Brunel and Roebling. Saw this girl, made
her acquaintance and told her mother — "When
Grace is a little older, I'm going to marry her.")

"She seems happy enough in her postcards," I
said to Mother.

"That could have been a front."

She's right. It could have been. I too have sent cheerful postcards to my parents — blue skies, "views." Cheerful letters as well. It's not so much that you don't want to burden them with things — or it wasn't, with me. I was always afraid that if I wrote it down then it might become fixed, permanent, real, that it couldn't be changed.

"You never tell us anything," my mother says, accusingly.

"You wouldn't listen if I did."

❧

Inside — the low ceiling made even lower by the exposed beams. A stone fireplace, dark furniture, a small piano with sheets of sentimental music underneath the seat: I would pick out the tunes with one finger: "Silver Threads Among the Gold," "There's A Long, Long Trail A Winding," "Sunday, Monday or Always." The boys at school had different words for this one:

> Won't you tell me, Dear
> The size of your brassiere.
> Thirty — Forty — or Fifty?
> If it's fifty-two, I'll go out with you
> Sunday, Monday or Always.

A photograph of my grandfather seated behind his big desk at IBM, surrounded by smiling secretaries and typists. THINK! said a placard on the desk; THINK said the monthly magazine.

On the back porch: gallon jugs of Chemung Spring Water, capped with fluted paper tops. Jars of grape jelly made from the grapes on the vine in the backyard. An old marmalade tomcat coming in and out the cat-door. Not a cat you could pet.

Years later, reading a book on schizophrenia and problems in perception, I came across this phrase:

"The word CAT cannot scratch you." (But if you are crazy enough, if you are convinced you have that power, then it's a different thing altogether.)

I tried to fix my tape-recorder myself but soon gave up.

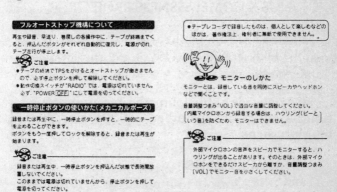

On my last day I visited the Dickens House on Doughty Street, washed my clothes and dried them, picked up my mended tape-recorder, bought a few more presents, including a large plum pudding for my sister at Fortnum and Mason's. My sister likes a big traditional Christmas with all the trimmings. By the time I had finished all this and had some tea it was getting on for five o'clock. I decided I just had time to visit the Coram Foundation Museum before supper.

I had taken the shortcut to Brunswick Square

many times before, even at night when you would be hard put to escape should someone confront you on the narrow, ill-lit footpath. Had taken the short-cut and seen the signs, with their arrows pointing to various buildings.

GREGORY HOUSE →
HOMELESS FAMILIES CENTRE →
THOMAS CORAM RESEARCH UNIT →
ST. LEONARD'S NURSERY SCHOOL →
THOMAS CORAM'S CHILDREN'S CENTRE →
KINGS X HOMELESSNESS PROJECT →

PEDESTRIANS ONLY
NO DOGS. NO LITTER
PLEASE

On one side of the footpath the various foundation buildings, on the other, a playground, fenced in. More signs.

CORAM'S FIELDS
and
THE HARMSWORTH
MEMORIAL PLAYGROUND

THIS IS A CHILDREN'S PLAYGROUND
IT IS *NOT* A PUBLIC PARK AND
THERE IS NO RIGHT OF WAY
ACROSS THE GROUNDS.
PARENTS, TEACHERS AND YOUTH
LEADERS ACCOMPANYING CHILDREN
AND YOUNG PEOPLE MAY COME AND GO
FREELY
NO OTHER ADULTS MAY ENTER EXCEPT

ON BUSINESS OR BY SPECIAL PERMISSION
OF THE COUNCIL OF MANAGEMENT OR
ITS OFFICERS

CYCLING, GLASS BOTTLES AND DOGS
NOT ALLOWED

Who needs a flaming sword when the Foundation is at hand? At night the gates to the playground are locked, unless there is an evening game taking place, but there is a space where the fence is pulled back creating a hole big enough for a large dog — or a small child — to come through from the square. All of these signs to keep out might easily lead one into temptation.

I hadn't used the footpath this visit because a new sign had been added after the storm.

DANGER. FALLING TREES
PEDESTRIANS USE THIS
FOOTPATH AT THEIR OWN RISK

Now the dangerous trees had been removed and only the usual warnings and thou-shalt-nots were posted. I wanted to do a piece, sometime, on interesting small museums in London. Whether the Coram Museum would turn out to be the kind of place tourists would wish to visit, I didn't know — even if not, there was a chance I could use it in a "human interest" piece for some magazine or other. "Two hundred and fifty years ago, in the area known as Bloomsbury, a prosperous sea-captain saw a baby lying on a dung heap." Not exactly the sort of thing for *Condé Nast Traveler*, but if I put it together with the Bethnal Museum of Childhood or the London Toy and Model Museum it might work. The last few years have produced a kind of sentimentality about children that hasn't been seen since Dickens's time. Whatever was inside would no doubt be tasteful as well as interesting. A clock was just striking the hour as I went in, followed by two workmen carrying boxes marked FRAGILE/THIS SIDE UP.

❧

The woman at reception said the museum was closing in half an hour so I bought a booklet about the hospital, some postcards and printed sheets about the paintings and various mementoes before I went up. I promised to turn out the lights and replace the baize covers on the cases when I was through. In the passageway in Reception was a painting called "The Pinch of Poverty."

Over 10,000 children were admitted during the first five years but many of them died. In 1760 Parliament passed a decree stopping the "general admission" and the number of children dropped to "about 400."

To gain a place for their child, the mothers had to take part in a kind of "Lucky Dip" invented by the Governors. Some coloured balls, either red, black or white, were placed in a bag. The mother who drew a white ball was given a place for her child. A red ball meant she might have a chance if any white ball child who had the first turn was found to be suffering from a serious illness, or unsuitable for any reason. A black ball meant that there was no place available, and mothers who drew a black ball had to be sent away with their child.

— *The Story of the Foundling Hospital*,
Maureen Boyd

The mother was asked to pin a token to the child's clothes; it might be a brooch, a coin or a letter or the baby's coral beads, or any small thing that only a mother would recognize.

— *The Story of the Foundling Hospital*,
Maureen Boyd

The children were usually admitted on a Saturday, and on the Sunday following would be christened and given new names in the hospital chapel. The Governors would choose the names and often called the children after famous people, such as "Thomas Coram" "William Shakespeare" or "Francis Drake."

	Breakfast	**Dinner**	**Supper**
Sunday	Broth	Roast pork or beef	Bread
Monday	Gruel	Potatoes	Milk and bread
Tuesday	Porridge	Boiled mutton	Bread
Wednesday	Broth	Rice/Milk	Bread and cheese
Thursday	Gruel	Boiled pork or beef	Bread
Friday	Porridge	Dumplings	Bread and milk
Saturday	Broth	Hasty pudding	Bread and cheese

On Founder's Day they had a holiday, with a special dinner of roast beef and plum pudding.

On the first landing was a terracotta bust of George Frederick Handel, who directed a performance of *The Messiah* at a concert in the chapel. The King was present and the hospital made £728.

"He shall feed his flock. . . ." On gruel, on porridge, on roast pork or beef every Sunday. Were the children happy here? (They are happy in the paintings.) Why does Dickens make Tatty Coram such a bitter, bitter girl, so angry and envious? He and his family attended chapel at the hospital; he saw the children; he heard them sing. Did he quiz them as well? Would that have been allowed — for someone as well known as he? And even if allowed, would the children have told the truth? What made Dickens think that Tatty Coram would have been so miserable as maid to the beloved "Pet"? She is already angry when she comes under the influence of Miss Wade, the Self-Tormentor.

I went up the original staircase of the Boys' Wing of the hospital, taken apart when the old building was demolished and reassembled, along with the court room, here at 40 Brunswick Square. After a small boy died, sliding down the bannisters, iron spikes were put in place to prevent such an accident ever happening again; the iron spikes had been removed. I try to imagine the child, not naughty but mischievous, seeing the long slide of polished wood, one leg up and over the bannister and then the thrill of letting go, whoosh, whoosh and then, unable to stop, out into the air, flying for an instant before he crashed, his head split open on the marble floor. Would his mother, if he had lived, have come to claim him? Did the hospital let her know her son was dead, or was he one of the ones left in a basket by the gate, early one morning, the mother quickly ringing the bell and then stumbling away into the London fog? Is his one of the trinkets or letters in the cases by the upstairs windows?

"A meddle of the King of Prussia is affix't to this letter and we your parents have each one of the same stamp."

Long glass cases against the far wall, like those in the manuscript galleries of the British Museum. Trinkets and mementoes, left in the bottoms of baskets or pinned to the infants' clothes. In case the mother could ever get back to claim her darling, her shame.

Coins with nicks in them, a mother-of-pearl heart, a few letters. And then, in the end case, the form. A small, hand-lettered card said DO NOT LEAN AGAINST THE GLASS but I had to write it down and I was alone:

> The Petition of (1)_____ of (2)_____ humbly sheweth that your Petitioner is unmarried (3)_____years of age and was on the (4)_____day of (5)_____ delivered of a (6)_____child which is wholly dependent on your Petitioner for its support, being deserted by the father. That (7)_____is the father of said child and when your Petitioner became acquainted with him was a (8)_____at (9)_____and your Petitioner last saw him on the (10)_____day of (11)_____ and believes he is now at (12)_____.
>
> Your Petitioner therefore humbly prays that you will be pleased to receive said child into aforesaid hospital.

296 / AUDREY THOMAS

In front of the marble fireplace there were two mannequins, a boy and a girl, wearing the early uniforms of the foundling children. The girl wore a long brown dress with a white apron and cap; the boy was all in brown except for a white collar. They were clean and clear-eyed, model orphans. Hogarth had designed the costumes. When the older children left the hospital and went out into the world, as servants or apprentices, did they leave the uniforms behind?

Les Misérables was playing in the West End. Every night there was a long line-up hoping for returned tickets. Set misery to music, provide a plot, and you'll have a smash-hit on your hands. On the way back from the National Gallery one day I talked to some punkers hanging around Trafalgar Fountain. All of them were, like, on the dole — UB40, did I, like, know what that was? One girl said there wasn't much point in lookin' for work, was there — what with the bomb about to drop and all.

"Or one of them nuclear leaks, like Chernobyl," another said.

The faces of the Coram mannequins were bright with hope. They would not have understood the kids in Trafalgar Square, kids who "hung out," kids with no moral centre. Entering the hospital as infants (the word itself means "speechless") they were given a set of new clothes, including "long stays," which was a bodice stiffened with whalebone, a kind of corset, to strengthen the baby's back; they were given a new name. Tatty Coram's name was Harriet.

"How did you feel about your adoptive parents?" I asked Lydia, in the darkness of the cabin. "Did you feel grateful? Did you feel love?"

"At first I was too lonely, too disoriented, to feel anything much but despair. They told me — at first — that I would be going home as soon as the war was over. They got me an English nanny — you probably remember her — I guess they thought that would make me feel more at home; but she was old, and snobby; she made fun of the way I talked — imitated me, told me over and over again how lucky I was to be in America. She made me drink big glasses of milk, which I hated, and made me sleep all alone in the dark, in that big, quiet house.

"The Armstrongs did their best, I suppose, but they weren't affectionate people — too well-bred for that. After Mr. Armstrong died, she — my mother — was warmer towards me. She may have been lonely herself, and besides, I was becoming more manageable and more 'American.' I remember hearing her friends saying, 'Emily, you've done wonders with that child.' By the time the war ended, I didn't want to go back any more. Don't forget, I'd never had a letter or a card or a birthday note from anyone. Mother told me they were all dead and I believed her."

"What makes you think they aren't?"

"Years of therapy, I suppose, plus the sense that she was lying — in order to make the transition easier for me, so I wouldn't look back."

"But the therapy didn't really help; you've said so yourself."

"Didn't help me to get back my memory — no. But it gave me some sense of identity. And it took away the guilt — that I was alive — that I had chosen to stay in America."

"But they abandoned you!"

"No. They sent me away so that I could have a better life — maybe to be sure I'd be alive at all."

"But why no letters? Nothing?"

"A clean break. You know, I searched for letters after Mother died, I searched for my birth certificate, for *something*. I think, if there was anything — she got rid of it."

"Maybe there was something she didn't want you to know."

"That I was illegitimate? But I already knew that."

"How could you?"

"I remembered some things, Charlotte, flashes of things before the night I was hit. I remember my Mother very clearly.

"My mother was pretty and she wore her hair in curlers during the day, underneath a bandanna — I suppose she would have called it a head scarf. She worked in a factory, making shell casings or something like that. And I'd seen, briefly, the long-form birth certificate."

"He might have been away at war, just like they told us in school. Just like *you* told us, Lydia. You told us he was a pilot."

"Well that was the most glamorous thing, wasn't it — a pilot? The most glamorous and the most likely to be killed."

"Why were you in Birmingham that night?"

"I don't know. I don't remember anything about that night — except legs sticking out of the rubble. I was put in hospital by somebody, and I woke up there I guess, but I don't remember any of that. I suppose people came to see me, but the first thing I actually remember is being on a train to Liverpool with a lot of other kids and we all had names pinned to our coats. Mine said HEATHER FULFORD but it didn't mean anything much. I still had a bandage on my head and I knew that underneath the bandage my head had been shaved. I worried that the other kids would laugh at me when the bandage came off. Then we were going up a gangplank and everybody was being very jolly — lots of big-busted jolly women, Scout-leader types, and nobody said, 'Wave goodbye to England.' I was seasick the whole way across, and cried a lot. By the time we reached Halifax I must have looked a mess. I'm surprised, now, that the Armstrongs didn't take one look and send me back. I could tell they were shocked when I was handed over, but they just said 'Hello, Heather' and led me to a big green car that smelled of leather and pipe tobacco, wrapped me up in a tartan blanket and put me on the back seat, where I fell asleep before we even left Canada. They told me later I said 'Madam, do you have a pony?' but I don't remember that."

"You'd probably been given something."

"Probably."

"You haven't even felt sick, have you, on this trip?"

"No — not even after I took off that patch."

"That patch was too dangerous — the nice doctors don't tell you that. Cognac is much safer. Also *wodka*."

"And it's been so calm. Like crossing a pond, not an ocean."

("Disappointingly calm," she called it. But she wasn't so calm inside; she had nightmares all the way across. "Wake up, Lydia," I would say, "wake up, my dear, you're having a bad dream." She would thank me and go back to sleep. In the morning she never remembered what the dream had been about.)

❦

The big boxes I'd seen being carried into the museum had contained wine glasses which were now set up on tables, along with plates of cheese and crackers and big bunches of green and purply grapes. Obviously a reception was about to take place. ("Friday: Porridge/Dumplings/Bread and Milk," but the Governors had no doubt always been offered something more *deluxe* when they met to discuss matters pertaining to the hospital.)

I thanked the receptionist, who seemed anxious to have me gone (it was after 5:30 when I covered the cases with their baize cloths and left the court room in darkness) so I did not linger but went quickly and turned left, back towards Mecklenburgh Square. I could see the sparks from the big bonfire rising up to the November sky and hear the chatter of parents and children as they gathered in the garden. I wished I had a small child to hold by the hand, a child excited to be out and about at night, just as my children had been at Hallowe'en or Christmas Eve. How quickly it went — their childhood, my active parenthood, parenting reduced now to friendly telephone calls, letters containing articles and cartoons clipped from newspapers and magazines.

Had I been a good parent — had I been *any help*? I thought again of my bumper sticker, LOVE YOUR MOTHER, and the violent reactions to it. Did *I* love my mother? Maybe, now that she had lost her power over me, now that she cast such a tiny shadow. Now that I knew for sure that I was not and had never been the real cause of her unhappiness. I knew she would continue to hang up on me when she was in one of her rages, continue to write those awful letters, continue to blame and judge, blame and judge, blame and judge, until, one day, she would go up in smoke. Ashes to ashes. Bonfire originally a bone-fire; Bone Voyage. If I could create for her one happy day, one day of even mild content, I would. Women think they can do that; we have been programmed to think we can do that — make other people happy. What I call the cruise director's attitude towards relationships: Are you happy? Are you having a *good time*?

I hesitated by the open gate; I have always liked bonfires, campfires, and I didn't really need a child in order to join the party. ALL WELCOME to this. But I went inside and up to my room to pack.

Even from my window in front of the desk, where I sat writing up my notes, sorting, labelling notebooks — "BATORY MATERIAL," "GREEN-WICH," "DICKENS HOUSE, MUSEUMS, CORAM'S FIELDS," "HASTINGS, SHREWSBURY, MORETON-CORBET," "NOVEL" — I could see the sparks from the bonfire and smell that spicy smell. Human bones don't smell that way — or, I should say, animal bones. In my Michael days we burnt all our bones in the woodstove, to keep rats and bears away from the compost heap. Bones have a bitter smell — they crack and sizzle.

I thought about Michael's kiln and how fire could create the beauty of glazes, how it could make clay strong. I thought of Shadrach, Meshach, and Abednego, and also of Guy Fawkes, whose celebration this was. I thought of my mother, as a small girl, seeing the men at Corbett, New York, stripped to the waist and feeding the fiery furnace in the acid factory.

A Catholic plot — Mother would say it served him right. Some of the children were wearing masks left over from Hallowe'en, which seems to be merging with, or even replacing, the traditional November 5th. Guy Fawkes just another hobgoblin, "downgraded," like Hurricane Len.

I dreamt that the annex was on fire and woke up to the radio playing "God Save the Queen." What does she think of *her* mother? I was disappointed the first time I saw Buckingham Palace; I suppose I was expecting something out of my fairy-tale books, not this drab rectangle.

Because I couldn't get back to sleep, I turned on the bedside lamp and decided to play the tape I had made of my latest conversation with my mother. I wished I hadn't finished the *wodka*; the empty bottle was soaking in the washbasin so that I could peel off the label and stick it in my notebook. Tomorrow night someone else would sleep here, perhaps a real scholar, not a scholar-gypsy. Someone who would be nicer to Dorothy Moore, whom I'd been avoiding like mad — putting her off with breezy little notes. I had ready, for her mail cubicle, a bar of Body Shop green-apple soap, as a thank-you for directing me to Thomas Cooper.

I pressed PLAY. The tape began to move, whirr, whirr, whirr, but nothing happened. I tried the other side: nothing. Somehow I had forgotten to press REC. when I began the interview. And of course had taken no notes. Fool!! She doesn't bother you, eh? Doesn't make you nervous any more?

"Nothing will come of nothing. Speak again."

❀

Letter from Lydia to Charlotte, sent Express

> B'ham The Wentsbury Hotel
> ("weddings and receptions catered")
>
> Her Majesty's Postal Service
> better be quick.

Dear Charlotte,

I've just had a very hot bath. The landlady — Mrs. Goodall — will knock on the
door any minute and give me a good
talking to as baths are <u>EXPRESSLY FOR-
BIDDEN</u> after 10 p.m. God, the English
love signs — always polite, of course, but
with a kind of controlled fury behind
them. Now I'm sitting in bed with all the
covers and coats I can find and drinking the
last of the wodka. I'm so <u>cold</u>. There's
something called a space heater but I think
the space it's meant to heat is not this cav-
ernous place. ("<u>Please</u> do not dry clothing
on the heater.") I'll be glad when Søren
arrives, tomorrow, and whisks me off to
someplace in the country with a roaring
fire. I'm soft, Charlotte, soft: can't image
how I ever lived here as a kid — and with
only a coal fire, no doubt.

I know I'm going to see you in twenty-
four hours or less but I feel I have to get
this down before Søren arrives and I start
changing things. We do that, you and I,

change things. So here's what I've found out and what I now remember.

Strangely enough — or is it — what I remember most are sounds, not faces or actual events before the bombing raid, although I feel that too may come. I remember the incendiaries now; they were noisier than the bombs. Bombs landing somewhere in the distance, I now realize, after my northern winters, sound like a load of snow falling of a roof. THUD. But the incendiaries were loud fireworks, right over your head. I never liked the Fourth of July.

The enclosed photo is of my cousin, whose name is *Heather*, and her husband. Yes — it's extraordinary, isn't it? Not only did we start out with the same name, we could be sisters. In fact we are. She is seventeen years older: Heather, my half-sister, known to the world as my cousin Heather.

My aunt helped with the barrage balloons and sometimes my cousin as well. I guess they took me along rather than leave me alone at home. For years I have remembered a humming sound, but thought it had something to do with the blow to my head; my cousin says it was the sound of the wires which held the balloons. The psychiatrists I've been to were all American. When I talked about the humming noise they just nodded, yes, I see, hmmm, and when they did that I would start to cry.

My uncle was away at war although he really was too old — thirty-six I think. Heather says he never bathed and slicked his hair down with brilliantine. He and my aunt ran a green-grocer's shop and once I was sent to live with them in Lichfield, which is outside Birmingham, we all lived upstairs. "Behind green baize curtains," I said to her, and she became very excited. But the peculiar thing is that I only remember the curtains and the sound of bombs and incendiaries and a few other things — the smell of coal smoke for example.

Heather says she took a bath in a tin tub every Saturday and that she used to let me wash her back. You'd think I'd remember that, wouldn't you — the black-out curtains and the lamplight shining on her long naked back, but I don't. I get a sort of D.H. Lawrence vision of it all but that's from literature and not the back of my brain or the front or wherever the warehouse is where memories are stored.

There was an Anderson shelter in the yard behind the shop, sunk into the garden. You stepped down into it. I don't remember this. Heather says I used to "make a big fuss and carry on something dreadful" when we had to go in it. "I don't remember," I said.

"Mum used to tell you to hush or the Jerries would hear you." "I don't remember."

But what you may remember, Charlotte, is that silly Arthur Godfrey song,

"I'm my own grandpa." I'm feeling a bit like that tonight. My cousin is really my half-sister; my uncle (dead dead dead and never called me daughter) was my father.

The night my mother was killed Heather and I were both in Birmingham. I wasn't supposed to be there but my aunt was poorly and I had begged to go along with my cousin and have a visit with my granny and my mother. Heather was at the art school on Margaret Street, part-time. She wanted to get her N.D.D. and then train to be a teacher.

(Fish paste on toast for supper. I remember that too.)

We'd gone to the art college and were on our way down to Gosta Green when the sirens went off, so we headed for the nearest shelter, which was by the Bull Ring. A bomb fell before we got there and Heather says she was pulling me along, holding her big portfolio over our heads because stuff was raining down on us and buildings were falling.

WHY DON'T I REMEMBER THIS?

("The management is not responsible for lost or stolen articles. Thank you.")

We started to run and a bomb fell right in front of us, only a few yards away. I was hit on the head by a great chunk of stone and Heather was thrown across the street. She thinks my mother and granny must have died just about the same time as I got hit on the head. They didn't tell me for days and then, because my memory was almost completely gone and I wasn't getting better, they let me go to foster-parents in America. Heather said they showed me where I was going, on the map, but I had no idea how far away America was because I could touch England with my thumb and New York State with my little finger. Why do I remember donkey-riding in Blackpool when I don't remember all this other stuff?

It wasn't my mother I must have seen, with socks on, crushed underneath a building. Somebody else's mother, no doubt, but not mine.

"We mustn't write to her," my aunt said, although they had promised me they would. "We must let her start a new life." Heather says my aunt wasn't a bad sort but she probably wanted me out of the way. Apparently she was furious that her younger sister had given me the same name as *her* child.

But not furious that I was her husband's child <u>because she didn't know</u>. My mother never told; it was my uncle, just before he died, last year, who told Heather.

Yes Charlotte, those are tears, not wodka stains. He was alive until last year. I could have seen him, touched him, <u>loved</u> him. He told Heather not to try and find me, but if she ever did see me again to say that he loved me and that he had loved my mother as well and he hoped it had all turned out for the best.

I can't go on. Will see you Saturday.
love,
Lydia

At the bottom she put a phrase from the Polish Fun Class:

"BYC ALBO NIE BYC OTO JUST PYTANIE"
("To be or not to be," by SZEKSPIR)

Then: P.S. I didn't find her, she found me. In a pub in Gosta Green — The Woodman. She has no idea why she decided to go there on this particular day. "Heather," she said, "Pardon me, is your name Heather?"

All flesh is glass. I, personally, was not an orphan, nor a foundling, nor was Lydia. Why, then, did I suddenly start talking this way at the table, when I was ten: "Pass the butter Mother, if you are my Mother." "Pass the bread Daddy, if you are my Daddy." I was not punished for this — sent away from the table or my mouth washed out with soap. That happened only once, when I said "fuck" at my grandfather's place, in order to get attention. It was tar soap and I can taste it still. That night my sister told me I would go to Hell. "Fuck," I said to her, "fuck you." I did not know what it meant but it rhymed with suck and I knew it was something bad.

"Mother," she called into the next room where our parents were sleeping on two army cots while we slept in the double bed, "Mother, she said it again!"

My sister said I would go to Hell. She also said that marmalade was made from goldfish.

As usual I had to buy another suitcase, at the last minute, from a shop on Southampton Row. Cramming in all the new notebooks, timetables, guide-books, souvenirs ("This is to certify that Charlotte Tipping has faithfully attended the Polish Fun Class . . ."), Christmas presents, not to mention the stuff I brought with me, which seemed to take up more space going back than it did coming over. I was tempted to chuck the Book of Begats — it alone weighed at least two pounds — but it didn't belong to me.

The trolley-wheels squeaked in protest at the extra load as I made my way to the Airbus stop, like any other thrifty tourist. The Tube was even cheaper but I didn't want to leave London like a mole, burrowing through darkness for miles and miles. Instead, once I had hauled my stuff up the steps and piled it on top of the luggage belonging to the people who'd been smart enough to get on at Euston, I went upstairs for a last look. I never feel that it is a final look; I always know that I will be back, so it's silly really. The route isn't particularly interesting, especially once we leave central London.

Sentimental — maybe hoping to spot Michael in the crowds?

The kids say he comes over regularly to see his mother, now that his father is dead. His parents stopped writing to me after a while; they weren't very big on letter-writing anyway, and once the children were old enough to write themselves, what was the point? At first I was hurt — I had wanted so much for them to approve of me — then I was angry, and then I really didn't care.

Even though I was a bit early, Søren and Lydia were already at Heathrow.

"Good God, Charlotte," Søren said, "what have you bought?"

"Just stuff," I said, "research."

"Charlotte's 'stuff,'" Lydia said, giving me a big hug, "fills her house. This will just be added to the midden." But smiled as she said it. She is very tidy. "Did you get my letter?" I nodded.

"Shall we find a place to have a drink?" I said, "after I get rid of all of this?"

"Actually, Charlotte," said Søren, taking over my trolley, "we were wondering how you might feel about changing your ticket and going home to Ontario with Lydia for a few days. I've been called back to Stockholm and she really needs to talk to you. Would you mind, or do you have to go straight home?"

Straight home to what? Leaving England has always made me weepy. Too many memories, too many might-have-beens.

"But I have a fixed ticket," I said. "I can't change it."

"Would you allow me to change it — to pay the difference? I really don't want Lydia to go home to an empty house."

Lydia was nodding and trying to look wan. Actually, she did look a little wan; maybe she shouldn't be alone.

"Why can't she go to Stockholm with you?" I said.

"She wants to go home. Please Charlotte, would you mind?"

One of the daughters was meeting me but that was easy to fix.

I nodded yes. There really wasn't any pressing need, other than the date on my ticket, to go home to Vancouver today.

"Very good. We will arrange this and then we will have a farewell drink."

In the V.I.P. lounge, as it turned out. And champagne as we took off.

"I've never travelled first class before," I said.

"You'll like it," Lydia said, clinking her glass against mine.

England grew smaller and smaller. The home counties, the white cliffs, the sea. The sea looked calm from where we sat — a bird's eye view.

The flight attendant asked if we'd like a bit more. We held out our glasses obediently.

"Lydia," I said, "the opium was incredible. I forgot to thank Søren, but I'll write him a letter."

"What happened?" she said, smiling. "Oh, Charlotte, I'm so *glad* to see you. You're my real sister, you know. I've missed you."

"Well," I said, "I was in the old church at Moreton-Corbet . . ."

As we zoomed upward towards Heaven I told her about the farmer, Jack, and his dog, Shep, and the ram looking over the fence, and Sir Chimes and the pears and then the church, the effigies, the helicopters overhead.

"And I knew this was the right place and the right time, so I took it, all of it."

"And —?"

"And they came to me, all of them. They came in and they filled every pew."

"What did they say?"

"They didn't say, they sang. They sang the first hymn that was posted on the board — last Sunday's hymn or next Sunday's, I don't know which.

"Then, after a while, after the last verse, they put the hymn books back and disappeared, just sort of dispersed, like smoke, like fog."

I shivered. "I'll never forget it."

Lydia looked at me and put her hand on my arm.

"Charlotte," she said. "That wasn't opium. We were too worried about you going off on your own and knocking back the stuff God knows where or when. So we made up something that looked like opium. What you 'took' my dear, was some water flavoured with anise and allspice."

"You're sure?"

"I'm sure. Oh, he got the opium all right, that wasn't the problem. *You* were the problem. What if you took it and it made you do something crazy? We'd never forgive ourselves."

She took out a bottle from her purse.

"If you still want to take it, we'll all take it. Stay until your birthday and we'll all take it. We want you to do that sort of thing among friends."

"Do you think," I said after a while, "that I could get some for my mother?"

"I don't see why not," she said.

"When I was walking out to the door with her last time," I said, "she stopped to introduce me to some old lady — I guess one of the ones she still speaks to. She said that I had come all the way from Canada and that I bring her all sorts of presents, a regular Santa Claus in disguise, and she just can't understand why I'm so nice to her."

I began to laugh. Two glasses of champagne and my usual plane paranoia had combined to make me slightly drunk. I could hardly speak for laughing.

"And this old lady . . . hee hee hee . . . this old lady looked at her and said '*Well*, you're the only mother she's got.'"

❧

August 1904. Ready or not, here I come. In the yellow light the children are hiding — behind haystacks, in hedges, at the corners of barns. Mama doesn't mind if they play with the farm children so long as they stay outside. Edna examines their heads for nits and checks their fingernails before their bath.

The farm boys swore, so did Lawrence and Cousin Marshall. Some of them smoked cigarettes; you could smell it on them.

Frances was happy happy happy. She was good at running, good at hiding. She could hear Betty calling for her but she didn't care.

They were all so absorbed in the game they hadn't realized the storm was directly overhead. And scattered like birds at the sound of a gun when the thunder crashed.

The drops fell, big as dollars. Cousin Marshall ran by with Betty on his shoulders. The horses whinnied in the barn. "Please God, please God." Frances had such hateful thoughts she was sure God would strike her dead. The sky lit up.

On the back porch they washed their feet in the enamelled pans of water, dried them quickly on a coarse towel and ran inside. The rain was pouring down, dancing on the dry earth. The world smelled sweet and cool.

Father sent Lawrence and Cousin Marshall to calm the horses. "Go to bed now," he said to the little girls. He had been standing quietly by the kitchen door. "Wash quickly and go to bed."

Frances wanted a bath in the big tub, with Edna singing to her and Betty and the cool water sluicing over her. She felt itchy and uncomfortable.

"Where's Edna?" she said.

"She's gone to bed."

Edna never went to bed until late; they often heard her down in the kitchen singing or making a cup of tea for Father. Mama went to bed early — to get her strength back.

Frances and Betty slept in a small room on the second floor. They had a blue candlestick that said Jack be Nimble, Jack be Quick. The house was electrified, but in summer they used candles and hurricane lamps.

Father lit their candle and let Frances carry it upstairs by herself. He did not kiss them. Frances was more afraid of lightning than she was of fire. She watched their shadows going up the stairs.

And when she awoke in the middle of the night she thought at first it was cows that had woken her. That the farmer next door had let his cows loose in the kitchen. Or the cows had broken down the door.

At first she was too afraid to move.

❧

In the village of Corbettsville they still observed the traditional rules for the tolling of deaths.

"It will ring for a few minutes and then toll — one for an infant, three for a girl, five for a boy, seven for a woman and nine for a man; it will then stop, and toll again the age — one toll for one year etc. It will also ring at the time for funeral."

Yesterday's storm had ceased and the air was cool and clean, like water. They would have been able to hear the bell from anywhere in the village, but no bell rang, no single round note to proclaim the death of the baby she had seen looking up at her from the ferny tops of the carrots they had had for supper.

Now Father had gone to town, Edna was gone away for good and Mama was upset. After telling them that Edna wasn't too well and had returned to the County Home to build up her strength, she put Lawrence in charge until Father came home and then retired to her room.

The bucket was on the back porch, just an ordinary bucket, empty.

Lawrence and Marshall, wearing their straw hats, as usual, had already been out before breakfast. Six cows had been struck by lightning in a nearby farmer's field; they wanted to go and have a look.

"No," Frances said, "we don't want to."

"Mother said we had to look after you, so you'll do as you're told."

"No," Frances said, getting down from the table and helping her sister down, "we aren't going to see any dead cows."

"Is Flora dead?" Betty said. "And Belle?" Her face turned red and she screwed up her mouth to cry.

"It's all right," Frances said, moving quickly to the sink for a damp cloth. Betty's face was smeared with jam; the wasps would be after her as soon as they stepped outside.

"We aren't going anywhere with them; we're going to pick a posy for Mama and then we'll go up to Grandfather's house and read books."

"You'll come with us," Lawrence said. He raised his hand.

"No," Frances said again, "we won't."

She had no idea where this new courage had come from but she wasn't afraid of her brother. Never again. She felt older than he, wiser, disillusioned. Lawrence looked like Father; he would grow up to be like Father.

Frances took their poke bonnets off the hook, grabbed Betty's hand and left the house.

"Stay away from the creek!" Lawrence yelled. She knew he wouldn't come after them; he and Marshall wanted to go off by themselves. If they drowned he probably wouldn't care. He'd pretend to care, but he wouldn't really. He said she was a goody-goody, a tell-tale, a pain in the neck.

"But I want to go to the creek," Betty said, jumping about while Frances tried to tie her bonnet strings.

"No," Frances said, "the prettiest flowers are up by the road. Don't you want to make a posy for poor Mama?"

"I want to go to the creek. I want to see if the water-baby is there."

Frances stood still. The air buzzed with insects and somewhere, quite far away, she could hear the whistle of a freight train. Her father's hands had been covered in blood.

"What water-baby?" she said, turning away from the path to the creek and towards the road. "I don't know what you're talking about."

"The water-baby we saw last night, you know."

"You had a dream, remember? It was only a dream."

"Anyway," she said later on, as they arranged the black-eyed Susans, the Queen Anne's lace, the goldenrod and flax into a bouquet Frances felt would be pleasing to poor Mama, "Anyway, if there was a water-baby they would have put him back in the water, wouldn't they? He'd be half-way to the sea by now."

All day she listened for the bell, but the only sounds were the usual sounds of summer.

"What I saw," says my mother, pulling at her fingers, "what I saw was a baby in a bucket, and my father looking up, from the bottom of the stairs. He had just come out of the hired girl's room and his hands were covered in blood."

Pull Pull Pull Pull

"And he saw me."

❦

Father sat at the head of the table, Mama to his right. The new girl's name was Ivy and she had a club foot. She stood still while they bowed their heads and closed their eyes.

"For what we are about to receive, may the Lord make us truly thankful."

Epigraph

Oh no, no, no, it was too cold always
(Still the dead one lay mourning)
I was much too far out all my life
And not waving but drowning.

— Stevie Smith